# DON'T BURN OUR BRIDGES

# DON'T BURN OUR BRIDGES

## The Case for Owning Airlines

Jean S. Holder

**University of the West Indies Press**
Jamaica • Barbados • Trinidad and Tobago

Caribbean
Development Bank

University of the West Indies Press
7A Gibraltar Hall Road   Mona
Kingston 7   Jamaica
www.uwipress.com

© 2010 by Jean S. Holder

All rights reserved. Published 2010

CATALOGUING-IN-PUBLICATION DATA

Holder, Jean S.
Don't burn our bridges: the case for owning airlines / Jean S. Holder.

p. cm.

Includes bibliographical references.

ISBN: 978-976-640-232-7

1. Airlines – Caribbean, English-speaking. 2. Airlines – Economic aspects – Caribbean, English-speaking. 3. Air travel – Caribbean, English-speaking – History. 4. Tourism – Caribbean, English-speaking.  I. Title

HE9828.5.A4H74 2010       387.7


Cover design by Robert Harris.
Printed in the United States of America.

This book is dedicated to my wife, Norma, my friend, supporter and confidante for more than fifty years.

# Contents

| | |
|---|---|
| Foreword | ix |
| Preface | xi |
| Acknowledgements | xvii |
| List of Abbreviations | xxi |

**CHAPTER 1**
The Case for Caribbean Carriers ..... 1

**CHAPTER 2**
A Brief History of Air Jamaica, Bahamasair, BWIA/CAL, Cayman Airways and LIAT ..... 6

**CHAPTER 3**
A Comparison of the Operational and Financial Performance of Caribbean and Major International Carriers ..... 16

**CHAPTER 4**
Options for Cooperation Between Regional Carriers ..... 42

**CHAPTER 5**
The LIAT Case Study ..... 60

**CHAPTER 6**
Why the LIAT–Caribbean Star Merger Was Necessary ..... 85

**CHAPTER 7**
Negotiating a Merger with Sir Allen Stanford ..... 95

**CHAPTER 8**
When an Airline Monopoly Is Justifiable ..... 113

**CHAPTER 9**
Deregulation, Yield Management, Fare Setting and
Hedging Oil Prices                                           130

**CHAPTER 10**
2008: The Worst Year in Civil Aviation History               149

**CHAPTER 11**
The Caribbean Reacts to the 2008 Crisis                      168

**CHAPTER 12**
Caribbean Tourism Performance, 2008                          177

**CHAPTER 13**
Air Transportation in the CSME: Beyond 2009                  186

**APPENDIX 1**
LIAT Shareholders, Board and Management, 2009                219

**APPENDIX 2**
LIAT Average Fares, 1998–2007                                222

**APPENDIX 3**
Fares and Taxes: Year-on-Year Comparison for 2007–2008       225

**APPENDIX 4**
Hedging Options                                              245

**APPENDIX 5**
Single Caribbean Airspace                                    253

**APPENDIX 6**
Caribbean Tourism Organization: Latest Statistics, 2008      257

**APPENDIX 7**
Caribbean Tourism Organization: Latest Statistics, 2009      266

**APPENDIX 8**
Register of Holders of Ordinary Shares in LIAT (1974) Ltd,
from 1999 to 2008                                            272

**APPENDIX 9**
LIAT Costs Distribution                                      283

**REFERENCES**                                               285

**INDEX**                                                    287

# Foreword

The cumulative effect of the ongoing discourse on the Caribbean air transport system and its impact on regional development has numbed many senses and bewildered more spirits. Welcome to chaos, one is likely to hear after making a discursive intervention. Experts and pundits alike have concluded that the discussion has crashed. Laypersons as outsiders are left to sift through the debris in search of evidence of conceptual clarity and unyielding commitment.

These were the glaring signs and immediate sensations I saw and experienced when asked by the author to prepare a foreword for this book. I had been in the author's corner for some time, urging him to reflect and to write, but I had no way of imagining or measuring the depth of the digging that would be required to unearth a text of this nature. I knew, of course, that an important book would be written, and that no other soul was more capable. But importance and excellence are altogether different concepts, and I knew where my preference is situated.

I feared for the author; why, I am not sure. It was not born of doubt. Neither was it connected to any anxiety about failure. It had more to do with my awareness of the enormous knowledge he possessed, carried like a lonely traveller for decades along pathways that led inexorably to the bottom line with little regard for intellectual process and development possibilities. The discussion about regional airlines has been framed and frozen within the accountant's gaze that visualizes no positive value in historical experience, political imperatives and the wider intellectual remit of community empowerment. This circumstance has fostered a festering perception that regional airlines represent black holes in blue Caribbean skies, and at a time when the prospects are looking rather brown for retreating governments and impoverished private sectors.

This perspective, of course, is misleading in its popularity, and has taken us nowhere fast. What has been missing among the chatter is reliable empirical data and sound recollection of historical trends and patterns. This is where we have now arrived. In a sense, this is where we can now begin a serious dialogue equipped with the critical tools for data analysis. This work, then, marks a new beginning; it is a seminal moment in the discourse of doubt and despair; it represents a voice and vision that presents a reasoned case for the regional airline enterprise. Critically, it carries as its counter reference the language of an affirmative Caribbean sensibility.

No one, I propose for your consideration, knows more about this subject than the author. Insights into a lifetime of professional journeys through every corridor of the tourism sector, comprehended by a mind steeled by rigorous academic training, now comes to us in a passionately presented narrative that speaks of values of commitment and dedication to the agenda of postcolonial nation-building. It takes business to care; and the author has been taking care of business. He has seen from all sides the world of travel that has been the pain and joy of what is a Caribbean reality cradled and crafted as God's special slice of paradise.

To read this text, furthermore, is to experience the labour pains and growing instability of a Caribbean construct as it is dismantled and re-engineered, elevated and relegated, in the never-ending quest for greater social relevance and economic effectiveness. In this regard, Caribbean people have shown that they know precisely what they need; stitching together the resources has proven elusive. Thankfully, what the author leaves with us is a road map that shows the way and urges that the quest must not be abandoned.

*Hilary McD. Beckles*

# Preface

This book is about air transportation, its important role as a bridge between the countries of the Caribbean and the external world, and between the countries themselves. By no means of less importance, this book is about ownership of airlines.

The Caribbean region for the purposes of this book is described as comprising an archipelago of over thirty islands in the Caribbean Sea as well as certain mainland territories that border the sea. They are normally referred to in various subgroups, such as the Commonwealth Caribbean, the French, Dutch and Spanish Caribbean, depending on their colonial histories and relationships with different metropolitan European countries. But what all those countries listed later have in common is a dependence on tourism and a close working relationship with each other in that industry for over fifty years. This resulted from their membership since 1951 first in the Caribbean Tourist Association and later, the Caribbean Tourism Organization (CTO) created by a merger of the association and the Caribbean Tourism Research and Development Centre in 1989.

The island territories are Anguilla, Antigua and Barbuda, Aruba, the Commonwealth of the Bahamas, Barbados, Bermuda, Bonaire, the British Virgin Islands, Cayman Islands, Cuba, Curaçao, Dominica, The Dominican Republic, Grenada, Guadeloupe, Haiti, Jamaica, Martinique, Montserrat, Puerto Rico, Saba, St Barts, St Eustatius, St Kitts and Nevis, St Lucia, St Maarten, St Martin, St Vincent and the Grenadines, Trinidad and Tobago, Turks and Caicos Islands, and the US Virgin Islands. The CTO mainland territories are Belize, Guyana, Suriname and Venezuela. While strictly speaking the Bahamas and Bermuda are not geographically in the Caribbean Sea, they are members of the CTO and have worked closely with the other territories in tourism matters.

The islands range in size from the very small ones like Anguilla, which is 35 square miles with a population of 10,300, to Cuba which is 44,218 square miles with a population of 11,050,729. The largest mainland CTO member state is Venezuela which is 352,143 square miles with a population of 22,576,000. At one time Costa Rica and Panama were member states of the Caribbean Tourist Association and Mexico of CTO.

The Caribbean Sea is an area of some 1 million square miles and the territories are scattered across its length and breadth, separated from each other by distances of water which cannot easily or quickly be traversed by small boats. From time to time there is discussion about using fast ferries as an alternative means of transport between the islands. This is more feasible between some territories than others. Where there are distances of more than 100 miles to cover and a high probability of deep and rough seas, both time and comfort are, in my opinion, factors militating against the widespread use of sea vessels as a means of everyday transport. This is here being contrasted to their use for sailing or cruising for pleasure and for carrying cargo. With respect to freighting, it will be argued that, with the necessary investment and a few adjustments, Leeward Islands Air Transport (LIAT) Airline could assist with freighter services between several countries of the Eastern Caribbean.

The Caribbean is therefore extremely dependent for both its business and social development on the existence of good air transportation services, both to the territories from foreign countries and between the Caribbean countries themselves.

More than 90 per cent of the tourism expenditure in the Caribbean comes from stay-over visitors who travel to the region by air. The wider Caribbean region has been described by credible sources, such as the United Nations World Tourism Organization, the World Tourism and Travel Council, and the CTO, as being four times more dependent on tourism for its socio-economic development than any other region of the world.

It is not difficult to understand, therefore, that air transportation, which may aptly be described as the glue that cements the tourism market to the destination, is even more critically important to the Caribbean than to many other places that are less dependent on tourism and are not separated by water. The symbiotic relationship between tourism and air transportation is clear. Any definition of sustainable tourism should therefore include, as a necessary condition, the existence of reliable and affordable air transportation access.

However, air transportation's importance extends beyond its role in the tourism sector. Fourteen Caribbean countries, all of which, except Haiti, were former colonies of Britain, are linked together in the Caribbean Community (CARICOM), which has the formation of a single market and single economy as its economic and social goal. For social and business purposes, the people of this sub-group need to travel often and easily between CARICOM states. This underscores the importance of intra-Caribbean air transport services for movement of both persons and cargo. In 2009, LIAT was serving the members of CARICOM except the Bahamas Belize, Haiti, Jamaica and Suriname, as well as eight other non-member Caribbean states.

Air transportation, therefore, may be described as an important instrument of trade, employment, defence and economic development generally. Its absence would reduce the population of several small island states, situated at some distance from each other across the vast Caribbean Sea, to being virtual prisoners on their island.

Since in the context of an archipelago, air transportation has been described as a bridge between the Caribbean countries, it can be argued that when a critical bridge breaks down, the natural first response often is how soon can it be repaired, rather than what will be the cost of repairing it.

The relevance of this comment will become more apparent when we discuss the cost of maintaining air transportation links between the Caribbean countries and offering fares that are affordable to the travelling public.

This idea of air transportation as a bridge was strongly supported by Lelei Le Laulu, president of Counterpart International, in addressing European aviation chiefs in Oslo in November 2007. He said "Without a rational aerial highways system lifting tourists in and flying goods and services out to global markets, the poorer countries will be sentenced to abject poverty." He argued that terrestrial highways, roads and bridges are recognized as essential components of infrastructure, responsible for turning new frontiers into thriving communities as goods and commodities are transported to markets.

He urged organizations like the World Bank and the International Monetary Fund, which fund large infrastructural programmes, to look at developing world airlines, not as money-losing ventures, but as an integral part of the infrastructure of poorer countries. "No one, he observed, ever questions whether a highway or a causeway is going to make money and added that tourism, the world's largest and fastest growing industry, represented the largest voluntary transfer of resources from the rich to the poor in history." He concluded that for those of us in the development community, tourism is the most potent and anti-poverty tool ever.

While there seems to be no disagreement about the critical importance of air transportation, there are stark differences of opinion, both in and outside the Caribbean, as to who should own, control and manage it in the Caribbean.

One school of thought is that Caribbean governments should not own national and regional carriers, nor should they support operations with subsidies. The feeling is that the public sector has neither the required expertise nor the financial resources, which over the years have proven to be enormous. Rather the solution to Caribbean air transport lies in a regime of deregulation, liberalization and privatization. It is held further that the market should decide, and that wherever there is a real need and an environment of open skies, private enterprise, most likely from abroad, will supply the services needed.

This view is partially grounded by the difficulties experienced by the Caribbean countries in meeting the cost of national carriers. But there is also an underpinning philosophy held by sources in the developed world and by many of the international development institutions led by personnel from that world, that regulation and government intervention are inherently bad. It is the religion of the New World Order in an era of globalization which has been taken to the extreme in the United States under Republican governments, for which words such as "socialism" and "liberal" are terms of abuse. It is a religion that may, however, lose many converts after the global economic meltdown of 2008 and the massive government bailouts of the private sector introduced by the Republican government of President George. W. Bush. This policy was greatly expanded by President Barack Obama, who was elected in November 2008 and took office in January 2009.

A contrary view is advanced in this book about ownership and control of air transportation in the Caribbean archipelago: the economy of the region is dependent on arriving tourists, the geography of the region means it is inaccessible by road or rail. The countries depend on air transportation services to connect them with the external world and with each other, and for this, they cannot rely solely on foreign carriers, which take decisions about services, routes, schedules and financial performance according to the best interests of their owners and shareholders. Such decisions will not, and cannot, always coincide with the best interests of the Caribbean states.

From time to time, the Caribbean has seen major foreign carriers that serve the region disappear without a trace at critical junctures, depriving the countries of links to the marketplace and endangering their tourism prospects. It is fear of this disaster recurring that has led certain Caribbean governments, even though they recognize that they cannot own all of the air transport services operating to and in the region, to reluctantly own or subsidize some national or regional carriers.

To those who say Caribbean governments cannot afford to do this, I reply that they cannot afford not to. Creative solutions are not easy, but they are possible and must be found.

Buffeted repeatedly by negative criticism about their national carriers, the Caribbean public has never, as far as I am aware, been given an adequate explanation of why their hard earned taxes should be spent on airlines. Caribbean people are constantly reminded of the losses incurred by government-owned carriers and their other deficiencies. But they hear little about the losses which private sector entrepreneurs, both local and foreign, operating airlines in this region have incurred or the subsidies they have received from governments. Few know of the subsidies that some Caribbean governments, which are opposed to subsidizing regional carriers, pay certain foreign carriers to fly into their countries. They are even less aware of the financial and operational challenges which a large number of airlines across the world, including the legacy carriers which are household names in the region, face every year, forcing some to close altogether and others to operate in a state of bankruptcy because of the high fixed costs they have to incur. They are unaware of the various types of subsidies which are provided to these international carriers by their own governments. This information gap is about to change. This book seeks to provide information on all the preceding matters and more.

It is hoped that the reader will have a better understanding of how difficult and complex airline management is and how the return on government's investment in air transportation should be seen in the context of its role in the economy as a whole. He or she should then be better able to view in a more sympathetic light certain Caribbean governments' persistence in supporting their national carriers.

Lastly, this book will have been a worthwhile venture if it gives some comfort to those of the Caribbean political directorate who have persisted in support of their carriers in the face of constant and widespread criticism and encourages those governments currently taking a free ride, to join the shareholders of regional carriers in keeping them aloft as a bridge over CARICOM.

As chairman of the board of directors of LIAT Airline, I have drawn extensively on the experiences gained from that association. However, this book also focuses on the experiences of all five CARICOM government-owned Caribbean carriers: Air Jamaica, Bahamasair, BWIA/Caribbean Airlines Limited, Cayman Airways and LIAT Airline, and compares their performance operationally and financially with those of the major international carriers in Asia, Europe and North America. It will be demonstrated that the Caribbean carriers do not suffer by comparison.

I hope that those who persist beyond the preface will find a great deal of interest and learn something new about air transportation in general. The facts and figures used are as they were at the time of concluding this book in October 2009.

*Jean Holder*

# Acknowledgements

I wish to acknowledge the encouragement and advice given by Professor Sir Hilary Beckles, principal of the Cave Hill campus of the University of the West Indies, to put into writing my knowledge and experience of Caribbean tourism and air transportation. This particular volume deals largely with air transportation and a separate book on tourism is in process of preparation. I also wish to express my indebtedness to Ms Vaneisa Baksh, well known in Trinidad and Tobago as a writer on Caribbean cricket, for her assistance with editing aspects of my work, and to Mr John Gilmore for sharing numerous developments in air transportation with me by e-mail.

I have drawn on publications such as the Caribbean Tourism Organization's (CTO) Caribbean tourism statistical reports, the CTO Caribbean Regional Airlines Functional Cooperation Study by El Perial Management Services, Port of Spain and Aviation Management Services, Miami, numerous eTurboNews reports, the IATA study done for the Caribbean Development Bank (CDB) on the costs of air travel in the Caribbean region, statements by the director general of the International Air Transport Association (IATA) on the state of international air transportation, the Speedwing Report commissioned by LIAT on the LIAT Recovery Plan 1999 issued by David Whitworth, Julian Ingram, Tony Liddard and Trefor Evans, a paper by Professor Andrew Downes entitled "Too Big to Fail: Economic Reality or Moral Hazard? A Global and Regional Perspective", a paper on a single Caribbean air space by acting LIAT CEO Brian Challenger, a paper by former LIAT CFO Alan Bryon on hedging oil prices, which was commissioned by LIAT's board, and from news reports in the specialist travel and tourism press, the financial sections of major UK and US newspapers, the general media and the Internet.

I have also referenced my other articles or chapters in such publications as *Practicing Responsible Tourism*, edited by Harrison and Husbands (John Wiley and Sons, 1996); *Tourism, the Driver of Change*, edited by Hall and Holding (Ian Randle, 2006); and *Production Integration in CARICOM*, edited by Benn and Hall (Ian Randle, 2006).

However, a great deal of practical hands-on airline experience has come from dealing with policy, financial and operational issues as chairman of the board of LIAT Airline since 2004.

I wish, therefore, first of all, to express my gratitude to the LIAT shareholder prime ministers and their ministers of tourism and civil aviation for the opportunity to serve. Special mention must be made of prime ministers, the Rt. Hon. Owen Arthur of Barbados, the Hon. Baldwin Spencer of Antigua and Barbuda, Dr the Hon. Ralph Gonsalves of St Vincent and the Grenadines, the Hon. Noel Lynch, minister of tourism and air transportation of Barbados on whose watch I was first appointed a director of LIAT and the Hon. Harold Lovell, minister of tourism and civil aviation of Antigua and Barbuda, all of whom recognized that the survival of LIAT was critical to regional air transportation and the Caribbean integration process. They were therefore unswerving in their support of the carrier.

I recognize also that the Hon. David Thompson, who succeeded Mr Arthur as prime minister of Barbados in January 2008 has continued in that tradition of support for the carrier.

Second, I wish to acknowledge the special role played by the Caribbean Development Bank, which at a critical time in merger negotiations between LIAT and Sir Allen Stanford came forward with a proposal to the LIAT shareholders for a loan of US$60 million to them to be invested in LIAT. The impact of this intervention will be treated at greater length in the body of the book. I could not also fail to mention the exceptional quality of advice received from Cameron McCaw in the area of finance and Karen De Freitas-Rait and Dr Adrian Cummins in the area of law during the negotiations with Caribbean Star.

I wish also to recognize assistance given by Ms Janelle Morris and Mrs Janelle Hunte of the LIAT Commercial Office and by Mrs Grace Holder-Nelson, whose computer skills I invoked in organizing tables, an area in which I have no competence.

Further, I wish to salute my fellow directors and members of the LIAT management team not only for their unstinting support to me as chairman, but also for all the things I learned from them about LIAT in particular and air transportation in general. Their names are listed in appendix 1. I wish also to acknowledge the support and contribution to LIAT of CEO Garry Cullen, who left in 2006, and CEO Mark Darby, who left in 2009.

Last, but by no means least, it is important to state that the views expressed in this book, especially those about the future direction of regional air transportation, are entirely mine and are not in any way intended to reflect the views and ideas of the shareholders, board of directors or management.

# Abbreviations

| | |
|---|---|
| BOAC | British Overseas Airways Corporation |
| BSAA | British South American Airways |
| BWIA | British West Indian Airways |
| CAL | Caribbean Airlines Limited |
| CARICOM | Caribbean Community |
| CASSOS | Caribbean Safety and Security Oversight System |
| CDB | Caribbean Development Bank |
| CEO | chief executive officer |
| CFO | chief financial officer |
| CIAH | Caribbean International Airways Holding |
| CTO | Caribbean Tourism Organization |
| EC | Eastern Caribbean |
| EDC | Export Development Corporation |
| FAA | Federal Aviation Administration |
| GDP | gross domestic product |
| GDS | global distribution system |
| IATA | International Air Transport Association |
| LCC | low-cost carrier |
| OECS | Organisation of Eastern Caribbean States |
| LIALPA | Leeward Islands Airline Pilots Association |
| LIAT | Leeward Islands Air Transport |
| LIFAA | Leeward Islands Flight Attendants Association |
| SFG | Stanford Financial Group |

# 1

# The Case for Caribbean Carriers

## Ownership and Control of Airlines

Countries in the developed world are very concerned about who owns and controls their airlines. Countries like the United States, Brazil and Australia do not leave matters to chance; they legislate against foreign ownership totally or prescribe the exact proportion of minority foreign ownership which is permissible.

Airlines constitute an important part of national security systems, and in many countries during times of war or other emergencies, private sector carriers (both air and sea) can be commandeered for military purposes in the interest of national security. The heinous acts of terror perpetrated on the United States on 11 September 2001 demonstrated the mischief that can be done even by private passenger aircraft when in wrong hands.

Airlines have been shown to be critical in times of national disaster; this was witnessed by the Asian countries when during the tsunami people had to be moved expeditiously by airlines under their own control. Caribbean and foreign governments have been able to call upon national carriers to make emergency flights to evacuate tourists and foreign students from countries hit by hurricanes as soon as it was safe to do so.

Apart from all this, the role of the airline industry in facilitating international tourism, world trade and diplomatic and international relations, generally, is self-evident; and its collapse on a global scale would take the world back into the Dark Ages. It is one of those industries which in the context of the worldwide economic meltdown of 2008 would be regarded as "too big to be permitted to fail" and would have to be bailed out by governments in defiance of existing market-driven philosophies.

If one applies the same arguments to a Caribbean situation, its geographical arrangements and its reliance on tourism, it is difficult to understand why so many people of apparently sound mind, both inside and outside the Caribbean, seem content that this region should depend solely on foreign companies for services which comprise its very lifeline.

Institutions like the World Bank have contributed to this line of thought. The World Bank has sought diligently to convince the Caribbean countries, which already own national or regional carriers, that they do not need to own an airline to have a successful tourism industry and that funds used for subsidies to keep them aloft would be better spent in other areas. To conclude, they should get rid of the ones they already have. Barbados and the Dominican Republic are prime examples proffered in the region for successful tourism industry despite not having any nationally owned airline; formerly both these nations had their own airlines but later closed them.

Unfortunately for that argument, in 2008, the Dominican Republic admitted that it made a mistake by closing its carrier. In March 2008, the Dominican Republic announced that in May 2008, its new airline, Air Dominicana, would begin operations, with flights to the United States, Mexico and South America, later expanding to other destinations. Government officials and business leaders stated that this was vital to the growth of their tourism. The executive vice president of the Association Nacional de Hoteles y Restaurantes (ASONAHORES), Arturo Villanueva, was quoted as saying that Air Dominicana will contribute remarkably to diversifying the tourism offer and increasing the number of visitors. The first plane, a Boeing 737, with a capacity of 180 passengers was scheduled to arrive in April 2008; and two others, a Boeing 737 and a Boeing 767, covering European routes would arrive by the end of 2008. The Government of Barbados owns close to 50 per cent of the shares in Leeward Islands Air Transport (LIAT) (1974) Limited, the major intra-regional carrier which provides lift for the Caribbean market, now of major importance to most Eastern Caribbean states.

The argument about ownership and control of the means of production in the Caribbean is an old one that extends far beyond air transportation. Most Caribbean countries have for hundreds of years survived by importing what they consume and many have been socialized to believe that foreigners always do everything better.

In earlier times a major issue with the tourism industry, on which the region became chronically dependent, was that it was an alien activity owned and managed by aliens in the interests of aliens. For a long time it was argued in the hospitality industry, that Caribbean people could not own or manage anything above a guest house or perform successfully in top management or specialist positions. Positions in the hospitality and tourism industry just above the entry levels were filled by the importation of labour.

Fortunately, the effluence of time, training and changed government policies and philosophies have, to a large extent, taken care of that situation. Few would now deny with respect to resort tourism, that Caribbean people, with Caribbean leadership, expertise and investment, must be counted among the greatest exponents of the skills required in the sector.

With respect to air transportation, an industry where there is a high rate of failure internationally, regional carriers like Air Jamaica, Bahamasair, British West Indian Airways (BWIA), Cayman Airways and LIAT have survived, not without difficulty, for periods of between forty and sixty years each, breaking international standards for longevity. They have been the bridges between Caribbean people and countries. It is now being suggested in this book, that before the region burns the bridges connecting its constituent parts, it should give the closest possible consideration to what it has achieved in the air transportation industry and to the human capital which its investments have created.

There are few businesses more difficult and complex than the airline industry. To operate a carrier, expertise and high-level skills are required in the areas of finance, maintenance, law, operations, information technology (IT), management, purchasing, human relations and industrial relations, industrial and other negotiations, buying and leasing aircraft, civil aviation, customer relations, press and public relations, reservations, sales, marketing and advertising, safety and security, pilots, ground handling, to name some. Over the years these skills have been honed at Caribbean carriers to the point where more than 90 per cent of employees are Caribbean nationals. If the region relied only on foreign carriers not only would these high-level skills be lost, but a number of high-paying jobs in the region would be lost as well.

But there is a great deal more; consideration needs to be given to the role of airlines as public transport, aerial infrastructure and contributors to the overall socio-economic development of the communities which they serve. Their benefits therefore cannot be assessed merely in terms of the colour of the bottom line on the balance sheet. This is not to say that the aim is not wherever possible to make a profit. But this cannot be the only yardstick by which the support necessary for their survival should be given. We need, therefore, to revisit the criteria by which we judge the return on investment with respect to our airlines.

None of the aforementioned is intended as an excuse for bad airline management by governments or even the Caribbean private airline sector. Regardless of who owns a carrier, there must be systems – at board and management levels – capable of monitoring financial and operational performance on an ongoing basis and of holding managers accountable. At the operational level, the skills of the locals must be equal to or better than those working with foreign carriers. Within these parameters, it should be possible to identify areas of inefficiency, mismanagement and any infelicitous financial practices, which must then be dealt with appropriately. Management must also be willing to take drastic and unpopular decisions, if necessary, to keep the airline operating. The main objective of management must be to increase revenues, reduce costs and drive customer loyalty through ever-improving and efficient customer service.

There can be no doubt that in the past, unrealistic expectations about the profitability of regional carriers were set up both among their shareholders and the public, only to disappoint them again and again. Governments which subsidize foreign carriers and almost every other aspect of their tourism industry with duty-free and tax-free regimes, have been made to feel a sense of misplaced guilt for subsidizing their own carriers. Regional airlines, left to struggle for long periods against impossible financial odds, have ended up with a mountain of accumulated debt and an annual haemorrhaging of cash, not necessarily because the management was poor, but because they were undercapitalized in the first place. This made it difficult to deal early and adequately with matters such as maintenance and fleet renewal, while being over-taxed and encouraged for social reasons to operate on a commercial basis in some routes that were not financially viable.

Given the role regional carriers play both economically and socially in the Caribbean Community (CARICOM) as a whole, it is suggested that if the time comes when any particular Caribbean government finds itself facing what seems impossible odds in keeping a carrier it now owns flying, CARICOM should be solicited to exhaust all other options in an effort to keep it in Caribbean hands before a foreign buyer is sought. This requires each member state to recognize the importance of owning some of the bridges over the community and to commit to meeting the costs of doing so.

# 2

# A Brief History of Air Jamaica, Bahamasair, BWIA/CAL, Cayman Airways and LIAT

It took hundreds of years for the Caribbean people to write about the history of sugar and slavery in their own countries. Far too little has been written about Caribbean tourism which since the 1960s has become the region's chief employer, earner of foreign exchange and government revenue. Even less is available in print about the history of air transportation and regional carriers although, judging from the extent to which they are daily discussed by the media and the public, their operations touch and affect the lives of a large number of people on a continuous basis.

This chapter therefore attempts to fill in some of the information gaps about the Caribbean carriers and to answer some of the questions often posed both by the travelling public and government officials. The brief historical account below focuses largely on Air Jamaica, BWIA, which was replaced by Caribbean Airlines Limited (CAL), and LIAT. It also provides information on Bahamasair and Cayman Airways. All five are government-owned carriers of the member states or associated member states of CARICOM.

# Historical Perspective

### Air Jamaica

In April 1969, Air Jamaica was launched with non-stop flights from Kingston and Montego Bay to New York and Miami. It was owned by the Government of Jamaica with a minority interest held by Air Canada. However, in 1980 it became wholly owned by the Jamaica government until the time it was privatized in November 1994.

Seventy per cent of the privatized airline was owned by the Air Jamaica Acquisition Group, comprising Jamaican business magnate Gordon "Butch" Stewart's interests, 25 per cent by the government, and 5 per cent by the employees.

The airline that was unveiled in November 1994 was a completely different airline from the government-owned carrier that existed before that date. The new owner, Gordon "Butch" Stewart, who had so successfully branded his Sandals hotel chain, applied the same magic to branding his airline. It was presented as a high-end product offering Lovebird hospitality, with a cabin champagne service and red-carpet counter service, intended to compete with, and surpass, the travel experience offered by the traditional legacy carriers serving the region.

It made a point of its *haute cuisine* prepared by special Jamaican chefs. It featured live fashion shows with Jamaican models on board. It claimed that its first-class service, designated "Top Class", was designed to offer passengers the ultimate luxury and comfort. Allen Chastanet (2003), vice president of marketing, declared, "While others within our industry are cutting services, we firmly believe that offering our passengers more than they expect can only enhance our reputation as the best airline to the Caribbean."

Air Jamaica prided itself on having the most modern fleet serving the region, and between 1994 and 2004, the fleet grew from nine to twenty. It made a clear decision about what kind of equipment it wanted and selected the Airbus. By 2003, Air Jamaica had four wide-body Airbus A-310s, ten A-320s, three A-321s, and three multi-class A-340s for the transatlantic routes to the United Kingdom and New York, with a total daily lift of over nine thousand seats.

Since Jamaica is a tourism-dependent country where the tourism industry earns more foreign exchange than all the other economic sectors combined together, it was no surprise that Air Jamaica positioned itself as the carrier that served the major tourism interests of Jamaica and other Caribbean countries.

While carrying ethnic traffic, it saw tourists as its major target market. It was said to carry 50 per cent of all arrivals to Jamaica and to contribute US$1 billion annually to the economy. Air Jamaica was owned by a man with an unsurpassed reputation for marketing, and every time a plane took to the skies, the airline was promoting Jamaica.

In support of the brand there was a powerful marketing and public relations campaign that kept both Air Jamaica and Jamaica before the eyes of the world. In this capacity it offered scheduled services with 330 direct flights a week from Atlanta, Baltimore/Washington, Boston, Chicago, Fort Lauderdale, Houston, Los Angeles, Miami, Newark, New York (JFK), Orlando and Philadelphia in the United States.

Air Jamaica provided more non-stop flights from its North-American Gateways to the Caribbean than any other carrier serving the region. It had also negotiated a code-share agreement with Delta Airlines and joint-fare arrangements and compatible schedules with United Airlines and other US carriers, thus extending its access to over 150 cities in the United States.

Air Jamaica also flew from London and Manchester in the United Kingdom to Kingston and Montego Bay in Jamaica and to Antigua, Barbados, Bonaire, Curaçao, Grand Cayman, Grenada, Nassau in the Bahamas, Providenciales in the Turks and Caicos Islands, Santo Domingo, and St Lucia.

The branding exercise could not be faulted and in many respects was reminiscent of that of Singapore Airlines. There was, however, a great difference; Singapore Airlines, which is also government owned, had access to very deep pockets whereas Air Jamaica did not. People saw money provided by the Jamaican government, not as an investment in Jamaica's tourism, but as a subsidy to a private entrepreneur. Air Jamaica's financial success did not therefore match its branding success. At the end of 2004, after sustaining major losses, private sector ownership reverted to ownership by the Government of Jamaica.

**Bahamasair**

Bahamasair, the national carrier of the Commonwealth of the Bahamas, came into being during the period of the energy crisis in 1974–75 when

British Airways stopped its service to the Bahamas and the government feared that other foreign carriers might also do the same. In fact, Pan American Airways had pulled out of the Bahamas in 1973. It was during this period that many of the foreign owners of large hotels in the Bahamas and Jamaica departed, leaving the governments to take over ownership simply to preserve jobs and keep the tourism industry going.

Like many Caribbean carriers, Bahamasair has had a turbulent history, both financially and operationally, and also had its fair share of industrial disputes with unions.

It provides service to four US destinations – Miami, Fort Lauderdale, West Palm Beach and Orlando – and to Jamaica, Dominican Republic, and the Turks and Caicos Islands. Domestically it also provides service to many islands of the Bahamas. It has a fleet of eleven aircraft which includes Boeing 737 jets and some turboprops.

Again there are ongoing discussions in the Bahamas about whether or not the government should sell or close the carrier which clearly provides a critical service to Bahamians in spite of all its difficulties. These are discussed in detail in chapter 13.

**BWIA/CAL**

BWIA was started by Lowell Yerex, a New Zealander, in 1940 and later taken over by British South American Airways (BSAA) in 1947. In 1949, BSAA merged with British Overseas Airways Corporation (BOAC) and BWIA became a subsidiary of BOAC.

In 1961, the Government of Trinidad and Tobago acquired most of the shares of BWIA from BOAC and owned the airline outright in 1967. In 1980 the airline merged with Trinidad and Tobago Air Services and became BWIA International.

In 1995, BWIA was privatized and the majority control turned over to a private group of US and Caribbean investors. At the beginning of 2000 BWIA was renamed BWIA West Indies Limited.

At the end of 2004 it was taken back from the private sector by the Government of Trinidad and Tobago which, at the end of 2006, closed its operations and replaced it by Caribbean Airlines, which is also government owned.

Trinidad and Tobago, in spite of Tobago's specific tourism orientation, is a state with oil and gas production as its largest industry and has an economy that is largely based on its manufacturing sector. In fact, for many years Trinidad, as opposed to Tobago, did not wish to be in any way associated with tourism. It treated BWIA, its former national carrier, largely as an instrument of ethnic and business travel, even if this point of view was not a publicly declared policy.

A review of BWIA's advertising revealed an emphasis on warmth, friendliness, familiarity and coming home. Unlike Air Jamaica, it never positioned itself as a luxury tourism airline product.

Before its closure, BWIA was carrying about 1.4 million passengers annually and significant amount of cargo, some 8,100 tons a year. At one time, BWIA served New York, Washington, Miami, Toronto, Manchester, London, with service to and from Trinidad and Tobago, Barbados, St Lucia, Jamaica, Antigua, St Maarten, and Suriname. More recently it operated a service to Costa Rica in Central America which was thought to have been dictated more by a strategy to strengthen Trinidad and Tobago's bid to be selected as the headquarters of the Free Trade Area of the Americas than to develop an additional tourism market in Central America.

The tourism policy has changed in recent years and Trinidad, like Tobago, has declared its commitment to tourism development as a major economic sector. It recognized that although oil and gas earn significant revenues, unlike tourism, they are not major employers of labour.

Ironically, it is Barbados and the Eastern Caribbean countries which have traditionally seen BWIA as their tourism carrier. Before its closure, BWIA was the largest carrier of passengers to Barbados. Those who based their arguments that a country does not have to own an airline to have a successful tourism industry and point to Barbados as proof are not, in reality, correct. Barbados's national (international) carrier was BWIA and under the CARICOM Community Principle it had been so designated.

It is not by accident that BWIA's commercial department was for many years located in Barbados. It is understandable, therefore, that when BWIA was shut down at the end of 2006 by the Government of Trinidad and Tobago and replaced by Caribbean Airlines, which cut several routes without consulting the governments of Barbados and the Eastern Caribbean, those countries were somewhat annoyed.

Over sixty-five years of its existence, BWIA's fleet has comprised a range of equipment: Lockheed Lodestar, converted Hudson Bombers, Vickers Viking, DC Dakota, Vickers Viscount, Boeing 727-100, Boeing

707-138, Boeing 707-227, Boeing 707-320, Douglas DC-9-50, Hawker Siddeley 748, Lockheed L 1011-500, McDonnell Douglas MD 83, Boeing 737-700, Boeing 737-800 and Bombardier Dash 8-300. In August 2006 the fleet comprised two A 340-300s and six 737-800s while Tobago Express operated five Dash 8s.

A wide range of equipment has many implications for maintenance, spares, pilot training, leasing arrangements and other operational aspects and an important question therefore arises: To what extent did this mix of equipment over the years negatively affect BWIA's operations and financial performance?

The view has been strongly advanced that in spite of their considerable dependence on BWIA's international services, Barbados and the other Eastern Caribbean States did not have to share BWIA's costs because the Government of Trinidad and Tobago has always preferred to own and manage the airline itself.

Whatever the accuracy of this view may be, it is arguable that the success of any future relationship between CAL, BWIA's successor, and any other Caribbean carrier will depend on whether it is seen as a genuine collaborative effort between equals, as opposed to an association between Trinidad and Tobago and suppliant Caribbean states.

As noted earlier, BWIA was replaced by CAL which began operations on 1 January 2007 as a carrier wholly owned by the Government of Trinidad and Tobago. CAL's performance since its establishment is discussed in chapter 13.

**Cayman Airways**

Cayman Airways is the national carrier of the Cayman Islands which is an associated member state of CARICOM. It was established and started flying on 7 August 1968. It was formed following the Cayman government's purchasing of 51 per cent of Cayman Brac Airways from Lineas Aereas Costarricenses S.A., the Costa Rican airline and became wholly government owned in December 1977. Apart from serving Cayman Brac, Grand Cayman and Little Cayman, it operates flights to Havana (Cuba), Honduras, Panama, Jamaica (Kingston and Montego Bay), and to O'Hare Airport (Chicago), Miami, New York, Orlando, Tampa, and Washington D.C in the United States. Its fleet comprises four Boeing 737-300 and two

DHC-6 Twin Otters. Throughout its existence arguments have raged in the Cayman Islands for and against keeping the airline which has consistently lost money, estimated in 2008 at about US$20 million.

## LIAT

LIAT stands for Leeward Islands Air Transport, a name that has long ceased to represent its reality. It began flying in 1956 as a small private airline with a single Piper Apache aircraft between Antigua and Montserrat. It was based in Montserrat and owned by Frank S. Delisle, later Sir Frank. It now flies to twenty-two destinations in the Caribbean and very much serves as the national carrier of Barbados and the Organisation of Eastern Caribbean States (OECS) territories which are among the world's most tourism-dependent states.

In 1957, BWIA owned 75 per cent of LIAT but sold it in 1971 to the British conglomerate Court Line. During this period, at least initially, no expense was spared by Court Line, even down to Mary Quant designer dresses for the cabin crew. LIAT began to expand its fleet and jet services were added.

Largely due to difficulties from the energy crisis of 1974–75, Court Line went bankrupt in 1974. LIAT was left with no financial resources and many of the islands served by LIAT faced the possibility of no air service. LIAT's employees experienced considerable insecurity as they faced the prospect of unemployment. A number of loans were negotiated, one with the British government, and in 1974 eleven CARICOM governments, including Jamaica, agreed to take equity participation in the carrier and LIAT Limited was born in 1974.

The 1980s witnessed a period of LIAT's route expansion, flying passengers and cargo to an increased number of Caribbean destinations.

Few airlines have had closer relationships than BWIA and LIAT. But difficulties beset the BWIA–LIAT relationship because after 1974, those who owned the two carriers had entirely different concepts of what the relationship should be; BWIA, the former owner of LIAT saw LIAT largely as its connecting service, feeding passengers to itself and other international carriers serving long-haul routes. These passengers were largely tourists, connecting from Caribbean destinations and travelling to markets in North America and Europe. This kind of relationship could easily have been established when BWIA owned LIAT and could plan an integrated service for the two, either as separate entities, or as one merged carrier. It is a concept that seems to have existed in Trinidad and Tobago since 1957, but is unlikely to be acceptable in 2009 to the owners of LIAT.

Barbados and the Eastern Caribbean countries, even those which are not shareholders in LIAT, have had an entirely different view of the BWIA/LIAT relationship from that held by Trinidad and Tobago. The OECS countries and Barbados recognize that LIAT has a very important role to play as a feeder service, hence the importance placed on striving to maintain the interlining arrangements between the intra-regional carrier and the long-haul international carriers. In fact, for the OECS countries, like Dominica and St Vincent and the Grenadines, which do not as yet have international airports, providing connections for their international visitors is one of LIAT's key functions.

But for the Eastern Caribbean countries, LIAT is much more than a connecting service for international carriers. It is something like the bus service between the countries of the Eastern Caribbean; currently, the bridge that connects nine countries of the community, except the Bahamas, Belize, Haiti, Jamaica and Suriname; part of the foundation on which the Caribbean Single Market and Economy must be built. It is a fundamental part of the infrastructure of these countries and it is important to hold that thought.

LIAT is often seen as a small carrier when compared to other airlines operating large equipment, which fly into the Caribbean. Since its establishment, it has used Avros, nineteen-seater turboprops, Dash 8s-100s (thirty-seven passengers) and Dash 8-300s (fifty passengers) which are more cost efficient for the network which it serves and more suited to land and take off at some of the small airports than the jets used by others.

The reality, however, is that although its largest planes carry only fifty passengers, even before concluding commercial arrangements with Caribbean Star in February 2007, it had a fleet of twelve planes which made more than hundred landings every day in twenty-one Caribbean countries. By the end of 2007, the combined LIAT–Caribbean Star fleet had grown to seventeen planes and the daily departures to 150. The fleet in 2009 has eighteen Dash 8s serving twenty-two destinations. The destinations served are the following: Anguilla, Antigua, Barbados, Canouan, Curaçao, Dominica, Dominican Republic, Grenada, Guadeloupe, Guyana, Martinique, Nevis,

Puerto Rico, St Croix, St Kitts, St Lucia, St Maarten, St Thomas, St Vincent and the Grenadines, Tortola, and Trinidad and Tobago. Antigua, Barbados and Trinidad are hubs. It operates charter services as well as Quikpak, an express small package service, with pickup and delivery available, to all the LIAT destinations plus Montserrat and Carriacou.

From a tourism perspective, Barbados is the largest tourist-receiving country in the Eastern Caribbean. People are always surprised to learn that of all the air services flying into Barbados every week, LIAT was, before the closure of BWIA at the end of 2006, the second largest airline in terms of passengers carried to that country. It had nineteen departures each day from Barbados alone. Since the closure of BWIA and its replacement by Caribbean Airlines which operates fewer routes than BWIA, the largest carrier to Barbados in terms of carriage of passengers is LIAT.

LIAT has always been, in every sense, the Caribbean airline, owned by Caribbean shareholders, largely governments at this time, and flying intra-Caribbean routes. Only 25 per cent of the 750,000 persons that LIAT carried every year before 2007 were connecting passengers from outside the region. Seventy-five per cent of its travellers comprised Caribbean people and other residents going about their daily business of trade and commerce, government and other meetings and conferences, vacation and recreation of various kinds, family visits, education and health matters, sports, securing visas and so on. These proportions did not change a great deal with the coming of the LIAT–Caribbean Star commercial relationship that commenced on 1 February 2007 and ended with the purchase of Caribbean Star's assets in October 2007.

In 2007, LIAT which operated as a separate company in spite of the commercial relationship with Caribbean Star, carried 708,242 passengers as compared with CAL's 849,298; and in 2008, after acquiring Caribbean Star's assets, it carried 1,036,308 passengers as compared with CAL's 1,600,000.

During the twenty years between 1974 and 1994, as with Air Jamaica and BWIA, ownership of LIAT had moved from public to private shareholders and back again without much noticeable change in its performance. In 2004, only three of the shareholder governments which had rescued LIAT in 1974 remained. These were the governments of Antigua and Barbuda, Barbados, and St Vincent and the Grenadines. They too seemed to be suffering from a certain shareholder burnout, but were fully seized of the importance of the carrier, from both an economic and social perspective, and therefore of the need to take all possible steps to help it to survive.

The intensity of the debate in all the territories about governments owning airlines, regarding the quality of the service they offer and the public funds invested in them for capital purposes or as subsidies, suggests that major philosophical differences exist in the society about the role and purpose of airlines in Caribbean countries which are known to be four times more dependent on tourism for their socio-economic development than any other region in the world.

The question that must be asked and answered by this book is why, in spite of all the debate about air transportation and the criticisms constantly levelled at regionally owned carriers, the only major Caribbean carriers which have survived in the region are those owned by the Caribbean governments. In 2009, they had together provided 237 years of unbroken service in air transportation.

In chapter 3 an attempt is made to compare the financial and operational performance of Caribbean and international carriers and to demonstrate how Caribbean carriers match up. Moreover, it will be seen that Caribbean carriers are quite often criticized for following practices which are in fact industry standards.

# 3

# A Comparison of the Operational and Financial Performance of Caribbean and Major International Carriers

It was refreshing to hear one of the region's celebrated journalists say that most of the media coverage about regional carriers is negative and they deserve better due to the service they have offered and the role they have played in developing the Caribbean over several decades. The criticisms have covered both operational and financial performance.

This chapter seeks to demonstrate that Caribbean carriers in terms of their performance do not suffer particularly by comparison with foreign international carriers which often escape the attention of local critics.

Like all Caribbean icons, regional airlines can be said to suffer from a love–hate relationship which Caribbean people reserve for their special people and things, although no attempt is being made here to pretend that the carriers have not often been at fault. It is, however, worth saying throughout this book that they do a difficult job, in difficult circumstances, and in fairness to all other airlines operators globally, to put it on the record that few enterprises are more difficult or complex to manage than air transportation companies.

With respect to operational issues, the complaints most often received by, and about, Caribbean carriers are related to poor on-time performance, cancellations, loss of baggage, poor customer service, a lack of schedule integrity, failure to work closely with each other and other inefficiencies. These conditions are often held to be exacerbated by government ownership of the carriers. They will all be addressed in the rest of this chapter.

## On-time Performance of Caribbean Carriers

On-time arrivals and departures and delivery of baggage are important indicators of an airline's efficiency. Historically, in spite of spurts of excellence, Caribbean carriers have not excelled in these areas and it is therefore not surprising that LIAT has been said to mean "Leave Islands Any Time" and BWIA, "Better Walk if Able" or "Better Wait in Airport". Air Jamaica, although no less culpable than the others, seems to have escaped this cynical use of its acronym, probably because the name "Air Jamaica" has so far defeated the creative imagination of even Caribbean people.

Both on-time performance and baggage delivery improvements are areas now being focused on by all the carriers with some success. But the public is due an explanation of why sometimes things go wrong in these areas for reasons other than bad management or employee inefficiency. The LIAT experience that follows is intended to be illustrative.

LIAT has peculiar challenges and here an attempt is being made to get a better understanding by the travelling public of what they are; it operates an inter-connected network of more than 150 relatively short flights a day; and if a few flights go wrong, it is easy to have a domino effect throughout the system. LIAT has been able to establish that the engines of its own Dash 8s, because of its schedules and routing system, work harder than any other fleet of Dash 8s anywhere in the world. However, these planes have proven over many years to be fuel efficient, safe and extremely reliable.

It is obvious, however, but nevertheless worth saying, that if a plane demonstrates any kind of maintenance defect before take-off, it has to be grounded or the flight cancelled until the problem is fixed. Unlike ground transport it cannot be pulled to the side of the road and fixed or changed. The disruption in service causes disappointment and even anger among passengers who have been inconvenienced, but the company cannot afford to take chances where people's safety is involved.

Some problems have to do with infrastructural or logistical issues at the airports over which the carrier often has no control. Serving the island of Dominica presents a good example of this; flights departing, for example, from Antigua to Dominica have, for good logistical reasons, to be scheduled to connect with passengers arriving from external markets in the afternoon. If there is a delay in take-off because the in-coming connecting flight is late, or for reasons of maintenance or weather, then ultimately the flight cannot go because it could be judged unsafe to land in Dominica where, at present, no night landing is possible. On a bad weather day, flights may have to bypass Dominica altogether, leaving disgruntled passengers both in the plane and on the ground.

Sometimes problems are caused by industrial action by persons whose work affects airline operations, but who are not the airline's employees. A good example of this is industrial action by airport security personnel or air traffic control staff.

Some of the delays experienced by the carriers have been due to increased security and the introduction of new security arrangements. It is worth noting that security arrangements now in place internationally, such as the Advance Passenger Information System, which requires passenger information to be collected during check-in and sent in advance of arrival can lead to delays at the counter. These delays have, however, been reduced by the acquisition of machine-readable passports and the installation of passport-readable machines at counters, which enable passengers' data to be collected more quickly than information collected manually. It should be noted that the Caribbean has not yet added those additional security measures to be found at several international airports, such as the taking of passenger fingerprints and photographs, which further lengthens the check-in process.

## Baggage Issues in the Caribbean

There are few things more annoying to a passenger than to arrive and find the baggage has been delayed or lost. In LIAT's case, the fact that it makes many short hops between several destinations increases the chances of mishandling the baggage. By changing its routing systems to more direct flights in 2006, LIAT was able to demonstrate significant improvements both in its punctuality and baggage delivery. Regretably, there was some slippage in 2007 for reasons related to some of the operational complexities that emerged during merger arrangements with Caribbean Star.

There are also problems related to the transfer of baggage from large international aircraft arriving at hubs, such as Antigua and Barbados, to the much smaller planes operated by LIAT, when passengers are transferred beyond the hub to off-line destinations. Many of those passengers would have boarded large aircraft, for example, in London, after checking in more than one piece of baggage. A first-class passenger may have checked as many as three pieces of baggage of 70 pounds each. The Dash 8 to which passenger and baggage is transferred will have only fifty seats and baggage capacity to accommodate fifty bags of 50 pounds each. If the LIAT plane has a full load of passengers, it is likely that with the extra baggage from the larger planes, there will be more baggage than can be safely carried on the Dash 8. The passenger boarding in London probably would not have been advised about the challenge he is likely to face with the baggage when he is transiting the hub after arriving at the first stop in the Caribbean. It then becomes LIAT's problem: Should it carry all the international baggage and leave that of local Caribbean travellers behind? Whatever it does is fraught with problems and attracts criticism.

When, before taking over the assets of Caribbean Star, LIAT was flying with poor passenger loads, a great deal more baggage could be put on flights. But it became a victim of its own success from 2007. This is a difficult problem to solve. Having larger aircraft would not necessarily solve all its problems, since some airports in the countries it serves cannot accommodate larger aircraft.

An interim solution considered was to fly a companion baggage plane when the loads are heavy, or to convert a few planes into a combination format, where part of the passenger cabin is configured to carry additional baggage.

There is another, though not a frequent scenario, where baggage has to be left behind in certain islands because, due to high cross winds, the plane cannot take off with a full load of passengers and baggage. In such cases a decision may be made to carry all the passengers and leave some baggage behind. Passengers claim that, more often than not, their complaint is that ground staff serving LIAT does not adequately communicate to them that the baggage is being left behind and the reason for it. There can be no excuse for this.

Sometimes the staff rendering the service directly to the customer is not under the control of the airline, but is employed by another company altogether.

Explanations are not meant to be justifications. They are given to impart information that might not otherwise be known. Nor is it intended to suggest that the carrier is totally free from blame. Whatever the cause of the problem, disappointed passengers will be inclined to hold the airline, with which they have a contract to provide service, responsible. It therefore has to come up with answers and solutions.

Perhaps, ultimately, it has to be conceded that flying is a stressful business and when both the passenger and the counter staff have had difficult days, there is a temptation for tempers to flare. It is then that the professionalism and training of staff or lack of it show. They must be able to keep a cool head and be empathetic even when confronted by difficult passengers.

## Operational Performance of International Carriers

All too often the problems of airline passengers detailed earlier are spoken of, both by Caribbean people and by visitors to the region, as though they do not occur with carriers other than those from the Caribbean or some other developing country. It is for that reason that the operational experiences of major international airlines and airports are shared later with the reader, so that there is a better understanding of the extent to which airlines around the world and their passengers have similar problems to those experienced by Caribbean carriers.

### Baggage

The book *Air Babylon* (2005), speaking of loss of baggage in England, states that while at most international airports on average two bags are lost in every thousand, at Heathrow, London, it is about eighty per thousand – some due to carelessness and some due to theft.

In April 2008, due to the problems following the launch of the £4.3 billion facility at the British Airports Authority's Terminal 5, British press reports spoke of "a national humiliation" in relation to the airport. Some of the blunders listed included the following:

- Lack of car parking space for baggage handlers
- Shortage of a British Airports Authority security staff to let baggage handlers into the terminal
- A programming "human error' that meant that staff could not log into the baggage handling computer when they finally got into the terminal building
- Inadequate training that meant baggage handlers did not know where they were supposed to go to take suitcases off the conveyor belts and out to the gates
- A breakdown of the transit system that is supposed to move passengers from the main Terminal 5 building to the satellite terminal 5B

Only two of twenty-six customer desks were open and British Airways announced that it was cancelling one-fifth of its flights. Hundreds of passengers were forced to sleep at the terminal after waiting for their luggage for up to six hours. All this had a negative impact on the airline's shares which were marked down 3 per cent, wiping £90 million off the carrier's value. In 2009, passengers were still complaining about problems at Terminal 5.

**On-time Performance**

In August 2006, British Midland Airways (BMI), for reasons which may be guessed at, published punctuality ratings for major carriers (with number 1 being best, and number 18 being worst) as follows:

1. BMI
2. Aer Lingus
3. KLM
4. Singapore Airlines
5. Finnair
6. Lufthansa
7. Cathay Pacific
8. Austrian Airlines
9. United Airlines
10. Swiss Airlines
11. Scandinavian SAS
12. Alitalia
13. Air France
14. American Airlines
15. CSA
16. Malaysian Airlines
17. LOT Polish
18. British Airways

An interesting footnote is that by November 2008, BMI was taken over by the German carrier Lufthansa and announced the closure of all its international flights, including those to the Caribbean, after March 2009.

In the United States, air transportation also had its share of operational problems in 2007 and well into 2008.

In September 2007, the *Wall Street Journal* carried an article recording that for two months in that summer, American carriers lost one million bags.

## Annual Airline Quality Report (US)

Brent Bowen of the University of Nebraska at the Omaha's Aviation Institute was quoted as saying of 2007 "it was the worst year ever for US airlines. Overall operational performance and quality declined to the lowest level that it's ever been".

According to the report, the industry posted declines in every area of the airline quality rating, amid rising fuel prices, safety problems and bankruptcy filings that shut down three carriers in one week in April 2008 alone. ATA Airlines, Aloha Airlines and Skybus stopped flying in early April 2008 because of financial pressures. On-time arrivals dropped for the fifth straight year, with more than a quarter of all flights delayed. The rates of passengers bumped from overbooked flights; and bags lost, stolen or damaged also jumped in 2007. Major airlines slashed jobs and passenger amenities while adding fees for second bags, travelling with pets and booking tickets by phone. Air Tran and Jet Blue took the top spots in the national survey of airline quality. Frontier, Northwest, Skywest, Southwest, United and US Airways showed declines in every area in the survey, although Southwest had the best on-time arrivals mark at 80.1 per cent.

The Annual Airline Quality Report released in Washington, DC, US, in April 2008, found that, overall, the industry did a poor job in 2007. There were more lost bags, more bumped passengers, more consumer complaints and fewer on-time flights than in 2006. The rate of consumer complaints in 2007 was up by 60 per cent, with US Airways having the most, and Southwest, the fewest.

On 15 April 2008, American Airline pilots were filmed demonstrating with placards at the American Airlines terminal at Los Angeles International Airport to call attention to the fact that American Airlines was placed last in the ranking among all network carriers for on-time performance.

In 2008, Southwest was accused of flying forty-six planes on 59,791 flights without performing mandatory inspections for fuselage cracks. The planes were mostly Boeing 737s and carried some 145,000 passengers. The matter became the subject of a Capitol Hill hearing. At that hearing on Thursday, 3 April 2008, head of the Federal Aviation Administration's safety division, Nicolas Sabatini, was told that his agency's performance was woeful, but he countered it by claiming that they had achieved 99 per cent safety compliance. It was decided in 2009 that Southwest would pay a fine of US$7.5 million.

In 2008, the Southwest issue led to a demand for comprehensive safety airline checks which grounded hundreds of airline services in the United States.

On 10 April 2008, American Airlines cancelled more than nine hundred flights to fix faulty wiring in hundreds of jets, marking the third straight day of mass groundings. Between Tuesday, 8 April and Friday, 11 April 2008, the airline had cancelled about thirty-one hundred flights after federal regulators warned that nearly half of American Airlines' fleet could violate safety regulations designed to prevent fires. This meant that a quarter of a million passengers were inconvenienced in one week alone.

The problems arose on the MD-80 jets, and other carriers operating similar aircraft left passengers scrambling for alternative means of travelling. Cancellations also occurred at Alaska Airlines, Midwest Airlines and Delta Airlines; and it was feared that further dislocations could follow.

In March 2009, the Air Transport Users Council reported that 30 million bags were misplaced by airlines in 2005, 34 million in 2006, 42 million in 2007, of which 1.2 million were irretrievably lost. It was being projected that the number of bags mishandled could grow to 70 million by 2019.

The preceding reports underline the sort of difficulties which all airlines face from time to time in what has to be the world's most challenging and stressful business.

## Caribbean Carriers' Financial Performance

Financial performance is the other area where Caribbean carriers have been heavily criticized. No one can deny that they have had a history of losses. The assumption on the part of the public nearly always is that this is because they are badly managed, and worse because they are owned by governments and managed by boards appointed by governments, presumably for all the wrong reasons.

What is often ignored, however, is the following: the private sector is often well represented on the boards of Caribbean government owned carriers; the same carriers have, at various times, been owned and managed by both local and foreign private sector entrepreneurs under whose stewardship the carriers' financial performance was the same or worse than under government ownership. Moreover, when under private sector ownership and management, they continued to need and to receive government subsidies.

It seems therefore a better approach would be to analyse why the losses were incurred, whatever the type of ownership, and once again to compare how international carriers across the world have fared financially over several years.

**Caribbean Airline Losses**

Below a look is taken first at the losses of the government-owned carriers – Air Jamaica, Bahamasair, BWIA, CAL, Cayman Airways and LIAT Airline – and then at Caribbean Star and Caribbean Sun, the privately owned Caribbean carriers.

*Air Jamaica's Losses*

In 1994, when public ownership first gave way to private ownership, Air Jamaica's accumulated debt was reported to be approximately US$131.8 million. Between the mid-1990s and 2004, under the private ownership of the Air Jamaica Acquisition Group, Air Jamaica reported losses totalling US$699 million, although government had made equity advances of close to US$400 million to the carrier. In 2004, the last year of private sector ownership, the carrier lost US$99 million. In 2005, the year in which Air Jamaica was returned to public sector ownership, it reported losses of US$131.5 million after receiving a government grant of US$21 million. In 2006, it lost US$128.4 million and received a government grant of US$27.7 million. In 2007, it lost US$171 million, with an interest subsidy of US$44.71 million and a government grant of US$25.41 million. At 2008, the carrier's losses were projected in the press to be likely to reach US$200 million and the accumulated debt was being put at US$1.1 billion.

## Bahamasair Losses

Bahamasair's losses are estimated to have been some US$86,222,701 for the three-year period 1999–2001, with the largest yearly loss being US$35,147,131 for the period ending 31 June 2001. For the period 2002 to 2007, losses were estimated at an average of some US$11 million per year.

In December 2007, it was reported that Bahamasair had an accumulated deficit of US$397.9 million and at the end of 2006 had sustained losses of US$19.9 million. In June 2008, after thirty-five years of operation and realizing no profit, the Government of the Bahamas decided to limit the annual injection of cash into Bahamasair to US$28 million, according to a statement in the House of Assembly made by the tourism and aviation minister, the Hon. Neko Grant.

## Cayman Island Airways Losses

Cayman Airways, after thirty-seven years, is yet to turn a profit, and its losses are in tens of millions of dollars. It has pragmatically recognized that the carrier is unlikely to make a profit, but is performing an essential service, and its operations will have to be subsidized. The only official discussion every year seems to be about the size of the annual subsidy and what relationship it bears to the overall financial performance of the tourism industry. This is not an unreasonable position to take, if one understands the role of regional carriers in the Caribbean tourism industry, which on an annual basis, attracts more than US$21 billion in tourist expenditure to the region.

## BWIA's Losses

BWIA's cheif executive officer (CEO), Peter Davies, speaking at a meeting of the Caribbean Tourism Organization (CTO) in Grand Bahama, in October 2006, said that in its sixty-six years, BWIA had only made a profit on three occasions, and added that in the past several years it had lost

US$30 million to US$35 million annually. He projected, however, that it was set to record a loss of US$50 million in 2006.

## Caribbean Airlines

The cost to the Government of Trinidad and Tobago for closing down BWIA at the beginning of 2007, and replacing it by CAL, fully capitalized, completely free of debt and still government owned, is estimated at over TT$3 billion.

On 29 July 2009, outgoing CEO of CAL, Philip Saunders, was reported by the Trinidad press as saying that CAL had made a profit of US$6.9 million at the end of 2007 (before formation, structuring and transition costs) and having committed to reach a breakeven point in 2008, had actually made a net profit at the end of that year. He gave the number of passengers carried in 2008 as 1.6 million.

## LIAT Losses

By 2004, LIAT had an accumulated debt of some EC$311 million (US$115 million). In 2005, LIAT incurred an operating loss of EC$33,976,828 (US$12,584,010). In 2006, the operating loss was EC$61,470,413 (US$22,766,819), and the operating loss in 2007 was EC$4,695,297 (US$1,738,998). In this year two events took place which were life changing for the carrier; it took over the assets of its rival Caribbean Star and received an investment of US$60 million from its three shareholder governments which went to pay off its accumulated debt and severance payments. Clearly, this is a story to be told at greater length later in this book.

In 2008, it made an operating profit of EC$2,016,753 (US$746,945) while airlines all over the world were recording heavy losses and even going out of business. Up to May 2009, it seemed set to make a small profit by the end of 2009, but considerable dislocations in its service and heavy costs due to industrial action in July and August, normally the highest revenue earning months, seemed likely to derail that achievement.

## Caribbean Star and Caribbean Sun Losses

The scale of losses of the privately owned regional carriers is much the same as that of those publicly owned, and in some cases even greater.

The cumulative losses of Caribbean Star and Caribbean Sun – owned by Texas billionaire, Sir Allen Stanford – over six and three years, respectively, were estimated at about US$156,296,629, probably twice those of LIAT.

## Financial Performance of International Air Transportation

Having seen the haemorrhaging of cash by Caribbean carriers, we need to now examine how international air carriers, particularly in Asia, Europe and North America, have been performing financially, during the period 2001–9, and how this compares with that of Caribbean carriers. Many of the problems with air transportation began soon after the horrific terrorist events of 9/11, but it will be seen that from as early as 2005, the rising costs of fuel is the major negative factor in airline financial performance everywhere.

**The Fuel Factor**

In 2005, according to Giovanni Bisignani, director general of the International Air Transport Association (IATA), the global airline industry faced a loss of US$6 billion, its fifth successive year of net losses. The fuel bill accounted for 22 per cent of the industry's total costs and jumped by US$39 billion in two years. These remarks were being made when oil had reached a price of US$67 a barrel.

Hedging, or buying forward, has been the mechanism used by prudent airlines to protect themselves against future fuel hikes. The financial success of U.S carrier, Southwest Airline, for example, has been greatly helped by its foresight in hedging long before the crisis of fuel prices reached its zenith in 2008.

In June 2005, however, *British Airways News* reported that, "the cost of hedging jet fuel for the next five years is near record high levels in Europe, threatening more pain for airlines in 2006. It is currently more expensive for airlines to buy jet fuel for delivery in 2006, than it is to buy fuel for use now. Prices for transport fuels are being driven by rising global demand, led by China and by a lack of spare refining capacity for distillation products like diesel, heating oil and jet fuel."

The price of fuel for the first quarter of 2006 was estimated at US$67 per barrel. In August 2005, Jim Rodgers, US commodities guru, had predicted that the price of fuel would eventually soar to more than US$100 per barrel, a prediction which at the time seemed unrealistic. Goldman Sachs, one of the biggest financial traders in the commodities market, expressed the view in 2005 that the price of oil would not fall below US$60 in the next five years.

In January 2006, analysts were predicting that if the nuclear dispute between the West and Iran dragged on, raising the possibility of Iran cutting production, oil prices could top US$70 per barrel, which then seemed an astronomical figure. By May 2006, a barrel of oil reached a high of US$74 and by July 14, it had reached US$78.40 and headed for US$80. By October 2007, it was over US$90. By July 2008, it had reached US$147.

Of course, the best of predictions can go wrong, especially about the price of oil. A number of airlines, like United Airlines, which hedged against rising oil prices, found in the fall period of 2006 that they were paying more for fuel than those who did not hedge. Against all the odds, the price of oil fell in October 2006 below US$60 per barrel.

In June 2008, with oil at more than US$130 per barrel, Giovanni Bisignani of IATA said that airlines faced a loss of £3 billion in 2008 unless oil prices turned. He said, "The situation is desperate and potentially more destructive than our recent battles with all the Horsemen of the Apocalypse combined. Over the past six months 24 airlines have gone out of business."

## Overall Net Losses

What can be said with certainty is that global airline cumulative net losses reached US$43 billion in the five-year period from 2001 to 2005. US carriers had net losses of US$9.1 billion in 2004 and were unable to hedge their fuel requirements significantly because of their weak finances and low credit rating.

Efficiency gains could not make up for structural problems in the United States, where labour costs remained high and low-cost competition had continued to drive down yields or average fares at leading hubs. Losses in 2005 were US$10 billion and although US carriers were able to shave some

US$15 billion in costs, it was predicted that they would need to shave a further US$10 billion.

In September 2005, Delta Airlines and Northwest Airlines joined a long list of US carriers seeking sanctuary from creditors under the US system of Chapter 11 bankruptcy protection. North West, which was losing about US$3.9 million per day, sought to reduce its costs by asking its employees to give back some US$1.3 billion in compensation and benefits. Delta only emerged from bankruptcy in 2007.

United Airlines, America's second largest carrier was there already. Its new strategy was to shift more capacity into international routes and to become a serious player in Caribbean air services.

US Airways which went into bankruptcy in 2001, soon after 9/11, came out in March 2003 and returned in September 2004. Internal costs weighed them down, with massive wage bills and commitments to pension funds proving difficult to meet.

If one looks at the losses of some of Air Jamaica's direct competitors, we see that in 2005, Delta's losses were US$3.8 billion, American Airlines US$861 million, US Airways US$537 million and Spirit US$110 million, for a total of US$5.3 billion.

Fortunately for US and Canadian carriers, Chapter 11, or some version of it, permits these companies to pay a fraction of their debts, while they keep trading and restructuring and convincing unions and employees of the need for severe pay cuts, layoffs and scaling back commitments to pension funds. By 2005, more than 50 per cent of American carriers by seat capacity were legally bankrupt.

In Latin America, where low-cost carriers (LCCs) like Brazilian carriers TAM and GOL were doing well, the majority of legacy carriers were technically bankrupt. In July 2006, the national carrier of Brazil, Varig, after sixty-seven years, was in serious trouble and there were fears that it might not be saved.

In 2005, European airlines saw a profit of US$1.4 billion, largely due to the success of the European LCCs, the severe pruning of costs of legacy carriers like British Airways and consolidation, like that between KLM and Air France which has helped capacity management.

In 2005, Asia Pacific carriers also saw a profit of US$2.6 billion, by having the competitive advantage of low labour costs, expanding economies in places like China, and high volume of passengers.

## Questions and Answers

We have seen the financial performance of both Caribbean and international carriers. Clearly, there are some international stars which have stood out before 2008, especially among the LCCs. But for the period 2001 to 2009, the majority of the international legacy carriers have turned in a financial performance which is certainly no better than those in the Caribbean.

This history of losses raises a number of important and relevant questions about the carriers. Are they simply badly managed or is it difficult to find a business model that works for an entity that people refuse to accept as a part of the infrastructural services?

If we were speaking only of Caribbean carriers the knee jerk reaction from many would be that bad management is the cause. The widespread nature of the problem, however, suggests the need for closer examination of the viability of different types of international air transportation and a differentiation of the various causes at work. Of particular interest is the evolution of the low-cost/low-fare carrier about which much has been written since the 1980s and which are often seen as the solution for air transportation in the Caribbean. Chapter 9 deals in more detail with the history of the LCC, but some of their basic operational characteristics is as follows.

**The Legacy versus the Low-Cost-Carrier Model**

From 2001 to 2009, several of the major legacy carriers, especially those in North America, have been in and out of bankruptcy. Serious questions have therefore to be asked about the sustainability of the legacy carrier model used by carriers like American Airlines, British Airways, Lufthansa, Delta and indeed by the Caribbean carriers. They operate hub and spoke networks covering extensive geographical areas both domestically and internationally, and are burdened by expensive collective union agreements, provident and pension funds, expensive distribution systems, generally speaking cater to different cabin classes, fly from expensive international airports and so on, and find it more and more difficult to compete with low-cost, low-fare, no-frills, non-unionized carriers which were unleashed in 1978 by deregulation.

## Is the Low-Cost Carrier Model the Answer?

Often when the legacy carriers are losing money, as was illustrated earlier, it is suggested that the LCC model is the answer and that all one needs to do to succeed in air transportation is to adopt it. In fact many legacy carriers tried to have it both ways by maintaining their traditional business model, while creating subsidiary LCCs of their own to compete with the major LCCs.

Caribbean carriers and the governments who own them are frequently advised that adopting the LCC model could be the solution to their problems; and in 2005 LIAT tried, with very limited success, to convert itself into an LCC. It is therefore useful to see what the LCC model is.

Following are some attributes of this model to provide greater clarity of what is normally involved:

- A single passenger class.
- A single type of aircraft which facilitates and reduces the cost of both training and maintenance (Boeing 737s and A320s are popular with large LCCs).
- A simple fare scheme – typically fares increase as planes fill up, which rewards early reservations by customers.
- Fares are paid in cash immediately to the LCC airline, which under the regime of the global distribution systems (GDSs) would receive its payments anything from thirty to sixty days after the customer had paid. Early cash payment helps cash flow, always a challenge for airlines.
- LCCs normally seek to schedule fast turnaround flights, allowing maximum utilization of the aircraft. This practice can, however, lead to problems of pilot burnout.
- There is an emphasis on direct sale of tickets, especially via the Internet, avoiding fees and commissions paid to travel agents and GDSs such as Sabre, Amadeus, Galileo and World Span, which are very expensive.
- LCCs seek to simplify route structures, emphasizing point-to-point travel transit more than hub and spoke networks, the complexity and costs of which are currently imposing huge burdens on legacy carriers.
- LCCs seek to operate from secondary airports where the taxes and other costs have traditionally been significantly less than that at major

international airports. (This is clearly not an option available to Caribbean carriers.)
- Passengers are made to pay significant penalties for excess baggage and while low base fares are cited, there is often a system of à la carte pricing for other services which can increase the costs to the customer significantly.

It is true that using the aforementioned model, some LCCs have been very successful. They have been able to reduce costs, while dispensing with a number of services which customers had come to expect, especially in business and first class. The jury is still out, however, on whether a sufficiently large number of people, especially business passengers, are willing to fly with only minimum services. It will later be seen that even Southwest Airlines, one of the world's most successful LCCs, which had always preached the gospel of the equality of passengers, found it necessary in 2008 to discriminate in favour of those designated as preferred passengers.

To some extent, the LCC model seems parasitic on the legacy model which continues, at great cost to itself, to meet customer needs, not only in terms of on-board service but also in relation to routes served.

Over time it has been seen that the probability of LCC failure increases as they are tempted to stray into the patterns of operation of the legacy carriers. Also, from time to time, situations from which they benefit change. For example, there has been a significant jump in the fees and taxes being charged by the secondary airports from which some of the LCCs have been operating. This has had a negative impact on their operating costs and it will be seen in chapter 9 that LCCs like Ryanair and EasyJet finally decided to take action against these airports.

However, it should be noted that as early as 2006, some of the major LCCs, for example, EasyJet, JetBlue and Spirit posted losses. During the first quarter of 2006, JetBlue reported a net loss of US$32 million and had to sell off some planes and cut back on its order for new equipment.

## Global Distribution Systems and the Low-Cost Carriers

It is a no-brainer that expensive fuel has been a great burden on the airlines. But another major cost item in airline operations is distribution, which has traditionally been done through the GDSs which comprise what must be called an oligopoly. The major players are Sabre, Amadeus, Galileo and World Span which control the business of making airline reservations. They receive the content of the product information from the individual carriers and store it on their systems. Carriers pay a high price whenever the customer gains access to this content on these systems, normally through the travel agent, to book a seat on an airline. The travel agent is often paid a commission, called an "over-ride" to sell product contained on the system, the terminals of which are often owned by the GDS.

One of the major challenges is that certain airline companies themselves own the major distribution systems and have other airlines as their clients. A major company was once quoted as expressing a preference to shut down the airline and keep its GDS since the airline lost money but the real source of its revenue was the GDS.

There have even been cases where the owners of these GDSs have been accused of manipulating the systems to give preference to the dominant carriers who own them. One of these cases hit the headlines in 1981, when it was alleged that a practice known as "screen bias" gave preference to American Airlines over other users of Sabre, which is owned by AMR Corporation, the parent company of American Airlines. In 1984, the US Congress outlawed the practice of screen bias.

In recent times there has been a kind of a revolt by carriers against the high price of making a reservation on these GDSs, and the LCCs have largely migrated from them to new and cheaper systems, like Navitaire, which LIAT now uses. Significant savings to LIAT's budget have been realized by the change but we shall see later that there has also been a downside to it.

In May 2006, during an airline distribution conference held in Dublin, Ireland, there was a distinct clash between the GDS and the LCCs.

Caroline Green, a former employee of Sabre and now services sales director for Ryanair, one of the more successful LCCs, described how 80 per cent of its tickets used to be sold via GDSs a decade ago and how, by moving to direct sales via call centres, they had brought this figure down to 60 per cent before coming up against a virtual brick wall. She claims that their real breakthrough was when they decided to do their distribution through the new Navitaire system and from that moment their business skyrocketed, not just in terms of number of passengers, but also in e-bookings. They now have 98 to 99 per cent Internet penetration, which is something that other airlines only aspire to.

Another Irish carrier, Aer Arann, a regional player in Ireland, claimed that after 9/11 its business using one of the GDSs had drained, but had been rescued by introducing radical changes, part of which was to change itself from a feeder carrier into a point-to-point airline, selling its seats from its own website.

Big carriers that are not shareholders in the GDSs can negotiate discounts with them. Small carriers are, however, normally trapped in the power of the GDSs, which have built-in annual price rises and make incentive payments to travel agents in many markets in return for volume sales. This motivates travel agents to continue using them and as LIAT was to discover, to shut out those carriers which try to opt out of the system.

It would be naïve to believe that powerful oligopolies would be prepared to lie down and die if and when airlines seek to leave their systems in favour of web-based systems like Navitaire. It was rumoured that there could be a pact between certain GDSs, normally fierce competitors, to back each other up, if either one lost the right to distribute a major airline's fares and content. Such arrangements would normally attract the attention of the US Department of Transportation, but any such battle is probably more likely to end in some kind of compromise where the GDSs give airlines a better deal than they enjoy and, by and large, retain their business.

**The Internet as an Alternative**

Thanks to the growing use of the Internet, more and more carriers have moved to direct sales or to only partial use of the GDSs, avoiding or reducing both GDS fees and travel agent commissions and thereby cutting the costs of doing business. The LCCs are therefore major users of the Internet and seek to motivate customers to use it. This development is understandably not popular with travel agencies and has had its own repercussions, as will be seen later.

**LCC versus Legacy Carrier Model**

The LCC model is clearly one which has revolutionized modes of travel and offers passengers an option to travel without some of the traditional services now regarded as frills. It permits the carrier to avoid many of the costs that have been associated with air travel in the past. Regrettably, one cost which they cannot avoid is that of fuel which reached astronomical levels in 2008. As slender margins disappeared, many resorted to a system of à la carte pricing where passengers were being charged for many of the things people had become accustomed to be included in the ticket price. Legacy carriers which had begun to argue that when one adds up all the LCC charges, the differential in costs to the customer disappears are now driven to follow their example. Only time will tell, therefore, whether one model will replace the other, or whether ever increasing costs and shrinking revenues will eventually force all carriers towards the lowest common denominator of service.

## Public Ownership: The Alleged Cause of Caribbean Airline Losses

This chapter on airline performance would not be complete without discussing the issue of public versus private ownership of carriers and the extent to which this factor affects the efficiency or performance.

Public ownership of the airlines is often offered by many in the Caribbean as the reason that the government-owned carriers have a history of losing money. There have even been some *a priori* arguments that government-owned businesses cannot, by definition, make a profit.

In 2006, a media attack on the Cayman Islands government, which owns Cayman Airways, stated the case very strongly for private sector ownership of airlines and boldly affirmed that their national carrier must be privatized, because a government, no matter how well managed or how democratic, cannot run a business at a profit.

This is simply not true. There are existing successful airline business models where governments are the owners. The airlines, Emirates and Singapore Airlines, spring easily to mind. They set a standard which the privately owned legacy carriers of Europe and North America envy and they offer interesting case studies for students of air transportation.

It is not widely known that Singapore Airlines, probably the most successful government-owned carrier of all time, is a 49 per cent shareholder in Virgin Atlantic Airlines, and in 2007 was considering selling the shares it bought eight years earlier for £600 million, back to Virgin Atlantic Airlines for £1 billion, on the grounds that the relationship with Virgin has not been as profitable as it had hoped.

There are, of course, abundant examples of government-owned carriers which perform badly. But often the businesses were not properly capitalized to begin with or effective management put in place and empowered to get on with the job of management. Where governments intervene to secure a social, rather than a commercial decision, they should be prepared to subsidize the carrier to achieve agreed social objectives.

The Caribbean reality is that Air Jamaica, BWIA and LIAT have been both publicly and privately owned and in both circumstances have lost a great deal of money. Looking back, it can be seen that over a period of fifty-three years in the case of LIAT, sixty-seven years for BWIA and some forty years in the case of Air Jamaica, these airlines moved between public and private ownership. CAL, the successor to BWIA at the end of 2006, continues to be government owned.

## Government's Position on Ownership

In the mid-1990s, the Caribbean governments which owned Air Jamaica, BWIA and LIAT, privatized them as a solution to the problem of escalating losses, and after a decade of monumental losses under private ownership, were forced to take over the carriers again, simply to save them from going under. During the period of private ownership, those same governments continued to pump subsidies into the carriers to keep them operating. It should come as no surprise, however, that contrary to a widely held view, not all Caribbean governments have taken the position that government ownership is the only, or even the preferred, solution to their air transportation problems.

## Caribbean Airlines and Ownership

The Government of Trinidad and Tobago, after announcing in 2006 that it intended to privatize BWIA, finally decided to liquidate it altogether and created an entirely new airline named CAL in January 2007. It was adequately capitalized and its cost structure reduced by cutting routes and staff. It was also able to free itself from the industrial controversies with which BWIA had been involved.

In July 2007, Prime Minister Patrick Manning of Trinidad and Tobago announced that as soon as Caribbean Airways was profitable, it would be privatized. It anticipated that within three years it would make a profit. The commitment to privatization has therefore been made, but finding a suitable investor, who is both willing and able to buy the carrier, clearly depends on CAL's prospects for turning a profit on a sustainable basis.

## Air Jamaica and Ownership

The Jamaica Labour Party which took office in Jamaica on 3 September 2007, after defeating the People's National Party at the polls, had made an election promise to seek a private partner for Air Jamaica and to make radical changes to its structure and operations. CEO Michael Conway resigned soon after the appointment of a new board and new chairperson, Shirley Williams.

In January 2008, Don Wehby, minister without portfolio in the Ministry of Finance announced that the Government of Jamaica had shortlisted four major airlines from which one would be chosen to take a stake in Air Jamaica within another year. Their names were not disclosed. He explained that the partner the government sought must be a major company with airline experience and a lot of capital to run Air Jamaica efficiently. A condition of the partnership would be keeping the Air Jamaica brand name. According to a Jamaica newspaper report, a new partner would be identified and the divestment concluded by March 2009. In February 2008, Prime Minister Bruce Golding said with even more urgency that the Jamaican government must divest all financial holdings in the state-owned airline because the ailing carrier was a drain on the cash-strapped island's budget. The losses of Air Jamaica for 2007 were US$171 million, the largest ever.

By May 2008, Air Jamaica announced that the Jamaican government was getting funds from the United States to help with its sale. Minister Don Wehby signed an agreement on 5 May 2008 for two grants totalling

US$820,180 from the US Trade and Development Agency[1] to assist with the Air Jamaica divestment process. To develop a state-of-the-art privatization programme, the Government of Jamaica engaged the services of the International Finance Corporation, the private sector arm of the World Bank. One grant for US$480,000 was to develop the appropriate legal framework and to tender documents for the privatization, and the second grant of US$340,180 was to fund the development of strategic options and financial modelling of the company's performance, as well as recommendations for environmental abatement measures that will help the airline to meet international standards for noise and air emissions.

In June 2008, in the wake of the world's worst oil crisis, as foreign carriers were cutting services, right, left, and centre from areas which include the Caribbean, questions were again being asked, especially by the Jamaican travel and tourism lobby and the labour unions about the wisdom of selling Air Jamaica to a foreign entity. However, in September 2009, the Government of Jamaica remained committed to a strategy of divestment and privatization.

## LIAT Shareholders' Views on Ownership

The situation at LIAT is slightly more complicated because there are three governments, Antigua and Barbuda, Barbados, and St Vincent and the Grenadines, which are the major shareholders and they do not necessarily hold identical views about the ownership of the carrier.

The expressed preference of the Barbados Labour Party government in Barbados in 2005 was that it had no real desire to own an airline, but

---

[1]The mission statement of the US Trade and Development Agency (USTDA) is: "It advances economic development and US commercial interests in developing and middle income countries. The agency funds various forms of technical assistance, early investment analysis, training, orientation and business workshops that support the development of a modern infrastructure and a fair and open trading environment. USTDA's strategic use of foreign assistance funds to support sound investment policy and decision-making in host countries creates an enabling environment for trade, investment and sustainable economic development. Operating at the nexus of foreign policy and commerce, USTDA is uniquely positioned to work with US firms and host countries in achieving the agency's trade and development goals. In carrying out its mission, USTDA gives emphasis to economic sectors that may benefit from US exports of goods and services."

had become involved with LIAT simply to prevent it from going under. Its preference, therefore, was to seek to improve the financial and operational affairs of the company to the point where private sector investors would be willing to invest in the carrier and run it as a successful commercial operation. Whether or not there was a shift from that position as time passed was never expressly indicated.

On 15 January 2008, the government in Barbados changed and the incoming Democratic Labour Party government indicated that its policy on LIAT would be made known after it had a chance to become fully *au fait* with the affairs of the carrier and to formulate a point of view on ownership and other matters, based on discussions with its other two partners. The reality is that the Barbados government has continued to support the carrier without any explicit statement of how it sees its future.

The other two shareholders, Antigua and Barbuda and St Vincent and the Grenadines, made no public statements about ownership; but knowing the relationship between LIAT and Antigua and Barbuda and the dependence of St Vincent and the Grenadines on LIAT, which currently has no international airport but is building one, it seems likely that they would be reluctant to see it pass to private or foreign hands, and lose total control over its operations.

It is clear that all three shareholder governments need to be able to guarantee their countries air access for their tourism, trade and social activities, and to be part of the decision-making process that ensures this happens. For them intra-Caribbean tourism is very important and given the economic meltdown in North America and Europe, the Caribbean market has assumed even greater importance in 2009 and beyond. They would be ill advised, therefore, unless they had no other option, to lose control over their daily bus service by ceding ownership of intra-Caribbean air transportation to foreign companies or countries.

## The Global Environment for Air Transport

Since the mid-1970s, several events have had a traumatic impact on international air transportation, which was said to have lost more money in 2004 alone, than it had lost in all its preceding years combined.

The first assault came with the energy crisis of 1974–75 when fuel prices escalated to heights formerly unknown. That catapulted LIAT's British owners Court Line into bankruptcy and brought LIAT closer to liquidation than it had ever been.

The second assault came with US deregulation of air transportation in 1978, as a result of which, several LCCs/low-fare carriers came into being. This forced all carriers, but especially the legacy carriers operating in a large network of routes and hub and spoke systems, to engage in suicidal competition with the LCCs. The customer benefited from the low fares, often below the cost of producing airline seats, but several airlines went out of business. In 2008, support for some sort of re-regulation came from no less a person than Robert Crandall, the legendary former CEO and chairman of American Airlines and a former champion of deregulation. Deregulation and its impacts are dealt with at greater length in chapter 9.

The Caribbean carriers have a range of responsibilities which includes air transportation services to their nationals on routes that few, if any, private sector, local or foreign operator would provide, guaranteeing service to tourists, offering competition to foreign carriers and ensuring security of service. They provide valuable socio-economic services to the community as a kind of "aerial infrastructure". There are not many highways, flyovers and bridges that make money in the sense of a bottom line performance, although it is clear that their contribution to the overall economy is enormous. It is therefore to the credit of Caribbean shareholder governments that so far they have decided that the value of their national carriers must be seen in terms of their contribution to gross domestic product (GDP), rather than in terms of a bottom line profit.

Caribbean carriers have faced a number of the following serious challenges:

- Gross under-capitalization.
- Major fixed and growing costs of inputs like fuel, maintenance, leasing of aircraft, security and insurance. The price of oil and aviation fuel has been the most worrying factor.
- Other costs such as labour, pension funds, and severance.
- Operating in an almost suicidal competitive environment in which passengers are seeking the lowest fares in markets where expansion

is limited. LIAT, particularly, has had to operate a complex intra-Caribbean network with small populations who have limited disposable incomes.
- Costly industrial action either by their own unions or by others, the work of which impacts the operations of the carriers. For example, industrial action by LIAT pilots in 2006, by its cabin attendants in 2007 and by the Antigua and Barbuda air traffic controllers in 2008–9 cost LIAT a total of about EC$3.5 million.
- Facing the challenges of online fraud which has grown with the growth in e-commerce and possible threats from the international illegal drug trade.

This chapter has presented the operational and financial performance of both foreign and Caribbean carriers and has done so against the background of the difficult environment in which they have been forced to operate. Caribbean people, having been presented with the facts, should cease judging their own people by a higher standard than that used by them to judge others, especially those from developed countries.

Caribbean political leaders, who are criticized by international agencies for providing financial support for their carriers, should answer their critics by citing the amount of losses incurred by the carriers of the developed world and the massive amount of subsidies of various kinds that those countries provide to support them. This book provides them with the ammunition to do that.

It is hoped that the prior analysis will assist people generally in better understanding why Caribbean carriers have continued to struggle. This does not resolve the dilemma in which certain Caribbean governments find themselves: on the one hand, wishing to sustain the existing carriers and to support them financially; on the other, finding it difficult, in the context of all their other pressing financial obligations, including massive debt, to meet the cost of subsidizing carriers. This dilemma, however, explains the never ending search for solutions, some of which are dealt with in chapter 4.

# 4

# Options for Cooperation Between Regional Carriers

Caribbean governments and Caribbean people have pondered long and hard on how to create viable, affordable, efficient and financially sound air transportation services to and between the Caribbean territories. This is by no means surprising in a region comprising largely an archipelago which is regarded as the world's most tourism-dependent area and of which some fourteen of the states are part of a community seeking to integrate its economies. Air transportation is therefore seen as an important factor in the regional integration process which itself seems to be something of a Holy Grail always hovering on the horizon, but most difficult to achieve.

Because the objective of integration is so desirable, many tend to underestimate the difficulties facing those who are actually entrusted with putting it into practice. This often results in a number of solutions being bandied about without any real understanding of the intricacies involved. Hence proposals for a single currency or freedom of movement of goods and persons are often suggested and the political leadership chastised for their failure to make quick progress. To this list may be added the creation of a single Caribbean carrier.

Creating a single Caribbean carrier should not be seen as an end in itself, although people often speak as though it is. The countries involved have to be convinced that such an entity would result in providing the region with more sustainable, efficient and profitable air transportation services than striving to recapitalize and improve individual Caribbean-owned carriers. The concept also has to be practically and politically feasible.

There are already factors which arguably favour abandoning individual country ownership; the region under consideration is poor and airlines complex and expensive entities to operate. As a result, the national carriers have, over a period of time, experienced considerable difficulties both in the areas of operations and finance. Logic would suggest, therefore, that some form of cooperation stands a good chance of reducing costs and improving efficiencies. Clearly, however, it has not been easy to achieve and it would be useful to examine why this has been so, in spite of several proposals about regional cooperation in air transportation over an extended period of time.

The Caribbean has been wrestling with the idea of regional air transportation at least as early as 1969. According to the Hon. Kamaluddin Mohamed (1969), minister of West Indian affairs of Trinidad and Tobago, "the integration process has for many years been hampered by the lack of fast, cheap and reliable inter-island transport ... this void is to a large extent filled by British West Indian Airways and its subsidiary LIAT. These are not regionally owned airlines. BWIA is wholly owned by the government of Trinidad and Tobago, which also has a controlling interest in LIAT. The airlines however provide a regional service, and efforts are now being made to have BWIA designated the regional Air Carrier with participation by the other regional governments."

In the same month, April 1969, when Minister Mohammed was calling for BWIA and its subsidiary, LIAT, to be recognized as the regional air carrier, Air Jamaica was launched.

Three years after the article by Minister Mohammed, the Commonwealth Caribbean Regional Secretariat Report (1972) expressed frustration with regional air transportation in these words: "there has been no progress whatever in developing a regional approach to air transportation. In this area, fragmentation, divisiveness and disintegration continue apace. Three member countries now have their own individual international airlines and the number of intra-regional airlines is multiplying daily. A UK company has acquired a controlling interest in LIAT because the previous company [that is BWIA] with a majority control, could not afford to infuse the new capital necessary for the improvement of the services offered by LIAT." The UK company referred to was Court Line.

## A History of Mistrust

This region suffers from a kind of schizophrenia about concepts of cooperation; it knows that the geographical realities and slender resources of individual countries are strong arguments for cooperation between the countries at various levels. But those very realities have fostered a tendency to seek relationships out of, rather than inside, the Caribbean, and the region's long social and colonial history has engendered and reinforced suspicions about trust and reliance on neighbours. The first great effort of political commitment, the West Indies Federation, ended in failure in 1962, as did the experiment with the "Little Eight" political arrangements which ended in 1966. These were traumatic events which created many insecurities and a great deal of suspicion between the participating parties which continue until today. Proposals for integration are therefore often viewed by some, even today, with ulterior motives and even when some form of cooperation has been agreed, gradualism is clearly preferred in some quarters to instant marriages. For all these reasons, trust and transparency are prerequisites for starting any process of unification in the Caribbean.

Priests often say during the marriage ceremony that marriage is not a state to be entered into lightly and yet the many proposals for airline marriages in the Caribbean are very casually made, without providing any specific details of how this might be done. In fact, except for the CTO Functional Cooperation study in 1993 done in respect of nine CTO member countries, there has never been any official feasibility study of the pros and cons of doing so which would examine the problems likely to be encountered and how those wishing to go forward should proceed.

Frankly speaking, little or no progress has been made due to some of the following reasons: the difficulties of doing it successfully have been underestimated by most of the proponents; the preparatory work needed has not been done; there is as yet no clear concept of what something like creating one Caribbean airline is intended to do. Most importantly, the political will has never been there, especially in Trinidad and Tobago and

Jamaica, to do so on terms that respect the sovereignty of all the partners needed to make it work.

If, however, the region is serious about the creation of the Caribbean Single Market and Economy, it will have, sooner or later, to seriously consider issues relating to the air transportation services of the community as a whole – the future socio-economic development of which depends on two critical factors:

- Moving people, goods and services to and around the community.
- Developing an efficient and internationally competitive tourism industry.

This chapter intends to examine various forms of cooperation between carriers, some of the steps taken in the past to implement them in the Caribbean, as well as the factors that tend to frustrate their implementation.

## Various Options to Consider

There are various options for airlines to work together, but the obvious ones are code sharing; functional cooperation between companies; creation of a holding company which involves transferring some functions to a central entity while maintaining the individual company identities; and a complete merger, which means creating one company out of many. These are dealt with in greater detail later, but it may be of interest first to explain some of the reasons why there is such reluctance, both at the country and the airline management level, to give up the identity of the national carrier.

**Ownership, Emotional Relationships and Branding**

*The Material Factor*

Those governments which are owners of Air Jamaica, BWIA/CAL, and LIAT, for example, are in a position to make decisions about the air transportation services performed by those carriers which they see as serving their national interests. They do not have to consult any other governments, whether inside or outside of CARICOM, on exactly what role they wished their carrier to play in national development. Jamaica wanted a carrier which was an extension of its tourism industry while carrying ethnic traffic also. Trinidad wanted a carrier that was largely business- and ethnic-travel oriented, while benefiting from the tourism needs of Barbados and the OECS states. The owners of LIAT wanted it to be the Eastern Caribbean's bus service as well as play a connecting role for international services.

So long as the services can be maintained at a national or sub-regional level, there really is no strong motivation for the owners to wrestle with other governments in the community, especially those which do not contribute to the operational or capital costs, to ensure that the current national benefits are delivered. It is when things begin to fall apart and supporting the national carrier becomes an unbearable national burden that national governments begin to cast around for other options. As with all regional services, national entities often wish it to be demonstrated beyond doubt, that there is more to be gained by working together than by doing it alone. One way of doing this is to demonstrate that ultimately the individual effort will fail or that there is a high probability of this happening.

*The Psychological Factor*

It needs to be stated that there seems to be another factor too, the psychological factor, which militates against countries easily giving up their national carrier. It is difficult to quantify this in a material sense, but in all countries there seems to develop a sort of emotional relationship between the people and the national carrier, which is associated with the branding process. As a result, the pride of national ownership and the fear of the brand disappearing is often stronger than the arguments in favour of collaboration. It must be understood that these emotions are probably more strongly felt by the populace than by the politicians.

Why, then, is the brand so important a factor?

*Defining the Brand*

Branding of a product is a critical part of its marketing, and those who have an interest in learning more about its importance, particularly with reference to airlines, may refer to Holder (2006).

When the livery of an airline is selected, there is an intention, through the design chosen, to forge a connection between look and operations, to present a certain image, tell a particular story and portray a particular culture. This is very important for national carriers.

By name and posture, airlines like American Airlines, British Airways Lufthansa and Air France, to name a few, have a global reach and seek to represent the power and pride of their very important countries. It can work against them, as it seems to have done, during the 9/11 event, when terrorists may have selected an American Airlines plane as a weapon against the World Trade Centre, simply because of what it represented.

Many carriers, whether local, regional or global, seek through their brand designs to capture something of the national culture of the country of ownership. This is reinforced in several ways, for example, by carrying life style magazines, stories, reports, news, music, *inter alia*, belonging to the country in the cabin.

These things add a touch of emotion to the brand that goes beyond functionality and can be used creatively in ad campaigns.

Three of the many important things the brand is meant to do are lay a special claim on the loyalty of those returning nationals who belong to the country or culture, by claiming to offer hometown comfort and familiarity from the moment they enter the plane in a foreign country; present to the visitor an experience of the destination to which he or she is travelling that begins with embarkation and results in a sudden and pleasant change of mood from whatever stress and turmoil he or she is leaving behind in the workplace; have a positive effect on the mood, spirit and loyalty of the staff through the use of the design and décor in the workplace.

However, a brand that has gone wrong can have a disastrous effect on an airline and its business, as was discovered by Bob Ayling, the CEO of British Airways who swapped the Union Jack on the tail of British Airways planes for a "pot pourri" of colours claiming that while it was proud of its British origins, the airline had to throw overboard the old-fashioned part of its British identity and instead take on the modern characteristics of the country. Virgin Atlantic was careful not to make this mistake. Ayling lost his job and the airline lost both money and the loyalty of many of its customers. It also cost a great deal of money to restore the Union Jack on its planes. Clearly, a national carrier that performs badly will also give a negative first impression of the country to visitors using it to travel to the destination of the owners.

It cannot be denied, however, that the loyalty of the Caribbean customers of Air Jamaica, BWIA and LIAT to the brand is unmistakeable and helps to explain why the governments who own them have been able, over many years, to continue to support the carriers financially in spite of haemorrhaging of cash and widespread criticism in certain quarters. A mother in the Eastern Caribbean was heard saying that her five-year-old son calls every air plane he sees flying in the sky, LIAT.

When LIAT and Caribbean Star were negotiating a merger, it was important to many people that the name LIAT survived rather than Caribbean Star. It was also with some difficulty that the people of Trinidad and Tobago tore themselves away from the BWIA brand after some sixty-seven years, and it will take sometime for CAL to evoke the same emotions. No government of Jamaica can easily shed the Air Jamaica brand without serious political consequences.

## A History of Competition between Caribbean Carriers

Based on what has been said earlier about branding, it was easy for these three carriers to see each other as competitors, especially as they were branded differently. In brief, they were seen by their owners as fulfilling different national purposes and took conflicting operational decisions. One clear example of this in the case of Air Jamaica and BWIA which both served international routes is that they used very different types of equipment. This would in itself have had a negative impact on several areas of cooperation. In fact, to anyone well-versed in air transportation matters, these two carriers had little in common except that they were owned by Caribbean governments and had accumulated a massive amount of debt. Air Jamaica found it far easier, for example, to code share with Delta Airlines with which they established a commonality of interests.

Air Jamaica and BWIA while competing with each other on international routes always considered LIAT the junior partner; the main role of which was to provide them with access into the Caribbean islands and serve as a connecting service to international passengers. At one stage each of them thought that it might even be better to perform this connecting role for themselves. Therefore, Air Jamaica, when under private ownership, and

BWIA, created intra-regional subsidiary airlines: Eastern Caribbean (EC) Express and BWee Express, respectively. These competed with LIAT and with each other in the Eastern Caribbean until a case of too many seats chasing too few passengers brought the inevitable result. The BWee Express/ LIAT competition took place, in spite of the fact that BWIA has always had various levels of ownership in LIAT. Between 1999 and 2002 BWIA was in fact LIAT's largest shareholder. In 2009, the BWIA Company, which survived the change to CAL, still owned 3.08 per cent of LIAT's shares.

In November 1999, Air Jamaica Express had applied on behalf of EC Express, to operate scheduled services between Barbados and St Lucia, St Vincent and the Grenadines, Dominica, Grenada, and Tobago. The proposed date of commencement was to be 14 February 2000, but due to problems with technical documents and other concerns, the commencement date was rescheduled to April 2000. Five provisional licences were finally issued on 24 July 2000, for commencement of services on that date. In November 2000, EC Express applied to operate other scheduled air services. A provisional licence was issued for a Barbados–Trinidad–Barbados route on 30 January 2001. But by 6 April 2001, a few months later, EC Express suspended operations until further notice to carry out the organizational and operational restructuring of the airline that had become necessary. It never reopened. BWee Express after suffering considerable losses also ceased operations.

For those who argued that the efficiency of LIAT's operations in 2008 suffered as a direct result of a lack of competition, it should be pointed out that LIAT is no stranger to competition. In fact, for years it seemed that every airline entering the arena in the Eastern Caribbean made it an essential part of its business plan that its success would be based on the collapse of LIAT. Some in fact stated so. From 1999, LIAT met the challenges posed by competition from various airlines such as BWIA, BWee Express, Air Jamaica and its subsidiary EC Express, Carib Express, Caribbean Star, Caribbean Sun, Air Caraibe, American Eagle and other smaller Caribbean carriers.

Caribbean Star had entered the arena in 2000 and was joined in 2003 by Caribbean Sun which was based in San Juan, Puerto Rico. Both of these carriers were owned by the Texan billionaire, Sir Allen Stanford. Caribbean Star provided what amounted to almost suicidal competition to LIAT, duplicating its routes, schedules and bringing down prices. When one adds the other competition listed in the previous paragraph, it is not surprising that so much money was lost by airlines in the Eastern Caribbean where there is no high volume of business to support so many airline seats.

## Different Types and Levels of Cooperation

The view has, however, been strongly held by tourism interests and some air transportation experts – cooperation between the carriers owned by Caribbean governments is desirable and air transportation services in the region would be greatly improved if some way could be found of doing so. What form however should this take? Following is an examination of a number of forms of cooperation.

**Code Sharing**

The term "code" refers to the letters approved by IATA by which a flight is identified in the schedule. It normally comprises two letters and this can be seen, for example, from the LIAT flight LI 754 or AA 1607 referring to an American Airlines flight. Code sharing between two carriers permits them to have a common flight number with several advantages; through an interlining agreement both carriers can sell seats on the same flight. On a thin route this can help to eliminate destructive competition. One major advantage offered is the convenience to the customer for connecting flights. If, for example, there is a code-sharing agreement between Delta Airlines and LIAT Airline, a customer wishing to travel all the way from Atlanta via Barbados to St Lucia, changing planes from Delta to LIAT at Barbados, travels under one company's code number. It assumes a coordinated schedule between the two carriers thus saving time and coordinated baggage handling. The customers can expect to have their baggage loaded in Atlanta and not see it again until they arrive in St Lucia. The passengers travelling in reverse can expect to board LIAT in St Lucia, change to Delta in Barbados and reach seamlessly any destination in the United States to which Delta travels. Code sharing also offers opportunities for joint marketing between the carriers.

Code shares give the impression of being direct flights and are therefore preferred options for travel agents, passengers and computer reservation systems over booking travel with separate carriers when a change of carrier is involved.

It is to be noted that the US Civil Aviation Authority, the Federal Aviation Administration (FAA), did not permit foreign carriers which did not have category one status, to code share with US carriers and this became a major reason for Caribbean carriers which had lost category one status, to recover it.

Carriers wishing to enter code-share agreements with each other need, however, to consider the pros and cons for their particular situation and business keeping in mind a number of important issues. Agreement has to be reached on the following, *inter alia*:

- Schedule alignment and arrival and departure times of the carriers.
- Fare rule alignment: How are pricing and prorating policy agreed?
- Who deals with seating assignment and the issue of boarding passes?
- Can seamless transfers be guaranteed?
- Can the baggage policy be aligned?

It is of interest that from February to October 2007, LIAT and Caribbean Star operated a commercial arrangement that involved code sharing. LIAT has also had code-share arrangements with BWIA and Air Caraibes but it is not a practice that has been widely followed between Caribbean carriers.

**Functional Cooperation**

Another form of cooperation is functional cooperation which has the following objectives:

- Achieving critical mass and economies of scale to reduce unit costs.
- Exploiting the combined marketing strengths and advantages that are unique to the carriers of the region so as to compete with the large external carriers.

It involves the carriers retaining their individual personas as companies, each with its own board of directors, but merging a number of functions with the aforementioned objectives.

The call for collaboration between the Caribbean government-owned carriers was made in 1993, but it did not come from the carriers themselves although almost all of them were members of the same Caribbean community. It came from the Caribbean tourism sector which argued that air transportation is the lifeline of the tourism industry and that a regional approach to air transportation would give clout and critical mass to small entities operating in a global arena.

In 1993, the CTO contracted Miami Aviation Services and El Perial as consultants to undertake a functional cooperation study covering nine Caribbean carriers. They were Air Jamaica, ALM, Air Aruba, Bahamasair, BWIA, Cayman Airways, Guyana Airways, LIAT and Surinam Airways.

The study was undertaken against a background where each Caribbean carrier faced major capacity differentials and tremendous marketing strength by extra-regional carriers, the most aggressive of which was American Airlines. The number of foreign international carriers competing on the Caribbean routes increased in 2007 and the competition became even fiercer than it had been in 1993 when functional cooperation was first discussed.

One of the factors driving the need for alliances was the fact that in the mid-1990s there was a major shift in the conception of the role of airlines. Air transportation, formerly seen largely as a public service, had become a cut-throat, survival-of-the-fittest, hard-nosed business because of deregulation.

The only future for small carriers seemed to lie in alliances. The strategy led by Transportes Aereas Centro-Americano in Central America, the AeroMexico acquisition of Mexicana and AeroPeru, the move by Lan Chile and Ladeco to merge, were all examples of carriers seeking possible alliances to survive. This seemed in the 1990s to be the way in which the Caribbean carriers should go.

The proposed 1993 Caribbean functional cooperation strategies took for granted two considerations: (1) the carriers would have strong government support in the region and (2) each carrier would continue to take all possible steps to put its individual house in order.

The study focused on four main areas:

- The "Miami opportunity" in which the carriers serving Miami would take advantage of the critical mass which their combined efforts at that gateway would offer

- Joint marketing
- Advantages made possible by cooperation in technical, operations and aircraft areas
- Regulatory matters

Action in these specific areas was considered by the consultants to be able to generate US$65 million in cost containment (US$34 million) and revenue enhancement (US$31 million) measures.

The following additional benefits were seen:

- Enhancing overall product and services
- Providing opportunities for private sector involvement in specific profit centres and subsidiary business activities
- Making the group more attractive for private sector investment and strategic alliances with extra-regional carriers

The 1993 study was never implemented and a number of the regional carriers invited to participate then, no longer exist.

There is nothing to suggest that many of the recommendations of the study are not as feasible now for the remaining government-owned carriers as they were in 1993, and could not be implemented if there were the political will and the willingness at the level of the boards of directors and senior management to do so. Achieving this is, however, a difficult task in the face of the vested interests involved and the different financial situations in which the carriers now are. The chances of success would of course be better if all the carriers started from a position of being entirely free of accumulated debt.

It was always felt that the best way to proceed in translating the idea of functional cooperation into action would be to establish a specific mechanism outside of the staffs of the existing carriers, with a small secretariat and budget, to examine all the relevant issues and to create and implement the programme of cooperation in consultation with the various boards.

**A Caribbean International Airways Holding Company**

Another and possibly a bolder proposal than functional cooperation, is the concept of the creation of the Caribbean International Airways Holding

(CIAH) Company. This was proposed in 2003 with respect to BWIA and LIAT.

The original idea was to create a holding company in which both BWIA and LIAT would retain their separate identities, but there would be major integration of many of their individual services and rationalization of their routes. This was seen as stopping short of a merger but possibly as a first step towards one, should the chemistry between the carriers after a while prove it to be feasible.

In May 2003, the governments of Antigua and Barbuda, Barbados, St Vincent and the Grenadines, and Trinidad and Tobago had actually agreed to the creation of CIAH to include the operations of BWIA and LIAT. The company was registered in Port of Spain, Trinidad, but the Government of Trinidad and Tobago withdrew from the process, for reasons which are unknown to the writer. The idea had progressed, but was dropped as suddenly as it had begun, allegedly by Trinidad and Tobago. Baffled by these developments, some concluded that there must have been internal differences of opinion about how to proceed between members of the Government of Trinidad and Tobago.

Ian Bertrand, of El Perial Management Services, who was one of the authors of the 1993 CTO Functional Cooperation Study, had also been engaged as a consultant to the CIAH project. Garry Cullen, CEO of LIAT from 2000 to 2006, also provided some technical input into the development of the idea in 2003.

Briefly, some of the ideas originally put forward on what form the CIAH involving BWIA and LIAT was intended to take were as follows:

1. There should be a good corporate fit between the carriers requiring the that

    - They share common competition
    - There be a common equity base
    - There be a common cultural and organizational fit
    - Agreement could be reached between the external shareholders about the CIAH
    - They could agree on complementary strategic objectives leading to a combined synergy

- Complementary operations with two fleet types of jets and turboprops could be designed and agreed

2. *Corporate structure and ownership.* A new corporate structure was envisaged as taking over the day-to-day management of the operations and business of the carriers involved. The existing airlines would maintain their legal entities, assets, structures and operations but the combined operation would fall under the direction of CIAH. There would have to be a rationalization of routes, especially those in the Eastern Caribbean and some adjustment to the total number of employees were logically dictated by the changes made. CIAH would combine all revenues and pay all bills.
3. *Commercial vision.* A comprehensive integrated market-driven schedule would have to be developed to meet the needs of the Caribbean ethnic market, the tourism industry and regional and international business and government travellers and shippers. Before the closure of BWIA and its replacement by CAL and the closure of the London services of both Air Jamaica and CAL, it had been thought that under a CIAH which included Air Jamaica, BWIA might have focused on the European routes (to include the United Kingdom), Air Jamaica on the North American routes and LIAT on doing what it has always done: feed the international services of the two carriers and any others and continue to serve as a bridge between all the countries of the community.
4. *Management, staffing and operations.* A CIAH would need a single management team and structure to run the network and the integrated business.
5. *Freedom of movement of labour.* Employees of the CIAH airlines would have to be included in the category of workers entitled to freedom of movement, and employment in all the territories of the Caribbean Single Market and later the Caribbean Single Market and Economy and the airlines would be seen as one entity for purposes of aviation-handling, landing fees, operating licences, route authorization and so on.
6. *Airline culture and work and rest rules.* Existing work and rest rules of the carriers would have to be revisited to ensure that they are consistent with today's competitive airline practices, while making sure that they meet the regulatory requirements and labour laws of the countries where the employees are located.

Pay and benefits of staff would be adjusted to suit the differences in the cost of living of the countries in which they are based, but these are matters to be attended to by workers' representatives.
7. *New investment and partnerships.* New investment would have to be invited into the CIAH to finance its rationalization and growth with respect to fleet, airport facilities, route development, livery, employees' training, systems and so on; and it is assumed that current shareholders of the three carriers would have first call on the allocation of new shares in CIAH.

**Implementing the CIAH Concept**

To those familiar with the challenges of implementing regional concepts, it is clear that making the CIAH happen among the airlines owned by individual Caribbean governments would not be an easy prospect, but it is possible. Such changes could not be achieved without some vested interests losing something it currently has and much resistance to the idea could be expected both from within and beyond the airlines themselves.

Again, it would certainly take a great deal of political will and support from the many unions which have great influence in the air transportation industry.

Unlike functional cooperation, implementing the CIAH would involve more than creating commercial relationships between boards and CEOs of the carriers involved. The total commitment to the idea and buy-in by the political directorate to a whole new direction, especially for those carriers which are currently owned by governments, would be absolutely necessary.

# Merging Caribbean Carriers

The ultimate form of cooperation would be to close down the existing CARICOM government-owned carriers and merge them into one airline. This has never been seriously considered by their owners, perhaps because it is seen as too radical a step in a region which has always shied away from the unification option.

When the Commonwealth Caribbean thought about political cooperation they chose federation over a unitary state. The only person ever to suggest such a radical step of a unitary state was Dr Eric Williams, prime minister of Trinidad and Tobago. But since he had given up on the federation in 1961 with the now famous statement, that 1 from 10 leaves 0, his offer lacked conviction. Only the Government of Grenada took his offer seriously, and he himself never responded to Grenada's expression of willingness to join Trinidad and Tobago in unitary statehood.

The events of the past forty years do not suggest that Caribbean governments, airline boards of directors and management and even Caribbean people can willingly create one effective and hopefully profitable carrier. But difficult times sometimes call for extraordinary decisions and radical and aggressive action, and no option should be ruled out in the search for solutions.

The years 2008 and 2009 have been years of operational and financial turmoil for the global airline industry brought on by the world's worst economic meltdown since the Great Depression of the 1930s. Chapters 10 and 11 set out in detail many of those experiences and underscore the fact that solutions for survival were often sought in cooperative arrangements and even mergers between established and seemingly powerful legacy carriers which had been competitors. Perhaps there are some lessons for the Caribbean to consider.

## Cooperation Reviewed

This chapter reviews a number of possible forms of airline cooperation and it can safely be said that none of them have to date been fully or seriously explored at a policy level between Caribbean carriers. The environment for cooperation might, however, be enhanced if there were a reversion to an old practice, when the chairmen and CEOs of Caribbean carriers met informally twice a year to compare notes about how their carriers were doing and to share suggestions about how they might find solutions to their common problems. That kind of exchange, however, works best where no carrier is more concerned with being the dominant carrier, than working with others to deliver a better total service. This should be possible in a Caribbean family. In that context it would ideally be better if Air Jamaica's ownership remained within the community which would leave decision making about air transportation in the Caribbean Single Market and Economy entirely in the hands of the community.

In the recent past, Caribbean carriers demonstrated that they can work successfully together. In preparation for hosting the 2007 Cricket World Cup in the West Indies, Air Jamaica, BWIA, later CAL, LIAT and Caribbean Star agreed to create the Caribbean Carrier Consortium and make a joint bid for transporting the teams, officials, media and sponsors around the region during the Cricket World Cup in 2007. They were awarded the contract and did a tremendous job in meeting the objectives set. They thereby earned the respect and congratulations of people who formerly had predicted gloom and doom for this exercise. Their cooperation sent a powerful message about the direction in which they could go in the future, if there was commitment at political and management levels to work together. With the end of the tournament, however, this idea of greater cooperation between the carriers lost steam as did many other such cooperative, one-Caribbean-space initiatives, started under the Cricket World Cup Sunset legislation.

**Challenges of Cooperation**

In conclusion, no one should underestimate the difficulties of inter-carrier cooperation and especially of taking that final step of creating one carrier out of the existing government-owned carriers.

First, the move from national ownership and control, to what I refer as community ownership and control, would require a sea change in the thinking of the region, not only among political leaders but also at the level of the people themselves. With all the difficulties Air Jamaica is facing in its search for survival, it is still possible to sense a deep popular prejudice in Jamaica against any solution that would involve Trinidad and Tobago buying the carrier. Such feelings have their origin in the history of inter-country relationships.

If one gets past the emotional barriers, those designing the model have a number of practical challenges to face. The model for one regional airline has to take into consideration the air transportation realities of the region with respect to geography, tourism, other business and ethnic social needs; and there needs to be a great deal of thought given to how it is to be positioned in the market to serve the interests of all; how the roles now played by the individual carriers will be distributed to serve the region; what will be hubs in the CARICOM countries and how they will work; what are the social commercial routes and on what terms and conditions they will be served; how the costs will be shared among the CARICOM members and what will be the civil aviation policy that governs the operations; how it will deal with the many unions now involved; and what will be the conditions of staff drawn from the participating territories. These are some of the questions to be answered to the satisfaction of those who will pay for the service.

Given all that has been said earlier about the difficulties involved in cooperation and especially of merging carriers, the fact that LIAT and Caribbean Star, two Caribbean carriers hostile to each other, one owned by governments, and the other by a Texan billionaire, Sir Allen Stanford, actually agreed to negotiate a merger of the two companies, seems an interesting story and one that needs to be told. It is even more remarkable that the negotiations ended with LIAT taking over the assets of Caribbean Star.

What to do about Caribbean carriers in the future, especially in the area of regional cooperation, requires much more knowledge about their operations and challenges over the many years of their existence than people know today. Many of those writing in the public media about airlines could benefit from a closer acquaintance with the facts.

The following four chapters are dedicated to providing this kind of information about one of the carriers, LIAT, about which the author has very intimate knowledge. They are focused on four different aspects of the LIAT experience; a case study of its operations and finances and the challenges faced in attempting to restructure it as an individual carrier; how and why the conclusion was reached that a merger with Caribbean Star, its greatest competitor, was its only hope of survival; the nuts and bolts of negotiating such a merger with Sir Allen Stanford, whose name has since made headlines around the world; and finally, the case for and against the resultant creation of monopolies which inevitably arise when mergers are discussed.

The information and the arguments presented are also used to support the case which this book sets out to make from the beginning; the Caribbean cannot afford to give up ownership and control over important aspects of its air transportation services and to achieve this, the region may have to defy some of the many established theories fostered by international agencies about government ownership, support of national carriers and monopolies.

Chapter 5 is a case study of LIAT, the fifty-three-year-old government-owned carrier.

# 5

# The LIAT Case Study

Unless one has had personal experience of managing an airline, it is difficult to imagine how complex a business it really is.

There are many issues to examine and resolve: how are they to be owned and managed; how are they to be financed or refinanced, as necessary; what legal matters are involved and how are they to be handled; what kind of fleet should they have; how should they be staffed; what should be their relationship to other carriers flying into the Caribbean; where should they fly, by what routes and according to what schedules; how should they brand and market themselves; what should be their pricing strategy; what kind of distribution and IT systems should they use; how do they manage their industrial relations; how do they develop and practise a successful customer relations policy; how do they survive the competition; what catering, if any, is to be done on board; with whom and how should they merge their operations; how are they to deal with maintenance and with safety and security issues; how should ground operations be handled; how are they to satisfy international civil aviation standards; what are their roles in the socio-economic life of their country; how are they to deal with crisis management, the press and public relations; what is the vision; how to handle the politics?

This is a sample of the issues which occupy the minds of airline boards and management on an ongoing basis and it is felt that having a look at a case study of one of the Caribbean carriers can help to reduce theory to reality.

LIAT was chosen as the case study by the author because as the chairman of the company he has an in-depth knowledge of its workings. However, there were two other reasons: first, although by international standards it is a small carrier, as one which serves a complicated network in a hub and spoke system, it exhibits many of the features and therefore the challenges which face major international carriers on a daily basis. Second, many of the post graduate students who are studying tourism and air transportation in the region select LIAT as a project and need more ready access to information about its history and operations.

## LIAT's Longevity

The first point to make is that by 2009 LIAT had survived for fifty-three years, which in airline years is a very long time. Since BWIA closed, it is in fact the Caribbean's oldest carrier. It owes this longevity, however, to the fact that over those fifty-three years, whenever it has been on the brink of collapse, certain governments and the people of the Eastern Caribbean have come to its rescue.

In 1974, after the collapse of its British owner, Court Line, there was a LIAT bailout which involved eleven CARICOM states.

In 1999, the Speedwing Report and Recovery Plan covering 1999–2004 was created, though never implemented as such. It however came to many conclusions on which future planners were able to build.

In 2000 and again in 2004, strategic plans were created. The first drew heavily on the Speedwing Report and the second merits particular attention because of its experimental nature.

In 2007, another strategic plan was created in which an equity investment of US$60 million was made by the three shareholder governments of Antigua and Barbuda, Barbados, and St Vincent and the Grenadines, through a loan to them from the Caribbean Development Bank (CDB).

During 2007 and 2008 LIAT made significant progress, although 2008 was a very difficult year in which many airlines either were forced to seek protection under bankruptcy legislation or actually collapsed.

As 2009 began it was still too early to say whether LIAT had achieved a sustainable situation and how the year would turn out in what was being described as the worst global economic meltdown since the Great Depression of the 1930s. The year 2008 has been described as the worst year for air transportation performance in the history of the industry.

## Airline Distress Syndrome at LIAT

To understand LIAT one must become familiar with its history. Regis Doganis of the Cranfield Business School speaks of an airline malady called airline distress syndrome, which exhibits the following symptoms:

- Under-capitalization and substantial losses
- Over-politicization
- Strong unions which tend to delay innovation and resist change
- Over-staffing and low productivity
- No clear development strategy, resulting in an over-extended historical network, inappropriate and aging fleet, and too many aircraft types
- Bureaucratic management, with a pyramidical management structure and reluctance to make decisions
- Poor service quality

A close study of LIAT over its fifty-three years suggests that throughout its existence it has suffered from a number of the elements of airline distress syndrome.

For example, it has been under-capitalized from the beginning. More often than not, financial support from whatever source has tended to come during crisis periods, and even then, much later than needed. By the time those funds came, more money was always needed to do the same job.

For its size, it deals with a large number of unions, some ten in all. And no single body represents those unions. There is the Leeward Islands Airline Pilots Association (LIALPA), the pilots union; the Leeward Islands

Flight Attendants Association (LIFAA), representing cabin attendants; the Managers Union; the Engineers Union; the Waterfront and Allied Workers Union in Dominica; the LIAT Workers Union in St Vincent and the Grenadines; the National Workers Union in St Lucia; the Antigua and Barbuda Workers Union; the Grenada Technical and Allied Workers Union; and the Barbados Workers Union. LIAT's management has therefore to undertake Collective Bargaining Agreements with each union, any of which could be complex and difficult of resolution and a breakdown of any one of which could lead to industrial action.

In the 1990s, LIAT employed more than 1,000 staff, which as a ratio of staff to seats or passengers carried, must be one of the highest in the world. This was usually attributed to political interference in the matter of hiring staff. LIAT's efforts to reduce over-staffing inevitably ran the risk of high severance costs or industrial action or both. Before its relationship with Caribbean Star in 2007, the number of employees had been reduced to 752.

In 2005, its three major shareholders, the governments of Antigua and Barbuda, Barbados, and St Vincent and the Grenadines, expressed their commitment to leaving LIAT to be operated by its board and management along commercial lines. Pressure, however, often comes from the public which sees the government-owned carrier as public property. This can mean, for example, that in matters such as fixing fares, the public frequently seeks to put pressure on governments to intervene to lower prices, with little consideration of whether this would result in the airline charging fares below the cost of operation.

Before February 2007 when LIAT entered a commercial arrangement with Caribbean Star, its financial situation was often made worse by the fact that it was forced to operate in an environment of intense competition from both foreign and Caribbean carriers leading to fare wars. It could expect no public consideration since in a region which is chronically dependent on tourism, both the public and private sectors, seem to prefer a situation where there is maximum airline competition and low airfares. This preference is, however, clearly in conflict with the mandate from shareholder governments to earn revenues that cover operational costs and not to come to the treasury for money to bridge the gap between revenue and expenditure.

## The LIAT Speedwing Study

By the end of the 1990s, LIAT was at one of its many crossroads; and Speedwing Consulting, which had been contracted at a cost of £40,000 plus expenses to prepare a LIAT recovery plan presented it in May 1999. It covered a five-year period from November 1999 to October 2004.

It found that a large increase in underlying cost levels since 1996 and losses of market share to new or expanding competition were reflected in the deterioration of LIAT's financial position.

It held that the level of losses in 1997 and 1998 were unsustainable for an ordinary commercial organization and that this put the viability of LIAT in question. These losses were EC$2,155,000 in 1996; EC$13,134,000 in 1997 and EC$15,653,000 in 1998 (US$1 = EC$2.70).

The conclusion was that the company was technically insolvent and able to operate only because of its default on outstanding payments to governments. Additionally, the launch of BWee Express by BWIA in 1999 posed a huge threat to LIAT's existing business.

The options presented by Speedwing were as follows:

- To close down LIAT
- To commit to large-scale, long-term subsidies of an unprofitable LIAT
- To embark on a process of substantial change to create a leaner, more effective LIAT that was profitable and self-financing

A review of LIAT's activities indicated general problems of low productivity, inadequate management, weak revenue generation and ineffective use of information technology. In the first year of reconstruction, the airline operated six Dash 8-100s and three Dash 8-300s. In subsequent years, it grew to eleven aircraft, with four Dash 8-100s and seven Dash 8-300s. The Dash 8-100 carries thirty-seven passengers and the Dash 8-300 carries fifty passengers.

Improvements in unit revenues were intended to be achieved by effective yield management, a pricing structure that segmented business and leisure travel better, a professional commission-driven sales force and initiatives and organizational changes to develop the Quikpak courier business.

It was concluded that improvement in unit revenues would not be enough to produce a satisfactory financial return and that it would be necessary to reduce the size of the operation. The smaller operation demanded that overheads be reduced to ensure that unit costs did not rise. It was assumed that the smaller operation required a smaller fleet and three aircraft could therefore be sold to generate a cash injection that would be used to pay off some of the loans. It proposed that all areas were to be downsized, with fewer staff employed in engineering, flight operations, ground operations and finance.

Table 5.1 sets out the LIAT then current manpower breakout by department and proposed reductions.

These target manpower levels were said to be based on improved, but achievable productivity. They called for scrapping existing working agreements for all groups of staff, reverting to a standard forty-hour week governed by applicable local labour law and applying Civil Aviation Authority operating limitations for flying crew. In some cases, more efficient and effective working practices were identified as increased night shifts and weekend work in engineering, and rosters which scheduled more flight hours from pilots, while also improving the morale of many of the more minor pilots. Other areas identified for improving processes were revenue accounting and ground handling at airports and in respect of the latter, buying in the service from an external supplier.

**Table 5.1** Manpower Breakout by Departments

| Department | Budget | Actual | Year 1 | Year 2 | Year 3 | Year 4 | Year 5 |
|---|---|---|---|---|---|---|---|
| | 1998–99 | 1999 | 1999–2000 | 2000–2001 | 2001–2 | 2002–3 | 2003–4 |
| Engineering | 169 | 159 | 123 | 106 | 106 | 108 | 113 |
| Flight Operations | 196 | 172 | 172 | 152 | 158 | 170 | 176 |
| Ground Operations/Cargo | 481 | 469 | 383 | 404 | 419 | 466 | 502 |
| Sales/Marketing | 33 | 23 | 30 | 30 | 30 | 30 | 30 |
| Finance | 88 | 80 | 69 | 69 | 69 | 69 | 69 |
| Support Areas | 35 | 30 | 28 | 28 | 28 | 28 | 28 |
| Total Staff | 1,002 | 933 | 805 | 789 | 810 | 871 | 918 |

The report proposed that a severance scheme be introduced, initially voluntarily, to reduce staff by 200. If this approach did not work, it was recommended that an involuntary approach be adopted, without the last-in–first-out principle applying. Instead, LIAT would retain the best staff who might be the more recent recruits. Avoiding the last-in–first-out approach would need the support of local governments, especially Antigua and Barbuda, and some enabling legislation.

Poor use of IT was identified in areas such as engineering, rostering and revenue accounting, where poor planning and low productivity were found. It was seen as the cause of higher wastage than necessary in engineering inventories and part replacements. In some cases, for example, yield management and cargo, there was a need for new IT. In others, the problem was that the existing systems were not properly used. A training programme was required, as well as a new IT culture throughout the organization. One recommendation was that the position of IT should be changed within the organization and a vice president of IT, who would report to the CEO, be appointed.

Further recommendations were for changes at both the departmental and top levels, to include setting up profit centres for the ground-handling operations at Antigua and Grenada, the engineering department, Quikpak and cargo. This would require establishing internal contracts, detailing standards, services and prices between these profit centres and LIAT. It was envisaged that the first three profit centres would ultimately be developed into separate businesses.

In 1998, the feeling was that LIAT lacked many of the skills in-house to manage this process. The proposed organizational chart included a president/CEO reporting to the board, supported by an internal auditor, a flight safety officer, an executive assistant and a communications advisor. The rest of the executive management team would comprise six vice presidents who would be responsible for the IT, commercial, operations, legal and human resources (HR), engineering and finance departments, as per the organizational chart (figure 5.1).

A number of positions were identified which LIAT was advised to fill externally for different periods of time, while putting in place a process of training to develop skills of existing LIAT staff and Caribbean nationals. There seemed to be a notion that Speedwing Consultancy would supply the necessary external expertise. The entire process was to be supported by

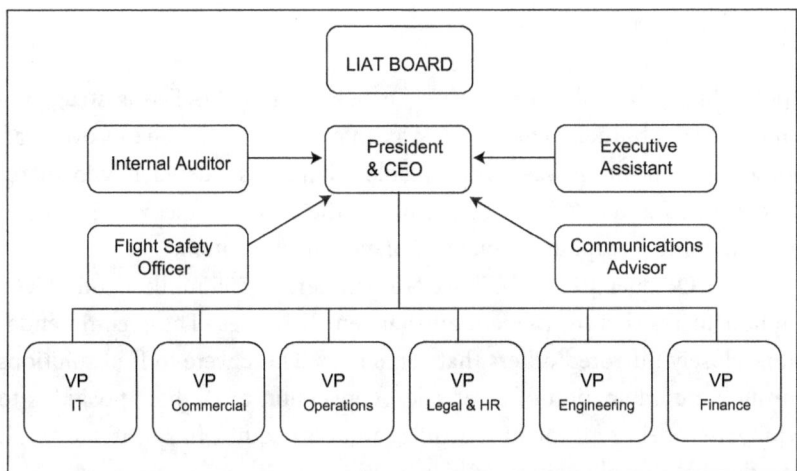

**Figure 5.1.** Organizational chart

a culture change programme aimed at inculcating individual initiative and innovation and a customer service and commercially focused approach. The staff to be brought in was as follows:

| VP commercial | minimum of two years |
| Commercial manager | minimum of one year |
| VP operations | minimum of two years |
| Chief pilot | ten days a month for six months |
| Hub development manager (Barbados) | three to six months |
| Manager ground services (Antigua) | six months |
| HR adviser | three to six months |
| VP engineering | minimum two years |
| Engineering planning manager | minimum nine months |
| Engineering purchasing manager | minimum two years |
| VP IT | minimum two years |
| Cargo consultant | three days a month for six months |

## New Schedule

A new schedule was proposed which concentrated on LIAT's best routes with a view to improving unit revenues. A decision was made that a number of journeys would be made by connections over Antigua and Barbados or by a cooperating airline.

## Financial Issues

Speedwing also dealt with LIAT's financial issues. LIAT was struggling under a heavy burden of debt with large interest payments, and its overdraft and creditor position was unsustainable. There was a deficiency in shareholder funds, and LIAT needed to support the proposed recovery measures by addressing its capitalization and balance sheet position.

On 31 October 1998, LIAT needed between EC$55 million and EC$60 million to restructure its debt and current liabilities. The recommendations closely mirrored others that came later. These were to find solutions through a combination of asset sales, conversion of creditor positions to equity, new debt repayment schedules and new equity. In specific terms, it was felt that the following should be done:

- Three surplus aircraft and engines should be sold, generating EC$20.8 million, which would provide cash injection of EC$9 million after repayment of associated loans.
- The remaining aircraft owned by LIAT (two Dash 8-100 and three Dash 8-300) should be sold and leased back. This would generate net funds of EC$14 million, after repayment of associated loans and payment of deposits for new leases.
- EC$14.3 million owed to existing shareholders for airport charges, which was projected to rise to EC$19.5 million by the end of 1999, should be written off, and if this was not possible, should be converted into preference shares. Such commitment from the shareholders was seen as likely to generate confidence of other parties for the re-capitalization to succeed.
- Further, amounts of EC$12.2 million owed to other creditors, such as travel taxes owed to shareholder governments, and amounts owed to non-shareholder governments and others should be written off or converted into a five-year loan with a two-year grace period for repayment.
- LIAT should try to secure agreement with the aircraft and engine manufacturers to convert their creditor position of EC$3.5 million into a medium-term five-year loan.

**Table 5.2** Profitability Targets (*in millions*)

|  | 2000–2001 | 2001–2 | 2002–3 | 2003–4 |
|---|---|---|---|---|
| Operating result | EC$18.6 | EC$21.5 | EC$22.6 | EC$21.8 |
| Net profit (after exceptional items) | EC$22.6 | EC$16.2 | EC$17.0 | EC$17.0 |

Speedwing argued that LIAT would still need a substantial overdraft facility to provide for any downside in the assumptions for the timing and achievements of the recovery plan and the re-capitalization proposals. It suggested raising additional equity capital to eliminate any overdraft and provide cash reserves. It felt that existing shareholders should be requested to subscribe EC$26 million for a new share issue on the basis of a 1:1 rights issue of existing ordinary shares. The new shares could be new ordinary shares in the same class, a new class of ordinary shares or redeemable preferred shares ranking ahead of common stock and receiving a fixed coupon dividend with conversion rights to ordinary shares.

It ended by stating that, "If the Board of LIAT grasps this opportunity, implements the Recovery Plan and Re-capitalization Plan in their entirety and funds LIAT adequately so that it can tackle the challenges it faces positively, then there can be a profitable future for LIAT."

The profitability targets established in the recovery plan were as shown in table 5.2.

It is now a matter of record that none of these financial targets were achieved since the assumptions on which they were made were never realized. Why was that?

# Why the Speedwing Recovery Plan Failed

To better understand the Speedwing Recovery Plan, one has to revert to an earlier period when LIAT was privatized, and to 1996 when the governments cut off all its subsidies. From 1996, LIAT jumped from one crisis to another to meet payroll, maintain safety standards and fend off one kind of competition or another. As a result of the privatization of LIAT, BWIA owned 29.58 per cent of the carrier.

People who were close to the LIAT issues at the time have offered several explanations of why the Speedwing Plan was not implemented. These are as follows:

- The LIAT board of the day neither endorsed nor rejected the Speedwing Report and Recovery Plan. Instead, it decided to distribute copies to shareholders, union heads and management, on receipt of which, each constituent element began to pick out those bits and pieces that suited their own interests.
- A number of governments focused on the level of staffing in Antigua and stated that they would make no commitment to address the debt write-offs until LIAT put its house in order in Antigua.
- The pilots were alleged to have concluded that the references to low productivity in the report applied to all staff, except themselves, and that the comments about weak management specifically applied to flight operations only.
- The Government of Trinidad and Tobago and BWIA objected to the view that the competition from BWee Express in 1999 was a major source of LIAT's problems.

The report therefore became a political hot potato and the Government of Antigua and Barbuda was put under considerable pressure. The then chairman, Aziz Hadeed, and the CEO, Ray Sawyer, left the company and John Benjamin became chairman for a six-month period. In the meantime LIAT went into further decline and seemed likely to go under. That was given as the reason that Prime Minister Lester Bird got into dialogue with Allen Stanford (later Sir Allen Stanford) and encouraged him to start Caribbean Star. Further to that, Robin Yearwood, a minister in the Lester Bird government, believing that LIAT could still be saved, got the support of the chairman of BWIA, Lawrence Duprey, and appointed Wilbur Harrigan to replace John Benjamin as chairman.

The Speedwing Report was quietly shelved and pronounced unaffordable in terms of the price tag (about £2 million) of the proposed Speedwing consultants, as well as the recommended level of investment and debt write-off. The major US consultancy firm of SH&E was then approached to review the situation, but their proposed fee was also considered too expensive.

In April 2000, chairman Wilbur Harrigan hired Garry Cullen, a former CEO of Aer Lingus as the LIAT CEO as well as Barbadian, David Stuart as general manager, marketing, and Rens van Eenennaam as chief financial officer (CFO). Cullen's contract made no reference to the Speedwing Report, but in preparing his own five-year plan he reviewed the Speedwing findings which he thought to be sound and incorporated many of them in his own document. He found the union leadership, led by Senator Humphrey of Grenada very useful in seeking to achieve the efficiency targets, especially since all union contracts had to be renegotiated.

It has been argued that the Speedwing revenue projections were totally invalidated by the arrival of Caribbean Star in 2000. The next three years were simply a struggle for survival, with the governments of the Eastern Caribbean continuing to argue that their help would depend on LIAT first "sorting out matters" in Antigua. It was these stringencies that led LIAT to have to raise a bond issue in 2002, which was backed by the Government of St Lucia in return for a seat on the LIAT board. This explains why St Lucia has a seat on the board without being a significant shareholder.

In reality, LIAT became largely dependent on the Antigua and Barbuda government until a government led by the Hon. Dr Ralph Gonsalves was elected in St Vincent and the Grenadines. Prime Minister Gonsalves became a strong supporter of LIAT and won the support of Barbados for the cause. Speedwing's call for EC$26 million from governments only yielded EC$2.6 million from St Vincent and the Grenadines. Prime Minister Gonsalves was also responsible for bringing other private sector resources on board. He later took the lead in the hiring of Zwaig Financial Consultants of Canada, whose sound financial advice, delivered largely through Cameron McCaw, was to prove a major turning point in the life of LIAT. By 2004, the Government of St Vincent and the Grenadines had become LIAT's largest shareholder with 25.26 per cent of the shares, ahead of Barbados with 22.19 per cent, and Antigua and Barbuda with 18.38 per cent.

The period from 2000 to 2004, which included the horrors of 9/11, was one of the most difficult on record for regional and international air transportation. Cost inputs into air transportation, especially those relating to safety, security and insurance, began to escalate exponentially.

The launch of Caribbean Star in 2000 had been followed by that of Caribbean Sun in 2003, operating out of San Juan, Puerto Rico, and also competing with LIAT on some of its routes. It was later discovered that both Caribbean Star and Caribbean Sun were suffering huge losses; but thanks to Sir Allen Stanford's deep pockets, seemed totally unaffected by these losses.

Between 2000 and 2004, LIAT's CEO, Garry Cullen, sought major changes at LIAT. His initial strategic plan called for an injection of equity capital of US$31 million. A strategic alliance between BWIA and LIAT had been agreed by the governments of Antigua and Barbuda, Barbados, Trinidad and Tobago, and St Vincent and the Grenadines, under which BWIA assumed responsibility for LIAT's marketing, sales, revenue management and advertising. For reasons about which the LIAT management claimed to be unclear, this arrangement with BWIA came to an abrupt end early in 2004. LIAT was not able to restore its own commercial operation until May 2006, when its commercial office was established in Barbados.

After St Vincent and the Grenadines paid the EC$2.6 million, none of the funds requested by Garry Cullen from the shareholders as a capital injection in 2000 were available until 2004.

In 2004, LIAT's shareholder governments (Antigua and Barbuda, Barbados, and St Vincent and the Grenadines) provided LIAT with EC$21 million; and in the first quarter of 2005, they persuaded the Government of Trinidad and Tobago, with the approval of the CARICOM governments, to provide LIAT with a grant of EC$44 million from the CARICOM Petroleum Stabilization Fund. This was a major achievement by prime ministers Arthur, Spencer and Gonsalves, since initially, Prime Minister Manning was adamant that his government would provide no further support to LIAT. What brought about the change of heart in a session behind closed doors would probably be very interesting to listen to.

By the end of 2005, LIAT had therefore received funds equivalent to US$25 million of the US$31 million the CEO had requested from its shareholders in 2000.

The period 2000–2005 found the company in debt to trade suppliers, banks, lessors, the Export Development Corporation (EDC) of Canada, regional governments and related agencies, and other debt holders and bond holders. Employees had not received a pay increase for more than seven years and creditors, generally speaking, were out of patience.

In August 2004, the board had received a report from Zwaig Financial Consultants on how dire LIAT's financial situation really was. As in 1999, liquidation of the company had once again been canvassed as an option. Another was to explore the possibility of seeking protection for LIAT under some kind of legislation similar to Chapter 11 in the United States. The reality was that such legislation did not exist in any of the countries of the Organization of Eastern Caribbean States, and LIAT (1974) Limited was registered in Antigua and Barbuda. There was further exploration of the possibility of taking such action in Barbados where the legislation existed, but where only one such bankruptcy protection case had been tested earlier.

Eventually, for good and proper reasons, that avenue was also abandoned and the only realistic remaining choice for LIAT's management was to meet with LIAT's bankers, creditors, unions, shareholders and suppliers once again and request their help and cooperation in restructuring the company. The approval of the shareholder governments was sought for dispensing with the bankruptcy option and meetings with the creditors began.

## Radical Changes at LIAT

Once the decision was made to go the route of seeking to restructure LIAT, a new strategic plan was presented to the board by CEO Garry Cullen. The twofold challenge was to deal with an accumulated debt of over EC$311 million and significant monthly losses, as well as to change the cost structure by introducing efficiencies in the operations and innovations that extended to a complete change of model.

It was conceived in two phases.

### Phase 1

Phase 1 of the LIAT plan was launched at the beginning of the last quarter of 2005 and was intended to accomplish the following:

- Renegotiate the company's debt with the Canadian EDC.
- Reschedule its debts with major creditors for spare parts and plane leases and so on.

- Reschedule its debts with banks and Caribbean governments.
- Negotiate with governments for the provision of reserve maintenance guarantees, which would remove LIAT from the need to pay large amounts of cash every month to be held in the escrow accounts of the lessors, against the proper maintenance of leased planes.
- Negotiate new collective bargaining agreements with staff and unions, which involved increased productivity incentives.
- Drastically reduce the cost of sales. This was to be done by the introduction of Navitaire to replace Sabre.
- Introduce ticketless travel.
- Introduce a new low-tariff system.
- Expand the fleet by increasing both the size of four of its planes and the number of aircraft. The initial plan was to move from eleven Dash 8s comprising 7-300s and 4-100s to thirteen Dash 8-300s by the end of 2005 and fifteen by the end of 2006. As was said earlier, the Dash 8-300s carry fifty passengers, as opposed to the Dash 8-100s which carry thirty-seven.
- Upgrade the marketing and public relations operations by creating a new commercial department headed by a chief commercial officer, to be based in Barbados.
- Introduce more non-stop and one-stop flights.
- Cut unprofitable routes.
- Introduce an extensive staff culture change programme.

It was an ambitious plan, with a Phase I target of reaching a break-even point by the end of 2005 and a small operating profit by 2006. At this point Phase 2 was supposed to kick in.

**Phase 2**

Phase 2 envisaged the pursuit of third-party equity financing to support company growth.

It assumed the following:

- Full implementation of the business model
- Full integration of the Navitaire system

- Continued enhancement of the quality customer service
- Efficient functioning of the commercial department in Barbados

## LIAT: A Legacy Carrier

To understand the radical nature of the plan proposed earlier, it has to be understood that for fifty years LIAT had operated along the legacy carrier model, using a hub and spoke system of routes and one of the established GDSs, Sabre, for making its reservations and interlining arrangements.

Sabre was tied into the terminals of almost all the travel agencies operating in the region and in many cases owned the terminals. The relationship between the GDSs and travel agents has already been explained in chapter 3. It was shown that both GDSs and travel agents have a vested interest in an airline maintaining the GDS connection.

Very importantly also, most of the international carriers with which LIAT had interlining agreements which affect the transfer of both passengers and baggage, used Sabre or some system compatible to their own. To transfer from Sabre to a system like Navitaire which was alien to these carriers was to take a major step which would later have a number of consequences for LIAT. The Cullen plan, however, involved having LIAT adopt the LCC model; and LCCs were using the Navitaire system to good effect.

The case presented by LIAT's management was that LIAT had operated the legacy model for fifty years with negative results and it was time to try something new. It was proposed to transform LIAT into a low-fare LCC and, for the purposes of distribution, to switch from Sabre to Navitaire which was used by LCCs and facilitated many of their processes with a positive impact on their costs.

## The Case for Navitaire

The arguments made in favour of Navitaire were many; it would save the carrier some EC$5 million a year in distribution costs; it would bring new ways of dealing with reservations, check-in, online bookings, revenue management and flight operations systems: one of the most attractive elements of the new business model was intended to be revenue enhancement due to its new and transparent pricing structure, ease of booking with its new website and enhanced revenue management capability.

It was a bold plan, but like all bold plans it also contained risks and disadvantages which were not either sufficiently communicated or understood up front.

Earlier in chapter 2, the main characteristics of the successful LCC were outlined. One of these was the ability to fly long distances point-to-point rather than operating in a complex network on a hub and spoke basis. As a relatively small carrier operating turboprop equipment comprising a fleet of fifty-seater and thirty-seven-seater aircraft flying short distances and with a substantial hub-feed market, LIAT was hard put to replicate the financial benefits LCCs receive from flying long point-to-point distances. Its model was at best a hybrid LCC.

More importantly, LIAT was to discover that to begin life as a legacy carrier and introduce radical transformation systems to become an LCC is a great deal more difficult than launching an LCC from zero. Legacy carriers come with a great deal of financial baggage and obligations to staff and unions.

There were also other realities facing LIAT. Given the region's economic structure and the generally high cost of inputs, it is easier to become a low-fare airline than a low-cost airline, and the geographical realities of the Caribbean determine that the islands form natural hubs and spokes. The number of multiple stops can be reduced, but never eliminated.

## Challenges of Changing to a New Business Model

LIAT, eager to introduce changes which were intended to cut losses, found itself during the last quarter of 2005 in a dilemma; problems which needed to be corrected were escalating rapidly and yet there was no time to invest in the preparation ideally needed for introducing so drastic a change in its business model. There were many challenges as follows:

- There was inadequate time to correct any kinks found in the new systems.

- There were costs and technical difficulties involved in the changeover from Sabre to Navitaire in terms of the old technology communicating with the new technology.
- There was resistance to change and opposition from some of LIAT's travel industry partners, the travel agents, who benefited more from the old distribution system of Sabre with which they were in an alliance, who operated Sabre's terminals in their offices and who therefore had their own reasons to prefer LIAT to keep the Sabre system in place.
- The time available for existing staff to become familiar with the new technology was short.
- More time was needed than was actually available for customers to get acquainted with the new online technology and ticketless travel.
- More time was needed using the new technology, to reinstate the interlining arrangements with the several international carriers which had been disturbed when Navitaire replaced Sabre.

When the new CEO, Mark Darby, arrived in July 2006, one of the priority tasks he was given by the board was to fix the interlining problems. Working with Navitaire's management, LIAT was able to find a technical solution to dealing with inbound interlining arrangements. But, as late as 2008, outbound passengers from off-line destinations wishing to book over the hubs in Antigua and Barbuda and Barbados through to the marketplace were still facing problems.

Agreement had been reached between the Grantley Adams International Airport and LIAT to seek to bypass the technical problems by administratively enhancing the facilitation process at the Barbados hub. The solution proposed was that connecting passengers who were booked through Barbados to off-line destinations could be permitted to clear immigration by a fast-track system, collect their baggage and place it on a carousel which would take it back to the in-transit lounge, to which they also would proceed directly without going through customs and back to an airline counter outside. This took longer to implement than was envisaged by those who proposed it and a new government which took office in Barbados after 15 January 2008 gave directions to the management of the Grantley Adams International Airport and other staff at the airport to resolve the logistic difficulties and implement the solutions already agreed upon.

The problems LIAT experienced with Navitaire were due to the fact that the system was created to deal ideally with airlines operating a point-to-point system, rather than a hub and spoke system and works very well for LCCs like Ryanair, JetBlue and others which operate largely on that basis.

However, Navitaire is a developing system which is introducing software solutions to the problems discussed earlier at a price. Discussions between LIAT and Navitaire in 2008 suggest that technical solutions can be found for complete interlining in both directions and for dealing with other challenges.

Having discussed the problems associated with the change to Navitaire, there are some arguments in favour of adopting this system. The new strategy permitted LIAT to switch from a strategy dependent on travel agencies and computer reservation systems to a high level of direct selling, which offers the public an easy, accessible booking and fare availability, while at the same time avoiding the punitive distribution charges of Sabre and similar GDSs. It brought new ways of dealing with reservations, check-ins, online bookings, revenue management and flight operations systems.

Initially when problems arose, switching from Navitaire back to a GDS was discussed, but decided against, once an interlining fix was identified. There would have been a costly penalty for breaking the existing contract with Navitaire and the fact is that GDSs remain expensive ways of doing business.

Moreover, at the time when the decision to switch to Navitaire was made, LIAT's interlining business had to a large extent been lost to its competitor Caribbean Star, which had won the business by offering unrealistic fares. It was later found that at those fares, the business simply increased its overall losses. These developments may have led management at LIAT, which recognized that 75 per cent of its business was operating as the intra-Caribbean bus service, to undervalue its role as a connecting carrier.

The fact is that the future of LIAT lies in maximizing both its role as a bridge between the Caribbean countries and as a connecting carrier to international services into the region.

The arguments for and against Navitaire are yet to be resolved and the board has taken a decision to have a study done on the basis of which a definitive conclusion can be reached, on whether it is best to retain the system or change it for a more trouble-free interlining-friendly mechanism.

# Continuing Challenges in 2006

In addition to the technological challenges which LIAT faced at the end of 2005, there were others which arose as if dictated by Murphy's law that whatever can go wrong, will. Mechanical problems, industrial action and charges by lessors all came together in 2006 to threaten LIAT's survival.

**Mechanical Problems**

Two of LIAT's planes went out of service for maintenance in December 2005, one of the busiest times for Caribbean carriers, and it was forced to transfer business to its chief competitor, Caribbean Star.

**Industrial Action**

During the first quarter of 2006, the board and management fought to put the recovery plan back on track, but experienced a major setback when the LIAT pilots went on a sick-out on 1 March 2006.

As part of the restructuring process, LIAT had been able to renegotiate salary and other benefits with all but one of its many unions. It had a long-standing dispute with LIALPA, the pilots' union, over both salary increases and issues arising from LIAT's termination of its provident fund in October 1997. LIALPA went to court arguing that such termination violated the terms of the individual pilot contracts with LIAT and the court found in favour of the union. LIAT accepted the financial responsibility imposed by the court, but argued for more time to repay it than the pilots were willing to agree to.

The first of March 2006 was a good day for making a protest through industrial action. It was the day when several people who had been attending Caribbean carnivals needed to return home and it was obvious that the absence of LIAT from the skies would create major confusion and inconvenience for travellers.

Once again, within a two-month period, LIAT found itself transferring business to its main competitor, Caribbean Star. It estimates that in actual and forward bookings, it lost some EC$1.4 million as a direct result of the pilots' sick-out. The negotiations with the pilots came to a sudden halt. On 11 March 2006, with a delegation of members of the board, the chairman of the board met with the executive of LIALPA for a frank and free exchange of views which resulted in negotiations recommencing.

### Reserve Maintenance Guarantees

At the beginning of 2006, LIAT had to make cash payments of US$20,000 per month per plane to one of its lessors, against the maintenance of its leased planes. An option had been to get two of its shareholder governments to put in place certain government guarantees requested by the lessor. These guarantees needed parliamentary approval and, given the continuing exchanges needed between the legal departments on both sides to get it right (governments and lessors), it took more than a year to put the guarantees in place.

### Financial Targets for 2005 and 2006

Needless to say, the deadline set in the plan for break-even in 2005 was not met and the prospects for an operating profit by the end of 2006 quickly receded. In fact, LIAT experienced quite a great deal of turbulence during the last quarter in 2005 which continued into 2006. It had been hard put to meet its basic costs of wages and salaries for December 2005.

## Barbados and Antigua to the Rescue

LIAT was forced to turn to its shareholders for financial support on New Year's Day of 2006. On that very special holiday, prime ministers Rt Hon. Owen Arthur of Barbados and the Hon. Dr Ralph Gonsalves of St Vincent and the Grenadines met CEO Garry Cullen and the chairman of LIAT at the Barbados Hilton Hotel to discuss how the crisis could be resolved. On that occasion, it was Prime Minister Arthur who came to the rescue of LIAT in its cash flow crisis by agreeing to an equity investment of US$10 million in the carrier.

Later in 2006, in the month of June, another shareholder, prime minister of Antigua and Barbuda, agreed to make a vital equity investment of US$6 million in the airline.

This kind of support from its shareholders in the face of much opposition represents more than financial assistance. It was a commitment to

LIAT and to regional air transportation, which sent important messages both to consumers and to competitors: that everything reasonable would be done by its shareholders to keep LIAT flying. There can be no doubt that it was these financial commitments that finally convinced Sir Allen Stanford, owner of Caribbean Sun and Caribbean Star, that it was not worth his time financially to wait for LIAT to collapse and leave the field.

## CEO Cullen Departs

To add to LIAT's many challenges in 2006: two of its three most senior officials, who would naturally be expected to drive the implementation of the business plan (which had got off to a difficult start), left the company. CEO Garry Cullen left at the end of March 2006, and the CFO, Roland Blais, left at the end of June 2006. Of the senior executive triumvirate, this left only Danny Oliver, the chief operating officer, a LIAT stalwart who himself later retired from LIAT in 2007.

The CEO's departure, although not entirely unexpected, could not have come at a worse time. He had originally come in 2000 for two years and had been persuaded to remain until March 2006. He brought a great deal of airline experience, knowledge and a calm disposition – an absolutely necessary requirement for anyone serving as the CEO of any airline. His diplomatic skills and awareness of how he was expected to relate to the shareholder governments were exemplary. At LIAT these qualities are needed in abundance.

His departure was soon followed by the CFO's announcement that he too was leaving. CFO Roland Blais had been identified to serve as officer-in-charge after Cullen left. His departure was unexpected and one could only guess that it was a case of LIAT burnout.

Their departure in the midst of an extremely challenging time for the carrier meant that matters which needed to be urgently fixed, like the interlining problems that arose after the introduction of Navitaire, were not attended to immediately.

Their departures also forced the board chairman to act briefly as an executive chairman, to whom all heads of department were now reporting directly. In addition to overseeing the operations of the company, he was faced with the need to preside over the recruitment of a CEO, a CFO and a chief commercial officer to fill the post of head of the new commercial department to be established in Barbados. Fortunately, the LIAT board of directors rose to the occasion and got the job done.

By the end of June 2006, candidates to fill the three vacant posts had been identified and appointed: Mark Darby, an air transportation partner in Unisys Consulting Firm was appointed CEO; Alan Bryon, acting CFO; and Leesa Parris, chief commercial officer. By July 2006, the new management team was installed at LIAT with the responsibility of urgently reviewing and revising as necessary, the existing restructuring plan created by Garry Cullen.

A major additional responsibility for LIAT was that during 2006 it had signed on as part of the Caribbean Carrier Consortium, which would be contractually responsible for transporting all the participating teams, officials, media and sponsors and all their baggage during the ICC Cricket World Cup Tournament in the West Indies in the spring of 2007, and it was important that it was financially and operationally able to carry out the responsibilities it had undertaken.

## Need for New Approaches

The existing restructuring plan was now put under the microscope. It had sought to tackle critical areas of LIAT's operations, such as labour, sales, ticketing and distribution; but major challenges remained and both the regional and international environment were becoming less favourable for conducting successful business in air transportation.

LIAT was never more convinced that a general case can be made for special treatment for small regional carriers for the following reasons:

- They operate in a capital-intensive industry with small margins, a perishable product and a high level of fixed costs, representing some 40 per cent of total costs. These relate to fuel, maintenance, insurance and other security costs, leases of planes and payments for spares and significant sums advanced as reserve maintenance guarantees. Over some of these, like the cost of fuel, the airline has absolutely no control.
- Buying aviation fuel in bulk or the ability to hedge against high prices by buying forward are two highly recommended strategies, the pros

and cons of which will be discussed at greater length in chapter 9. These strategies are, however, normally beyond the ability of small carriers. In fact, the smaller an airline, the higher the premium it has to pay for everything it needs.

- A niche carrier can only succeed if it has special features and lower unit costs than its competition. The LCCs – Southwest, JetBlue, Ryanair and GOL – have demonstrated success in this way.
- Since the Caribbean operates an "open skies" policy, even where no formal "open skies agreements" have been signed, the competition from foreign legacy carriers, LCCs and charters has always been fierce. This policy is driven by the region's reliance on tourism, which seeks to achieve a high level of reliable air service and relatively cheap fares. The downside of this policy is that too much capacity on the routes dilutes business and drives down fares, which benefits the travelling public in the short term, but causes many an airline to go out of business. Low fares can lead to withdrawals of service by some of the carriers, which can lead to monopolies and to the return of higher fares than before.
- Unless some means can be found of getting rid of massive accumulated debt, the interest payments remain as a mountain to climb every month.
- The ongoing threat of terrorist activity has meant increasing airline costs in insurance and security generally.

In 2006, LIAT had its own specific challenges as follows:

- First, between Caribbean Star, Caribbean Sun and LIAT alone, there were thirty Dash 8 planes flying the Eastern Caribbean routes in July 2006, with Caribbean Star matching every route, schedule and price that LIAT offered.
- Fares got lower and lower as a result of the LIAT–Caribbean Star fare wars and when in July 2006 oil reached US$78.84 per barrel, it represented too high a proportion of the carrier's costs.

According to the preceding view, a suggestion was made to the shareholders that LIAT would either need an annual subsidy built into the budgets of its shareholders, like that provided for Air Jamaica by its government, or there should be some sort of regulation by Caribbean authorities to prevent predatory pricing or both. When neither proposal was positively received it became clear to LIAT that it would be unable to survive much longer while the haemorrhaging of cash continued. It was not, however, aware at the time that Caribbean Star was in very much the same situation and was looking for a way out.

However, a serendipitous meeting in the Cayman Islands between the chairman of LIAT and the president of Caribbean Star and Caribbean Sun on 7 July 2006 led to historic developments which surprised the Caribbean region. In the process, cooperation between Caribbean carriers was redefined and taken to a new level. Chapter 6 explains why the LIAT–Caribbean Star merger was necessary for LIAT's survival.

# 6

# Why the LIAT–Caribbean Star Merger Was Necessary

## The Caribbean Star and LIAT Relationship

There was nothing friendly or fraternal about the Caribbean Star/LIAT relationship from 2000 when Caribbean Star was introduced into the Eastern Caribbean. Of course, they helped each other out, as all airlines do, in a crisis, especially if it meant accepting each other's passengers. But beyond that, it was usually competition to the death and it was no secret that Caribbean Star duplicated the LIAT schedule, country by country and fares wars were the order of the day.

More often than not Caribbean Star and LIAT left airports within minutes of each other with half empty loads because of the excess capacity on the routes.

## Overcapacity in the Region

Between 2000 and 2006, the excess supply of airline seats over demand in the Eastern Caribbean had reached ridiculous proportions. Even during the months of July and August, when travellers around the world were normally having great difficulty in finding enough airline seats, there was never any such constraint in the Eastern Caribbean, however, late the time of booking. Sporting, church, festival and other groups wishing to travel had many half empty carriers from which to choose. Moreover, LIAT's fares in 2006 were 25 per cent lower than they had been in 2005. An examination of graph and tables (appendix 2) showing the average fares of LIAT between the period January 2000 and January 2007 reveals that its fares fell consistently after January 2000 when Caribbean Star first came on the scene. The fare level obtained in January 2000 was reached again for the first time in January 2006.

It was this excess capacity and low fares in the Eastern Caribbean that had caused BWee Express, Jamaica Express, Carib Express and others to go out of business. Caribbean Star and Caribbean Sun were able to survive simply because of the deep pockets of their billionaire owner, Texan, Sir Allen Stanford.

While this state of affairs continued, LIAT, Caribbean Star and Caribbean Sun were losing vast amounts of money. Sir Allen Stanford was thought by everyone to be more likely to hold out than the public sector shareholders of LIAT. But even billionaires must have limits to how much money they can afford to lose, especially on a venture which is not part of their core business. To make matters worse for Caribbean Star which was LIAT's direct competitor, every time LIAT seemed on the brink of collapse, its shareholder governments, Antigua and Barbuda, Barbados, and St Vincent and the Grenadines, would come to the table and bail it out. This must have surprised and frustrated Sir Allen Stanford.

This brief background to the relationship between the two carriers and their subsequent close relationship demonstrate some important truths; first, it is a great incentive to competitors to talk to each other when both of them are losing large amounts of money; and second, there is little room for emotion in commercial business. Not to be ruled out, however, is the need for the right opportunity to present itself.

## Contacts with Caribbean Star

During the first quarter of 2006, while Garry Cullen was still CEO, there had been some conversations particularly at the level of Danny Oliver, chief operating officer at LIAT, and his opposite number at Caribbean Star, about ending some of the suicidal competition which was clearly damaging both carriers. It does not seem, however, that Sir Allen was privy to these conversations.

On 7 July 2006, the Latin American and Caribbean Air Transport Association held a meeting for CEOs in the Cayman Islands. It was also attended by the CEOs of Air Jamaica, CAL, Caribbean Star and Cayman Island Airways. The chairman of LIAT attended only because the new LIAT CEO, Mark Darby, had been on the job for four days only and needed to concentrate on other priorities. He made an intervention at the meeting on the topic of functional cooperation between Caribbean carriers and also circulated an executive summary of the study that was done for CTO in 1993 by El Perial and Miami Aviation Services when he was the secretary general of that organization.

It was Skip Barnette, a former veteran of Delta Airlines and at the time president and CEO of Caribbean Star and Caribbean Sun, who raised the possibility with the LIAT chairman on that day of Caribbean Star and LIAT entering some sort of cooperation along the lines outlined at the meeting. They spoke frankly about the losses of the two carriers and the need to do something to stop them. Within half an hour, six years of baggage between Caribbean Star and LIAT had been left behind. Skip Barnette promised to speak to Sir Allen Stanford and get his agreement to explore closer working relationships between the two carriers; and LIAT's chairman undertook to discuss the subject with the three shareholder prime ministers of LIAT.

So began the dialogue that led first to the Caribbean Star–LIAT commercial agreement commencing on 1 February 2007 which was initiated by the CEOs of the two carriers and ultimately led to the purchase of Caribbean Star's assets by LIAT (1974) Limited in October 2007.

By mid-2007 it was clear to the board and management of LIAT that a collaborative venture with Caribbean Star was the only option likely to create an inter-regional carrier which had a chance of achieving sustainability and profitability, while permitting Caribbean governments to maintain some element of control over intra-regional air transportation. The LIAT shareholders were therefore strongly advised to proceed in that direction.

Once the LIAT–Caribbean Star discussions about a merger began, they took on a life of their own and by the summer of 2007, had reached a conclusion never anticipated by either party when the conversations began in July 2006.

The story of how this was done is, in many ways, the reverse of the direction in which so many things in the Caribbean have gone, and holds out hope that wider rationalization of air transportation services in the region could be possible if there was a will to make it happen.

In August 2006, Sir Allen Stanford called the chairman of LIAT and confirmed his wish to negotiate a merger of Caribbean Star and LIAT. He was assured that the LIAT shareholders had been briefed and that he could expect a definite answer after LIAT's CEO, Mark Darby, who had only taken up his post in Antigua at the beginning of July 2006, could make a formal presentation to them.

He was told further that under the relevant companies act, a pre-condition of LIAT entering any merger would be its ability to first liquidate its enormous accumulated debt of over EC$300 million. LIAT's next first step would therefore be to identify a financial institution from which it could borrow the funds needed. The conversation ended with Sir Allen Stanford agreeing to consider making such a loan to LIAT from the Stanford Financial Group (SFG).

## Meeting of LIAT Shareholder Prime Ministers in Kingstown

In September 2006, Prime Minister Ralph Gonsalves invited prime ministers Baldwin Spencer and Owen Arthur and their delegations to a meeting in Kingstown to review all the strategic options available for LIAT's survival.

Owing to illness, Prime Minister Arthur could not attend the meeting and the Barbados delegation was led by the minister of tourism and international transport, the Hon. Noel Lynch. LIAT was represented by chairman Jean Holder, CEO Mark Darby and acting CFO Alan Bryon.

## Financial Position of LIAT at September 2006

The numbers presented at the meeting by Mark Darby in September 2006 showed LIAT's financial situation to be difficult. Losses for 2005 had been

EC$47,803,993 (net) and EC$33,976,828 (operating). In July 2006, LIAT's estimated losses were already EC$37 million, with losses to year end being projected to be more than EC$60 million. The new CEO's analysis of the problem areas was as follows:

- Too much capacity
- Irrational competition
- 2006 fares too low (some 25 per cent lower than that in 2005)
- Some revenue losses sustained due to post-Navitaire loss of interline arrangements with long-haul carriers
- Business model too inflexible
- Aging fleet leading to expensive maintenance
- Restrictive labour agreements leading to difficulties and expenses in reducing the workforce
- High cost base

He informed the shareholders' meeting that the existing situation called for another financial bail out in which the shareholders needed to inject cash of about EC$54 million by October 2006 (US$20 million). Of this sum, EC$24 million was needed to cover projected estimated losses for the months of August–December 2006, and the rest, EC$25 million, was required to settle a debt with the EDC of the Government of Canada. This sum was far less than that was actually owed to Canada, but the original amount had been considerably reduced due to an extensive process of negotiations between LIAT and the EDC, assisted by the Canadian high commissioner, HE Michael Welsh, based in Barbados, and Prime Minister Ralph Gonsalves of St Vincent and the Grenadines. It was hoped that Antigua and Barbuda might find the EC$54 million (US$20 million) needed from a possible loan for this amount which it was negotiating with the Government of Venezuela for investment in LIAT.

The meeting in St Vincent, which lasted five hours, reviewed the options of voluntary winding-up, liquidation, bankruptcy, continuing the restructuring process in isolation and finally, a merger with Caribbean Star. It came to the following conclusions:

- *Voluntary winding-up.* Under voluntary winding-up, the shareholder governments would be able to shed all long-term commitments to LIAT and would finally be out of the airline ownership business. However, the costs to them of a voluntary winding-up of the company would have been EC$249 million, which presumably few commercial banks would wish to lend them or they would wish to borrow for such a purpose. Job losses at LIAT would have numbered 752. The commitments made by LIAT to the Cricket World Cup Tournament scheduled for the spring of 2007 for teams, officials, media and sponsors could not have been honoured. There would be nothing to show for the shareholders' previous investments in the carrier, and Caribbean Star would have the market to itself – altogether a political mess. This was not an option.

- *Liquidation.* Another alternative would have been simply to liquidate the company, meeting certain shareholder debt, but avoiding many other outstanding liabilities, like severance payments to staff. This would have had serious repercussions for the Antiguan Commercial Bank with which LIAT did business. The estimated cost of doing this was EC$93 million, but it would have been a political nightmare, especially in Antigua and Barbuda, and would have brought with it some of the disadvantages of the voluntary winding-up process mentioned earlier.
- *Bankruptcy protection.* After the 2004 experiment of unsuccessfully exploring court protection for LIAT by going the bankruptcy route, this recourse was not seriously considered again in 2006.
- *Continuing the restructuring process.* Perhaps the easiest option for LIAT in September 2006 would have been simply to keep on doing the same old thing; trying to source the EC$54 million needed to survive a little longer, continuing the implementation of the individual restructuring process started in 2005 and competing with Caribbean Star. If this sum of money could be found, this plan would have guaranteed, for a while, the availability of a great deal of seat capacity at low, if commercially unrealistic prices, and would almost certainly have appealed to those who were receiving LIAT services, but did not have to contribute to its costs.

Realistically, however, this course of action presented no solution to the fierce competition from Caribbean Star, no solution to the need for a major capital injection to put the airline on a commercial footing, no solution to paying off the accumulated debt, no solution to the shareholder governments having to make repeated future injections of cash into the carrier and, in any case, would have been an unsustainable situation.

## LIAT–Caribbean Star Merger

There was really no credible option left on the table, but the formerly unthinkable merger between LIAT and Caribbean Star. This was, however, to become a matter of considerable controversy throughout 2007 and the beginning of 2008, for a number of reasons.

In September 2006, many were sceptical about Sir Allen Stanford's motives in agreeing to discuss a merger between LIAT and Caribbean Star. It was assumed that he personally had initiated the merger talks with the intention of taking control of LIAT and creating a monopoly for himself in the intra-Caribbean air transportation business. While the idea of a merger was first broached by Skip Barnette, Stanford's president and CEO of Caribbean Star and Caribbean Sun, there seems good reason to believe that initially Sir Allen Stanford was very opposed to working with LIAT and had to be persuaded for this course of action, based on the argument that there was otherwise no end in sight to the haemorrhaging of cash by his two carriers.

Second, a number of people who had always vehemently objected to Caribbean governments' giving financial support to LIAT to keep it operating were now equally appalled at the idea of it falling into Sir Allen Stanford's hands. They began to argue in support of governments continuing their financial support to LIAT so that it could avoid merging with Caribbean Star. It was assumed that in any merger talks between LIAT and Sir Allen Stanford, LIAT would get the worse of the deal.

This scepticism was further heightened when it was later made public that LIAT had under consideration an option to borrow money from one of Stanford's banks to pay off its accumulated debt. There was a strongly held view that the shareholders would not be able to repay the money and Sir Allen Stanford would simply take possession of the merged carrier, thus, achieving in the peace, what he had been unable to achieve in the war.

Fortunately, the shareholder governments were not persuaded by any of these arguments to shelve the idea of the merger. Shareholders, board and management agreed that without it, it would be a matter of time before LIAT in its then weak financial situation would exhaust government subsidies and be made bankrupt by the daily competition from Caribbean Star. Further, they had no means of knowing the true financial situation of Caribbean Star, which was a private company; the affairs of which were known only to a few persons close to Stanford.

One may ask why billionaire Sir Allen Stanford did not simply wait for LIAT to collapse and then operate his carrier in a market free from competition and at fares required to meet his costs. There are probably four reasons:

- Caribbean Star was actually haemorrhaging cash very badly.
- Based on LIAT's history of survival, he could not be sure that the airline would actually be allowed to go under, however close it came to that point.
- Sir Allen Stanford must often have wondered why he got into a business which had nothing to do with his core business of banking and finance.
- He was rapidly coming to the conclusion reached by others before him, that the quickest way to become a millionaire is to be a billionaire and buy an airline.

**Kingstown Agreement**

The meeting in St Vincent ended with an agreement among the shareholder governments to authorize the board of directors to start the merger talks with Sir Allen Stanford formally. This was ratified by the LIAT board at its meeting in Barbados in October 2006.

**Oversight Negotiating Committees**

LIAT's next step was to create two oversight negotiating committees, one to conduct the negotiations with the SFG and the other to conduct union negotiations concerning personnel matters relating to the staff of both LIAT and Caribbean Star resulting from the merger of the two companies.

The two LIAT oversight negotiating committees were chaired by the chairman of LIAT and reported to a three-man shareholder committee comprising prime ministers Owen Arthur, Baldwin Spencer, and Dr Ralph Gonsalves. Board members Brian Challenger, George Goodwin, Miguel Southwell of Antigua and Barbuda; Grantley Smith and Irvine Best of Barbados and Isaac Solomon of St Vincent and the Grenadines were members of the oversight committees. From time to time alternate directors, Valerie Brown of Barbados and Godfrey Pompey of St Vincent and the Grenadines were involved.

CEO Mark Darby and CFO Alan Bryon were *ex officio* members of the committee and interacted on an ongoing basis with the corresponding officials of Caribbean Star.

## Committee Advisers

The committee formed to conduct the negotiations with the SFG was advised by Canadian Cameron McCaw from Zwaig Financial Consulting; Barbadians Anthony Ellis, accountant, Dr Adrian Cummins, QC, and Oliver Browne, QC, of Carrington and Sealy Law Firm in Barbados; Attorney-at-law Stacey Richards-Anjo of Richards and Co, Antigua; solicitor general of Barbados, Jennifer Edwards; deputy solicitor general of Antigua and Barbuda; Karen DeFreitas-Rait and Camillo Gonsalves representing the attorney general's offices of St Vincent and the Grenadines. Jackie Blackman of the Ministry of International Transport of Barbados served as secretary to the committee.

Sir Allen Stanford had his lawyers and financial experts drawn as needed from his companies, and headed by Skip Barnette, the president and CEO of Caribbean Star and Caribbean Sun and supported by Michael Henne, Caribbean Star's CFO.

## Trade Union Council

For the purpose of negotiating on human resource merger matters, the ten LIAT unions created a trade union council comprising representatives from the various unions, under the chairmanship of Senator Chester Humphrey of the Grenada Technical and Allied Workers Union.

The LIAT committee established to handle the union negotiations was advised by Burns Bonadie, an experienced trade unionist from St Vincent and the Grenadines and Edward Bushell, then consul general of Barbados in Miami, but formerly a human resources director and very experienced negotiator in industrial matters on the management side.

In January 2008, negotiations between the shareholders of LIAT and Caribbean Star began with a view to merge the two carriers.

# 7

# Negotiating a Merger with Sir Allen Stanford

The commencement of the LIAT–Caribbean Star talks had immediate beneficial effects on the operations of both carriers. Caribbean Star agreed to put an end to the operational practices which had resulted in losses to both companies during a six-year period of fierce competition. As early as November 2006, an end was put to the fare wars and LIAT was able to return its fare levels to those that existed before 2005. This meant that although LIAT was not able to avoid entirely the cash flow crisis forecast by the LIAT management at the September 2006 meeting in Kingstown, the need for funds by December 2006 was not as great as had been anticipated. It was now projected that an injection of EC$8.1 million (US$3 million) in December 2006, would suffice, as opposed to the sum of EC$24 million, which management had stated in September would have been needed. The funds were paid by the shareholders, but the message from them was clear: run this carrier along commercial lines and do not come back to us for any more money as a subsidy. It should be noted for the record that since that date until October 2009, when this book was completed, management had not requested or received any further subsidies from any government. This however had implications for the LIAT fare policy.

## Unionization of the Merged Carrier

The basis on which the talks commenced was that a merger of the two carriers was on the table in which the two existing airlines would disappear and be replaced by a new entity. As soon as the talks began in November 2006, they ran into their first hurdle relating to whether or not the new carrier resulting from the merger would be unionized.

The LIAT negotiators and Sir Allen Stanford were totally divided on the question of unionization. Caribbean Star was not unionized and the attempts of its staff to become so through all its years of existence had not succeeded.

Sir Allen Stanford was opposed in principle to having unions, arguing that it was better to employ people and pay them well than to have one's businesses repeatedly disrupted by industrial action. He was particularly concerned about LIAT having some ten unions. His position could not be supported by the Caribbean shareholder governments, given the history of the region's social and political development. They were firmly committed to the merged entity being unionized and Sir Allen Stanford was adamant that it should not be. This disagreement was seen as a possible deal breaker.

Inevitably, the unions in the countries served by LIAT began to make their voices heard in support of free association of workers and asked for a meeting with the chairman and the CEO of LIAT to discuss it. At a meeting held in Barbados they were given the assurance that the shareholders were committed to unionization and the negotiating team would work to get Sir Allen's agreement. Fortunately, he was persuaded that this was not an area where there could be any compromise on the part of our political leaders. His yielding on this point sent a clear message that he wanted the merger to succeed and it was possible to confirm the commitment of both sides to continue the talks.

It was at this point in January 2007 that LIAT was approached by CAL of Trinidad and Tobago to end the talks with Stanford and consider an alternative offer from CAL instead.

## Caribbean Airlines' Proposal

On 10 January 2007, the chairman of LIAT was contacted by CAL, which had recently replaced BWIA. It was mentioned that the prime minister of

St Vincent and the Grenadines, Dr Ralph Gonsalves, had visited Trinidad and Tobago and explored the possibility of a LIAT–BWIA alliance and that the call was related to that visit.

The call was followed by a letter indicating CAL's vision to become the regional carrier of the Caribbean and stating that CAL had been designed and capitalized with that intent to leverage operational and financial synergies throughout the region. One of the reasons suggested for the slowness in one viable regional carrier being created, was the lack of a stable host airline with efficient operating processes. It was indicated that this need would now be filled by CAL which, with the support of the Government of Trinidad and Tobago, would explore a solution. This would involve the liquidation of LIAT, including the settlement of staff severance liabilities and other commercial and official debt, and the assumption by CAL of some or all former LIAT routes.

It was further suggested that LIAT suspend negotiations with Sir Allen Stanford and put off all arrangements with any other airline, including CAL itself, until the end of September 2007. The reason given was to accommodate the Trinidad and Tobago Carnival 2007 season, the ICC Cricket World Cup taking place between March and April 2007 and to get beyond the months of July–September 2007, seen as their "super peak" passenger travel period.

The shareholders of LIAT realized that if they did nothing between January and September 2007 to save their carrier, having given up the Stanford option of a LIAT–Caribbean Star merger, LIAT, starved of funds, would have gone out of business and the Eastern Caribbean would have been left with only Stanford's Caribbean Star service. Further, nothing had been shared with LIAT about CAL's business or operational plan and how the air transportation needs of the Eastern Caribbean would be met once LIAT had been closed down.

With respect to the funding required by LIAT to settle its debts, there was a suggestion that it could once more approach the CARICOM Petroleum Stabilization Fund which had helped with a grant of EC$44 million in 2005. But the liquidation costs of LIAT in 2007 would have been in excess of EC$311 million, and access to the Petroleum Stabilization Fund depended not on Trinidad and Tobago's agreement alone, but on the approval of the grant by all CARICOM states. LIAT had no guarantee that a second dip at the well for what would have been a very large sum of money would have been approved by the CARICOM states, themselves needing finance from the same source for a number of projects.

CAL's offer might have been considered by the LIAT shareholders had the Stanford option not been available. In the existing circumstances, however, the LIAT shareholders had no choice but to reject CAL's offer and to continue discussions with Sir Allen Stanford. They appointed the Rt Hon. Owen Arthur, prime minister of Barbados, to represent their interests in meetings with Sir Allen Stanford, and the first meeting took place in late January 2007 at the Barbados Hilton. It ended with the signing of a memorandum of understanding which formalized the commitment of the parties to the process.

## LIAT–Caribbean Star Commercial Agreement

A very important development in January 2007, already referred to, was the agreement brokered by the CEOs of LIAT and Caribbean Star, that from 1 February 2007 the carriers would enter into a commercial arrangement to operate almost as one carrier, although remaining two separate companies with their own operational divisions. Under the terms of the agreement, reservations and distribution generally would be executed through LIAT and check-ins would be done by LIAT at LIAT counter space in all destinations, except Curaçao, which had been served by Caribbean Star but not by LIAT before 2007.

This arrangement enabled both carriers to accelerate the cooperative arrangements. Caribbean Star began to dismantle some of its operations, including selling some of the planes it owned (as opposed to leased), and closing down its counter service, except in Curaçao. LIAT maintained its fleet, while wet-leasing from Caribbean Star the additional equipment and crew needed to adequately maintain the intra-regional service. Things were happening between these two former competing carriers at a speed to which the region was definitely unaccustomed.

## LIAT–Caribbean Star Merger Proposal

By February 2007 the specifics of the merger proposal were ready for presentation to the LIAT board and shareholders of both LIAT and Caribbean Star. CEO Mark Darby and the chairman met Sir Allen Stanford; Skip Barnette, the president and CEO of Caribbean Star and Caribbean Sun;

and Michael Henne, their financial adviser in Houston, Texas. The proposal presented by LIAT's CEO in a broad outline was as follows:

- LIAT and Caribbean Star would merge to form a single intra-Caribbean airline, under the joint ownership of the current shareholder governments and Sir Allen Stanford, chairman and CEO of the SFG.
- A new company named "LIAT, Star of the Caribbean", would be created into which the usable assets of LIAT and Caribbean Star would be transferred. Governments would own 47.5 per cent of the shares; Sir Allen Stanford, 47.5 per cent and the LIAT staff, 5 per cent.
- Selected members of the two companies' staff would be invited to join the new company, and severance would be paid to the staff being replaced.
- The new company would commence by operating in essentially the same footprint as the two carriers, with new routes being determined only by proven demand.
- The new company would be capitalized through a loan from the SFG, with the prospect of being profitable from day one.

Sir Allen Stanford, after listening to the presentation, expressed his confidence in the new carrier showing early profitability and expressed the view that the merger should be followed quickly by a public offering of the company in the marketplace, leading to privatization of the carrier. He proposed the full involvement and cooperation of his financial companies in helping to make the initial public offering successful.

## Early Opposition

As soon as the commercial agreement between the two carriers, in February 2007, began to take hold and regional airfares began to rise to a level reflecting the two airlines' real costs of operation, serious opposition to the LIAT–Caribbean Star arrangement arose in several quarters, but especially among elements of the regional tourism–hotel sector.

The Caribbean Hotel Association, which blamed the increased air fares as the reason for falling regional hotel business, described the proposed merger as "the worst thing that ever happened to Caribbean Tourism".

The reality was however that had LIAT been forced out of business by Caribbean Star, which was the only serious alternative to merging or an asset purchase by LIAT as ultimately happened, the surviving privately owned carrier would have had to raise fares to remain commercially viable. It is unlikely that such an entity operating with very little competition would have been as subject to political pressure or public opinion as LIAT proved to be. Of course, no one could have foreseen that in February 2009, the assets of Sir Allen Stanford would have been frozen by the US authorities. These would have included Caribbean Star which is registered in the United States and the Caribbean region's intra-Caribbean air transportation service would have come to a sudden halt.

The Caribbean hotel industry kept making the point that in international travel involving long distances, one paid much less per mile than one did on the island-hopping LIAT; and it saw this as an unfair practice. This suggested a lack of understanding of the economics of air transport. The case for the fares was, however, made very strongly in a letter sent by a member of the travelling public to the shareholders as follows:

> it is really a matter of the simple lessons of economics – fixed costs, variable costs and the law of decreasing marginal costs/increasing marginal returns. As I understand it, every time LIAT takes off, that is a particular fixed cost incurred, irrespective of the number of passengers. Add to that the fact that, relatively speaking, the distance between our islands is short. So we have high fixed costs to fly a few passengers short distances between islands. Our pilots and maintenance crew are specialist skilled workers who would require certain levels of remuneration. The support staffs also do not come cheap. Add to this the increasing world oil prices. Wherever did we get this notion that regional air travel was cheap? That is one of the realities of our smallness. It is my view that such fundamental economics of air travel in the region needs to be understood and appreciated by those entrusted with the task of governing our respective islands and managing their economic development. (*Grenada Voice*, 17 November 2007)

One of those fixed costs is fuel; and an airline like LIAT which operates one thousand flights a week, with all the attendant take-offs and landings, burns a great deal of fuel. In early 2008, LIAT's fuel bill jumped almost unnoticed from US$250,000 a week to US$350,000 a week. Our average price of fuel has jumped from US$2.48 per gallon in May 2007 to US$3.90

per gallon in June 2008. In every part of the economy, it is understood that some aspects of the rising cost of fuel must either be passed on to the consumer or absorbed by the government.

Meeting its daily recurrent operational costs was only one of LIAT's challenges. From a strategic sustainable development perspective, the region needed to be able to guarantee the existence of some element of regional air transportation and the greatest probability of doing so depended on LIAT's survival. That road to survival, however, could only begin with its ability to liquidate its hundreds of millions of dollars of accumulated debt.

The long standing debt of more than EC$300 million which existed in 2004, was not one out of which the company could trade. Financial rescue packages which the shareholder governments had made from time to time simply went to fill the gap between costs and poor revenues caused by low fares. The LIAT shareholders were not able to play the kind of godfather role which the Government of Trinidad and Tobago, flush with oil revenues in 2006, was able to play for BWIA, by providing a cash injection of over US$350 million to liquidate its debt before closure. LIAT had to find a way to deal with its debt and it did so.

## Clearing LIAT's Debt

### Obligations to the Export Development Corporation of Canada

LIAT's debt with the EDC had been incurred through a loan to purchase three Dash 8 planes. Shareholder injections of cash, up until that time, had gone not to pay debt but to meet various cash flow crises. The debt with the EDC was settled through a bridging loan from the SFG which would not have been available outside of the merger negotiations. This proved to be a double win for LIAT since, in paying off the loan, it took ownership of the three planes which were security for the loan and considerably improved its asset value.

### Other Debt

A number of various stratagems were now employed to reduce the core debt even further: various negotiations were pursued, including debt forgiveness, debt for equity swaps, reduction in the amount of severance to be paid by retaining staff and so on, until the debt was reduced to about EC$129 million.

At this point it was accepted that to wipe out the remaining debt, the LIAT shareholders would have to make a commercial loan of between US$50 million and US$55 million to invest as equity in the carrier. Banks were not lining up to lend US$55 million to LIAT. Sir Allen Stanford was approached and confirmed that the SFG was prepared to lend the money.

The loan originally discussed with Sir Allen Stanford was US$35 million, in the expectation that the additional US$20 million needed would come through the loan which the Antigua and Barbuda government was discussing with the Government of Venezuela. When several meetings between the governments of Antigua and Barbuda and Venezuela ended without a firm decision on the matter, it became clear that the additional US$20 million would have to be sourced from elsewhere.

With this understanding, the merger talks were taken to a new level and the lawyers and financial advisers on both sides began to get into the details of the negotiations.

It cannot be stated too often that LIAT was particularly fortunate in having the Government of Barbados retain the team of Dr Adrian Cummins, QC, assisted by the Hon. Oliver Browne, QC, CHB, of Carrington and Sealy, attorneys at law in Barbados, to serve both as its legal adviser and LIAT's and the CDB retain the services of Cameron McCaw of Zwaig Consulting as financial adviser. Together they provided the Oversight Negotiating Committee with excellent legal and financial advice which resulted in, what I believe will be seen in retrospect as, a very successful negotiation.

## Objectives of the Merger

### Background

Between the year 2000 and 2006, LIAT and Caribbean Star had lost a considerable amount of money. A very common assumption in the region is that the private sector company was performing financially much better than LIAT. Yet Caribbean Star's financial performance is instructive as an example of how difficult it is to run any airline, especially an intra-Caribbean airline, at a profit, whoever owns it. Its losses between 2000 and 2005 were EC$333 million, and by October 2006 a further EC$75 million had been lost.

When the figures on both sides became available, it was clear that if both carriers had continued to operate as independent entities, neither of them stood much chance of a turnaround, as long as they both continued to fly the same intra-Caribbean routes in the same way. They both faced the challenges of lack of liquidity, cut-throat pricing, excess capacity, inherent inefficiencies associated with a lack of economies of scale and escalating fuel costs. One of them would have had to go and we may speculate from this vantage point of hindsight which of them would have been the first to go.

It can be argued, therefore, that the three shareholder prime ministers and Sir Allen Stanford made a historic and farsighted decision in agreeing at the end of 2006 to enter merger negotiations.

In the months that followed Sir Allen's meeting with Prime Minister Arthur in January 2007, the Oversight Negotiating Committee explored a range of options in the area of mergers and acquisitions.

In the beginning the aim was to achieve a merger conceived with the following objectives:

- To stop the significant monthly financial losses suffered by both airlines.
- To position and maintain the new LIAT as a solvent and viable enterprise that, in due course, would be seen in a favourable light by potential investors when and if an initial public offering were floated through the capital markets.
- To better serve the needs and expectations of the travelling public with respect to interline connections, and the regional tourism industry through the delivery of timely, reliable and sensibly priced services.
- To improve the airline's overall cost efficiency and effectiveness.
- To eliminate the heavy reliance placed upon the shareholders for direct financial support.
- To minimize the merged airline's overall debt burden.
- To improve the airline's overall capitalization.

- To implement realistic strategic operational and financial plans that enhanced the new airline's capacity to consistently generate sustainable profitability and liquidity.

**Merger Options**

There were three potential scenarios of how the merger could be structured, each of which was fully explored:

- *Scenario 1: share transaction through creation of a holding company (Holdco).* Under Scenario 1, Holdco would become the parent company through a share transaction, with existing ordinary (common) shareholders of LIAT and Caribbean Star exchanging ownership interest in each airline for new shares of Holdco. Initially, Holdco would have two wholly owned subsidiaries: LIAT and Caribbean Star. Concurrently, or shortly thereafter, the two subsidiaries would be amalgamated pursuant to the Antigua and Barbuda Business Corporation Act (1995).
- *Scenario 2: winding-up and starting over.* Each airline would liquidate its respective legal entity, sever all employees (pursuant to applicable labour codes) and start up an entirely new airline with no history and no legacy issues.
- *Asset purchase transaction.* Under an asset purchase option, one of the two airlines would purchase only those segments of the other airline's business that would be needed for the "new" airline's future success and prosperity. Such assets would include cash, various spare parts inventory, some fixed assets and both assets and liabilities related to the leased planes that would be transferred as part of the future operations.

    If an asset purchase was going to be the option chosen, it was of critical importance politically for LIAT to persuade Sir Allen Stanford that the surviving carrier should be LIAT. At a meeting with Sir Allen at his headquarters in Texas, the CEO and chairman argued the case for LIAT's survival based on the strength of its brand, the commercial value of the emotional attachment which intra-Caribbean travellers held for the airline and the political capital for the shareholder governments, if LIAT were not seen to have been taken over by Caribbean Star.

As had happened before, when we discussed unionization and the commercial arrangements between LIAT and Caribbean Star, Sir Allen Stanford showed willingness to compromise. We ended by agreeing to call the surviving carrier "LIAT, the star of the Caribbean", which seemed an excellent compromise.

**The Choice**

It is now a matter of historical record that the deal was settled not on the basis of a merger, or of winding up the two companies and starting all over again, but on the basis of the purchase of Caribbean Star's assets by LIAT. Following are the reasons for this.

*Share Transaction*

Mergers bring their own baggage, whether organizational, emotional or legal, and in the highly charged political climate in which LIAT operates, a benefit of the share transaction contemplated was that there were no perceived winners or losers. The "statutory amalgamation", which was provided for by the companies acts of Antigua and Barbuda and Barbados, would not have triggered the massive severances LIAT feared, except that the merger would have involved some downsizing and severances.

However, we were legally advised that under the statutory procedure we were contemplating, an amalgamated company is a continuation of each of the amalgamated companies as one and the same company. The relevant act provides for the amalgamated companies continuing as one, with all the property of each of the amalgamated companies belonging to the amalgamated company. The amalgamated company then becomes liable for the obligations of each amalgamated company and all liabilities, claims, causes of action and legal proceedings by or against any amalgamated company (whether civil, criminal or administrative) may be continued against or by the amalgamated company. Convictions, rulings, orders and judgments in favour of or against any of the amalgamated companies may similarly be enforced by or against the amalgamated company.

It is of interest that LIAT's decision not to choose the amalgamation option proved to be correct. When the two parties were at the point of concluding an asset purchase deal, some Caribbean Star pilots who had brought a case against their company for wrongful dismissal, succeeded in getting a stay order from the court to stop the negotiations until there was clarity that any judgment brought against Caribbean Star would be settled before that company was liquidated. Even after LIAT completed the asset purchase agreement, persons who felt they had a grievance against Caribbean Star when it was still operating, have sought to ascertain if the new LIAT was now liable for any claims against Caribbean Star.

*Pros and Cons of Winding Up and Starting Over*

Given all the baggage that Caribbean Star and LIAT brought to the table, winding up the two companies and starting over with an entirely new company seemed a far more attractive scenario than amalgamating the two companies and carrying forward their joint obligations and liabilities, some of them unknown. However, it would have been very costly, especially in terms of severance payments to staff. This may not have been a problem for Sir Allen Stanford at the time, but it would certainly have been one for LIAT.

## Asset Purchase Deal

After a rather protracted meeting in February 2007 in Atlanta, Georgia, between our financial adviser Cameron McCaw and Caribbean Star's financial adviser, Michael Henne, among others from the Stanford Group, it was agreed to recommend to the two companies' shareholders that the matter should proceed on the basis of a clean asset purchase deal. It was proposed that under this arrangement Caribbean Star Airlines Limited would remain behind to be wound up by, and at the expense of, Sir Allen Stanford; and LIAT would acquire from Caribbean Star in return for equity in LIAT, only those assets and business that it needed to continue operating.

The deal suggested was as follows: the money borrowed from the SFG would come to LIAT as government equity. The assets coming over to LIAT directly from Caribbean Star would include some cash, a hangar, inventory, deposits and maintenance obligations on five planes being leased by Caribbean Star and wet-leased by LIAT from Caribbean Star under the commercial agreement. Measures would be required to ultimately transfer the leases on the planes to LIAT; in return, Sir Allen Stanford would get a shareholding of 47.5 per cent in the shares of the airline to be named "LIAT, Star of the Caribbean".

It was agreed that Caribbean Star's negotiators after their meeting with Cam McCaw in Atlanta, would brief Sir Allen Stanford on the details agreed at their level and that the next step would be a meeting between the three prime ministers and Sir Allen. This meeting took place on 7 March 2007 in Antigua with the purpose of seeking to reach agreement among the four shareholders on the matters discussed in Atlanta.

The meeting had a number of interesting outcomes:

- When the meeting began, the Caribbean Star Group proposed that LIAT, instead of purchasing some of Caribbean Star's assets, as had been discussed by both our financial advisers in Atlanta, should purchase the entire company.
- The governments proposed that Sir Allen Stanford should accept 35 per cent rather than 47.5 per cent of the company's shares in return for the assets coming over to LIAT from Caribbean Star.
- LIAT requested Sir Allen Stanford out of the proposed US$55 million loan to advance a bridging loan of US$11 million directly to LIAT to be used for the purposes partly of paying US$6 million in debt and having US$5 million of working capital.

Sir Allen Stanford agreed at the meeting to accept the 35 per cent of the shares proposal and to advancing the US$11 million bridging loan and a memorandum of understanding relating to the loan was signed. These matters were, however, further reviewed by the legal and financial advisers on both sides after the meeting and new concerns were raised.

LIAT's financial adviser, Cam McCaw, who had represented the company in the Atlanta meeting, when briefed on the discussions at Antigua meeting, recommended against the proposed change from a clean purchase of selected assets of Caribbean Star, to buying out the entire company. He argued that such a purchase could expose LIAT to several obligations, financial and otherwise, attaching to Caribbean Star, of which LIAT would not be currently aware and could not easily anticipate. This led to the reopening of many issues that had been presumed to be concluded in March 2007.

As the arguments flowed back and forth, there was another development. Sir Allen Stanford advanced the view that the 35 per cent interest in LIAT to be allotted to him should be attributed solely on the basis of Caribbean Star exiting the market. In other words, he wanted the transaction viewed as a zero net assets deal and would be based strictly on an intangible asset: "the value of Caribbean Star going out of business". There would be no cash, no other tangible assets coming over to LIAT. LIAT would have to purchase separately all the additional assets it needed to carry on the business after Caribbean Star left the field.

This was, of course, unacceptable to LIAT which argued that in the Atlanta talks between the financial officials of the two sides, it had been agreed that in return for Stanford's equity in LIAT, there would be a transfer of tangible net assets worth about EC$27 million to EC$28 million to LIAT. If this were not the case, LIAT felt that it could not justify, either on commercial or political grounds, giving Sir Allen Stanford 35 per cent of LIAT.

The governments and LIAT were at pains to separate the two transactions of the asset purchase and the proposed loan of the SFG to governments which was an entirely separate arrangement made with a financial banking entity on commercial terms. The interest rate offered on the loan was the London Interbank Offered Rate (LIBOR) plus 100 basis points, with a grace period of twenty-four months which could be extended to sixty months under certain circumstances. After this, the full loan, including accumulated interest, would become payable. It was held that the sovereign guarantees offered for the loan rendered the terms not much different from normal market terms and not as generous as the Caribbean Star group was suggesting.

In April 2007, these differences threatened the conclusion of the asset purchase deal with Stanford and therefore the survival of LIAT. It was the intervention of the CDB which presented an alternative to raising the funds from the SFG which saved the day and almost certainly saved intra-regional transport in the Caribbean.

LIAT's financial adviser, Cameron McCaw, had never been comfortable with Sir Allen's proposal to go to the market with an initial public offering after only twenty-four months of performance of the new LIAT. He doubted that with so short a track record, LIAT could attract the cash investment it needed. CDB was also concerned that Sir Allen's 35 per cent shareholding interest would be on a fully diluted basis and not be part of the initial public offering. In that case, should the offering be unsuccessful, default provisions in the loan agreement with him could be activated. But even if the initial public offering were successful, while the governments would recover the money they had invested in LIAT, they could end up with no ownership interest in LIAT and have either limited or no ability to influence the strategic direction of the airline in terms of social or economic needs of the region. A possible outcome was that Sir Allen Stanford could end up being the single largest shareholder in LIAT or even owning the carrier, a situation which might not have been acceptable to the public, judging by the ubiquitous public comments for LIAT to remain in Caribbean hands.

In April 2007, the LIAT negotiating team met a high-level delegation from CDB at the Barbados Hilton Hotel to discuss the LIAT shareholders applying to CDB for a loan of US$60 million which would provide them with an alternative to Stanford financing. The meeting was chaired by the Rt. Hon. Owen Arthur, prime minister of Barbados. At this point an agreed Stanford offer of US$55 million was already on the table and LIAT had no certainty that the CDB directors would approve such a loan.

In fact, there was a high probability that they would vote against it. First, certain key non-Caribbean directors of the bank were thought to be unlikely to support the bailing out of LIAT with CDB financing. They had doubts about the carrier's ultimate viability and were probably philosophically opposed to public financing of airline operations.

Even some Caribbean directors from non-shareholder countries were not overly excited about supporting such a loan. All this became clear when the idea of CDB support for the LIAT project was first broached during the annual general meeting of the bank in Venezuela in May 2007.

From a LIAT perspective, however, it was clear that a loan from CDB would completely change the equation; it would divorce the asset purchase negotiations with Stanford from the SFG loan, and permit LIAT to negotiate with Sir Allen Stanford from a strong position.

Judging from the way events unfolded in 2008 with foreign carriers abandoning the region in the face of the world's worst oil crisis, the CDB's action clearly helped to preserve LIAT as one of the few options available to Caribbean countries for intra-Caribbean travel. This however is a matter of hindsight. In 2007, the shareholder prime ministers understood that getting the loan approved at the July 2007 CDB board of directors meeting in

Barbados would be an uphill battle and that a winning strategy would have to be put in place. They had to convince their CARICOM prime ministerial colleagues of the need to support the loan application and to persuade the principals of non-Caribbean directors of the need for their representatives on the CDB board to at least come with an open mind to discuss the issues at the board meeting.

Prime ministers Baldwin Spencer, Owen Arthur and Dr Ralph Gonsalves were vocal champions of LIAT's cause at the July 2007 CARICOM Heads of Government meeting in Barbados. The session had been so heated that one prime minister was reported as having said that, up until then, possibly no other matter had ever caused such a high level of bitterness among heads as did their differences on the LIAT matter.

At the end of the CDB board meeting in July 2007, after a heroic struggle by LIAT supporters, it was announced that a US$60 million loan was approved for the shareholder governments to invest in the LIAT reconstruction, plus a US$500,000 grant for capacity-building in the LIAT company. The projected use of the loan was to meet indebtedness to commercial banks, bond obligations, repayment of the bridging loan made by Stanford, accounts payable/accruals, transaction costs and working capital.

The first disbursement of funds by CDB did not take place until late November 2007, justifying the wisdom of sourcing a bridging loan from the SFG at an early stage.

It was an incredible achievement by the CDB team which worked on the LIAT project, and the carrier's management was therefore conscious of the need to repay their trust by seeking to mount a successful operation into the future.

The CDB loan was in every aspect a better deal than the loan offered by the SFG. It consisted of the equivalent of an ordinary capital resources (OCR) portion of US$45 million at a variable interest rate currently set at 6.26 per cent, and an amount of US$15 million from CDB's special funds resource at an interest rate of 2–4 per cent. Repayments were to be over a period of twenty to twenty-five years inclusive of a grace period of three years. The OCR interest rate of 6.25 per cent was then equivalent to LIBOR plus eighty-eight basis points. The bank worked closely with LIAT's in-house team in executing the due diligence exercise and it was agreed that after the loan was made, CDB would have a representative (voice, but no vote) on the LIAT board of directors for the duration of the period of the loan. By 2009 a study was in place to examine how the grant of US$500,000 was to be used to upgrade the organization, systems and financial operations of the carrier.

From as early as May 2007, when discussions began with CDB, it was uncertain whether Sir Allen's interest in being a LIAT shareholder would be maintained if the CDB loan were approved, removing the need for governments to borrow money from the SFG. In July 2007, when a shareholders meeting was called for the Crane Hotel in Barbados to agree on what specific assets LIAT would be purchasing from Caribbean Star, and to define how the purchased assets would be linked to his 35 per cent of the company, Sir Allen suddenly and without explanation announced that he was pulling out of the share option and settling for LIAT purchasing the Caribbean Star assets for cash.

Between July 2007 and October 2007, several versions of the asset purchase agreement and related schedules were prepared and discussed by the lawyers on both sides, with each side seeking to ensure that no advantage was taken by one over the other. The valuation and transfer of assets from one airline to another is by no means a simple process. The asset purchase agreement included a transfer to LIAT of leases on five planes which Caribbean Star held with a number of different lessors. Since these negotiations involved the lessors as third parties, LIAT was unable to determine how soon they would be transferred, but it expected the transaction to be completed by the first week in November 2007.

The asset purchase agreement also included the transfer of a hangar which would have to be dismantled by Caribbean Star and moved and reassembled by LIAT. The transfer of this asset generated an unexpected amount of discussion after it was discovered that it was owned by an SFG company, other than Caribbean Star, and that its lawyers wanted to put cast iron clauses around the transfer which would protect Sir Allen Stanford from any conceivable possibility of financial injury by LIAT. As late as January 2008, LIAT was forced to take the hangar off the list of assets it wanted to buy from Caribbean Star, since it had concerns that after dismantling, transferring and reconstructing the building, it would not be worth either the trouble of doing so, or the sum asked, in comparison with constructing a new hangar.

In October 2007, the legal arguments about what seemed small things continued to drag on, and getting to the point of the asset purchase agreement being signed seemed like something that would never happen. Signing the agreemement was, however, a condition precedent to the disbursement of the CDB loan, and without receiving funds from CDB, LIAT could not repay Sir Allen Stanford the bridging loan. The president of Caribbean Star and chairman of LIAT persuaded their shareholders that it was in their mutual interest to cut through the legal clutter and bring the matter to a conclusion to meet a disbursement date of 31 October 2007. This decision issued in the birth of the new and expanded LIAT totally owned by Caribbean shareholders. It was immediately dubbed a monopoly, and the following chapter will address the question of whether LIAT is a monopoly and if so, whether monopoly status can ever be justified.

# 8

# When an Airline Monopoly Is Justifiable

The *Concise Oxford Dictionary* describes a monopoly as the exclusive possession or control of the trade in a commodity or service. More often than not the word is given a pejorative meaning as something that benefits a few and disadvantages many. It is a term which has been applied to LIAT since its purchase of the assets of Caribbean Star, resulting in that carrier ceasing to operate. Some people claim that most of what is wrong at LIAT is a direct result of monopoly status. Perhaps it needs to be explained that while LIAT is now the sole carrier on a number of Caribbean routes, strictly speaking, it is not a monopoly. It continues to compete on certain routes with Caribbean, American and French public and private sector carriers. It has now however shed itself of major competition from Caribbean Star, a carrier which mirrored its every move and up to 2007 competed on price on twenty-one of twenty-two routes. LIAT's new status may, however, be said to be close to that of a monopoly and the question that therefore arises is, Can monopoly status be justified?

The answer is not as simple as it seems to many. LIAT itself also perceives both gains and losses from its present status and ultimately, like with many other Caribbean situations, one sees that solving one problem often results in creating another.

A number of operational problems being experienced by the carrier in 2008 gave rise in several quarters to a clamour to have more competition on the routes served by LIAT. No thought was given, however, to what would result from more competition; if that would produce a desirable result, and how, in specific terms, the level of fares and customer service would be impacted.

There seems to be an assumption that "airline competition is inherently good" and "monopolies bad"; but certainly in the case of LIAT, it would be useful, before coming to a judgement, to have a scientific study done about particular travel markets to see what level of competition, if any, they can bear. Even casual observation of regional air transportation will reveal that many intra-Caribbean carriers have come and gone equally swiftly over the years creating monopolies by default. People, with interests to promote, often suggest the level of fares they would like to pay or which would nicely complement their tour package if bundled with their hotel room rates. They, however, show little interests in the airline's costs, except to make facile and unscientific statements about how they should be reduced.

There are, of course, clear cases where monopolies do not serve the public interests. These are where major companies set out to dominate local and international markets and use their market dominance to control supply and prices.

But this is clearly not LIAT's situation. It has never sought a monopoly status. For fifty years it struggled in competition with local and foreign carriers which set out to put it out of business. Owing to the unstinting support of its three shareholders and the fierce loyalty of the people of the Caribbean, it saw off the competition and finally took over the assets of its most fierce competitor. This book is about why the survival of LIAT and other Caribbean carriers is in the best interest of the Caribbean public, and even to the most casual observer it is clear that LIAT and Caribbean Star could not have both survived in the circumstances existing in the Eastern Caribbean.

In this chapter, the case will be made that there are good arguments on both sides but, on balance, it can be shown that certain types of competition in the region's existing circumstances will almost certainly lead to carriers going out of business and a return to a monopolistic situation for the carrier with access to deepest pockets.

There are times when LIAT has reason to regret its present status. These are where industrial action or mechanical problems disrupt service and inconvenience hundreds of passengers in circumstances where they have no choice of carrier. In those cases LIAT incurs major costs and takes the full blast of public criticism. But, however, there is another reality, that if it did not have some sort of monopoly status on a number of thin routes, with no access to external financing, it would only be a matter of time, given the region's economic realities, before some other carrier replaced it as a monopoly.

## Beneficial Outcomes of the Asset Purchase

The cooperative arrangements between LIAT and Caribbean Star which began on 1 February 2007 and ended in October 2007 with the acquisition of Caribbean Star's assets, together with the CDB loan, which was associated with that process, led to LIAT's financial and operational improvements and freedom from government subsidies as detailed below:

- A debt of more than EC$300 million was reduced to EC$10 million. Some of the debt had been negotiated away by the company. The rest had been paid off through the CDB loan of US$60 million to the LIAT shareholder governments, which they invested in LIAT as equity. Two-thirds of it went to settle the company's external debt and the rest to pay off a provident fund debt which LIAT had owed the staff for over a decade. None of it went to support day-to-day operations.
- LIAT was able to reduce its operating losses from EC$61,470,413 in 2006 to an operating loss of EC$4,695,297 in 2007.
- In spite of 2008 being the worst year on record for airlines which on a global scale, according to IATA director general and CEO Giovanni Bisignani lost US$10.4 billion, LIAT made an operating profit of EC$2,016,753 and a net loss of EC$2,843,453 (US$1.00 = EC$2.70).
- In 2006, LIAT still leased all its airplanes. By 2008 it owned six airplanes outright.
- It carried some 1,008,632 passengers in 2008 instead of the 728,155 it carried in 2006 and 704,768 it carried in 2007.
- It received a technical assistance grant of US$500,000 with which to address some of its structural weaknesses.

Most importantly from 1 February 2007 LIAT was able to take the tough decisions it needed to survive; it reduced the excess capacity created by the fact that together the two carriers had thirty Dash 8s on the routes; it reduced the baggage allowance which up until then had been one of the cause of excess baggage and customer complaints; it returned fares to the year 2000 level which was needed simply to cover its costs and it reorganized its routes and schedules, making more day-returns and direct flights possible.

These actions incited an unprecedented level of criticism from politicians, the tourism industry, the business traveller and the public, but now directed solely at LIAT. Considerable courage was needed to hold the line amid a deafening silence about realistic solutions as to how to ensure that the losses of previous years would not reoccur. It will be noted in chapter 10 that when the world of international air transport fell apart in 2008 and 2009, measures similar to those taken by LIAT in 2007 were also taken by a large number of major airlines around the world to survive.

From 2007 LIAT's increased fares were blamed on its monopoly status and became an easy target for those seeking an explanation of their reduced business. But certainly, even if it is admitted that they contributed to reduced flows, there were certainly other causes that were ignored; some loss of stay-over business would have resulted from a change of LIAT's schedules to include more day-return flights. While this would have injured hoteliers in the receiving country, it would have benefited those business travellers who could do a day's business in another island and return the same day to sleep in their own beds; there was increased competition from the cruise industry, which in 2007 was targeting Caribbean passengers more aggressively than ever; Caribbean leisure passengers were, like the rest of the world, also suffering from reduced disposable income due to a global deteriorating economic situation; increased government taxes and other add-ons by airports, which are included in the ticket price and in some cases approach 30 per cent or more of the fare charged, were certainly a factor and travel agents were now adding service fees to ticket prices to make up for reduced commissions from airlines. (Tables of taxes on each of LIAT's routes are attached as appendix 3.)

The global travel statistics in 2009, in fact reveal a situation in which cutting fares is not leading to increased passenger flows, but rather to serious airline financial losses. A growing phenomenon is fewer people travelling first and business class, and a drift of passengers from premium to economy, as the economic crisis continues.

From a service perspective, the initial arrangements of the LIAT–Caribbean Star commercial agreement had brought a few negatives of their own since, until the actual closure of Caribbean Star in November 2007, two separate airlines existed side by side, often taking directions from two parallel management departments. This, however, was seen as something that would end with LIAT's completion of the take over of Star's assets.

When Caribbean Star closed on 15 November 2007, however, LIAT experienced unexpected difficulties in getting hold of the planes it needed from them to operate efficiently. It started with twelve planes of its own, but needed seventeen, fully crewed, to operate the routes according to the published schedules. It had been agreed that leases on five planes which Caribbean Star held with certain lessors would have been transferred to LIAT by the first week in November 2007. This did not happen. There were various delays for a number of reasons; some of the planes which came across to LIAT needed maintenance before they could be released into operation, or required security related structural changes, such as bullet-proof doors, before they could be permitted to fly into American territories; others were not transferred to LIAT until mid-December 2007, because of outstanding matters between Caribbean Star and its lessors, which had nothing to do with LIAT.

Pilots and cabin crew that were being transferred from Caribbean Star to LIAT for the purpose of operating the planes were required to be retrained and recertified as LIAT crew under regulations of the Eastern Caribbean Civil Aviation Authority. This resulted in several operational challenges; one was that the shortage of crews led to some dislocation of LIAT services. Another was that the training had to be done in Canada and, to take the place of those being trained, LIAT had to bring in crews on short-term contracts and therefore at higher rates of pay than those obtaining for the regular crew. This may have been one of the causes of the industrial action that followed.

## Industrial Relations

The state of industrial relations also has a bearing on the question of whether or not there should be competition on LIAT's routes. For example, as the Christmas season approached in 2007, the union of the cabin attendants, LIFAA, took industrial action. On 19 December, twenty-four cabin attendants reported sick, thus grounding thirty-five of LIAT's flights on that day. The action by LIFAA threw LIAT into a state of turmoil, probably never experienced by the carrier to that extent before. There was now no alternative carrier to which the passengers could be transferred.

When Caribbean Star existed, LIAT was able to recover relatively easily from any disruption in service by transferring business to that carrier. Now that LIAT was often the sole carrier flying, with full loads in December, passengers and baggage left behind because of the sick-out could not be transported on the following days. CAL, which had replaced BWIA, was now operating fewer flights than BWIA did. Efforts had to be made to get passengers and baggage home for Christmas by whatever other carriers could be found to assist, including charters. Most, however, had to be accommodated in hotels for two or three days at LIAT's expense. Costs were assessed at something of the order of US$520,000 (EC$1.5 million). The entire episode was an operational, financial and public relations disaster.

The sick-out by LIFAA and subsequent industrial action by LIALPA throw into high relief the embarrassment which both the carrier and its shareholder governments face when industrial action is taken and disrupts an essential service of which, on some routes, they are the sole provider.

In the case of LIAT, it is a service used by the entire Eastern Caribbean region. In these circumstances there is a danger of LIAT's management being made to operate under constant threat of industrial action, should a union choose to employ such a strategy. Strike action could be bolstered by the belief that in the absence of another carrier, neither shareholders nor management would risk the complete closure of the carrier, depriving the region of air transportation services.

This argument taken to its logical conclusion could be self-defeating, since, if demands are made of the carrier which it is unable to bear, it will collapse anyway under the weight of its financial difficulties.

Faced by such a dilemma, the shareholders may have no option but to sell the intra-Caribbean airline to a foreign company or to do what was done by the Antigua and Barbuda government in 2000, that is, invite another foreign carrier on the route. Alienating this service to foreign ownership is not an option to be recommended, and it could have consequences, such as loss of jobs, not currently anticipated.

Out of concern for the reoccurrence of unstable industrial action, LIAT sought the status of an essential service in Antigua and Barbuda in 2008, which would require that, in case of industrial disputes, at least agreed proper grievance procedures would have to be followed. This request remains under consideration by the Government of Antigua and Barbuda. However, it seems that Caribbean governments with a long pro-union history are reluctant to introduce legislation which restrict industrial action. Even where such legislation exists, unions have found ways of getting around it by staging "sick-outs" or by "working to rule", thus finding ingenious ways of disrupting the company's services. It is critical, therefore, that, in the best interests of both management and unions, and even more important, the travelling public, a better way be found for dealing with industrial disputes than that which currently exists.

Following the LIFAA industrial action in 2007, the council of LIAT unions, formed during the LIAT–Caribbean Star merger negotiations, met under the chairmanship of Senator Chester Humphrey of Grenada to seek improved methods of negotiating. They sought to develop escalation mechanisms for disputes that would avoid future unofficial action and would also reduce the complexity of the relationships which currently requires LIAT to deal separately with a large number of unions or associations. This meeting was followed by one between the unions and Prime Minister Ralph Gonsalves, CARICOM's lead prime minister on regional transportation, which it was hoped would lead to a memorandum of understanding establishing agreed procedures about future industrial practices. This continued to be a work in progress at October 2009.

However, the value of pre-strike consultation was seen when industrial action which threatened at the beginning of 2009 was avoided or at least deferred, by the timely intervention of an honest broker while negotiations commenced.

In July 2009, disagreements between LIAT and LIALPA during collective bargaining negotiations escalated into industrial action which caused massive dislocation of flights, unhappiness among passengers, embarrassment to the shareholder governments and a major loss of revenue to the company. In August 2009 at a meeting of shareholder prime ministers, attended by board representatives, management and union leaders and chaired by Prime Minister Gonsalves in Kingstown to resolve the issues with LIALPA, a definite decision was taken that the long discussed consultative mechanism between

LIAT and its ten unions would be established in an effort to pre-empt a similar breakdown in negotiations in the future. It was also agreed that many of the outstanding issues would go to binding arbitration and an attempt made to settle them by the end of September 2009.

Because of longstanding disagreements between LIAT and LIALPA and the pilots union, the public has the impression that there is a constant state of upheaval in the industrial relations at LIAT. Throughout 2009, collective bargaining negotiations with all ten LIAT unions were in progress and the company's initiative in bringing in external negotiators to lead the negotiations seemed to have worked well.

## Customer Service

Another charge often laid at the door of monopoly status is poor customer service which covers a multiplicity of areas. The more obvious ones are counter service at check-in, communications with the passenger generally, on-board cabin service, passenger safety and comfort, delivery of baggage intact and with the passenger, and on-time arrival according to the published schedules. These cover the major areas of complaints received daily by management, but the weight of evidence is against any correlation between the number of complaints and the monopoly status of the carrier. In fact a close examination of the experiences of all types of carriers, local and foreign, which were discussed earlier in chapter 3, suggests that most airlines receive similar complaints on an ongoing basis. What, then, is responsible for this?

It is possible that while everyone wishes to arrive, few persons actually wish to fly. Passengers therefore bring a nervous tension to the counter which easily erupts into conflict when things go contrary to expectation. Unless the counter staff is well trained and in fact was from the beginning fit for the job, tempers rise easily on both sides. Sometimes the persons interacting with the passenger are not direct employees of the carrier, but are the staff of a ground handling company on contract to the carrier. The customer should, however, be able to identify easily who served him or her by a name tag and be able to identify the person serving for reward or discipline.

Aggression, however, can take place on both sides of the counter. Some customers bring a sense of self-importance to the counter and expect to be exempt from rules that are set by management for staff or by civil aviation authorities for the carrier. Many of the procedures, especially those relating to security and transport of drugs, through which passengers are now put, are prescribed by international agencies or by the aviation administrations of countries to which these passengers happen to be flying. It is the management that decides how much baggage is allowed per person and at what weight, not the counter staff. The amount of weight a plane carries affects the safety of all the passengers on board and depending on the wind there may be times when it is advisable not to try to take off with what would at other times be a safe weight. In such cases baggage gets left behind. Rules like payment for excess baggage or fees for change of date of travel are again out of the hands of the staff serving the customer at the counter. The problem is that this information comes as bad news and a disappointment to the traveller who vents his or her irritation on the messenger.

What is important in all these circumstances is the need for transparency, courtesy, patience and communication skills on the part of the staff. Passengers charged for excess weight must receive an official receipt which they can reproduce at any time they wish to prove its authenticity. Staff should never seek to match the anger of customers with their own. There are times for calmly stating company policy and referring the complainant to the manager on duty or, where necessary, as far up as executive management.

When there are significant delays, cancellations, loss of property or liability to charges, the company's policy, especially relating to compensation, should be well known to and understood by staff and should be clearly indicated in some written form available to the passenger at the time of purchase of the ticket. No airline wishes to be late or to cancel a service which often incurs serious costs and may cause it to lose future business. Travellers must always understand, however, that unlike with ground transport, it is necessary on each and every occasion before take-off to make sure that the equipment is safe. Delaying or cancelling a particular flight often saves many lives. Frequently when there has been a major or fatal aircraft accident, it has been demonstrated, regrettably too late, that there had been trouble with that particular aircraft or aircraft type, which was not addressed before take-off.

Often people who have been inconvenienced by LIAT report that what was wrong was not the fact that there was a problem, but that it was communicated poorly – either not at all or with an attitude that was seen as unhelpful.

In 2009, LIAT has more than nine hundred employees stationed in some twenty-two Caribbean countries. They speak among them four different languages and operate some one thousand flights a week on behalf of the company. For fifty-three years they have delivered a safe and essential service, most of the time efficiently and courteously. The problem is that only a few passengers bother to call or write to the company to say when service is excellent.

LIAT's board and management place a very high value on good customer service. An important aspect of the re-engineering of the carrier has been the intensification of training programmes, the introduction of change management initiatives and the creation of a new customer service department headed by someone at the director level.

However, achieving changes in behaviour is neither easy nor short term. While those employees who consistently offend against the company's standards should be disciplined or dismissed, the unions will ensure that it is done according to the book. Ultimately, however, what is needed is a means of inspiring pride in an employee to the extent that he or she buys into the company's brand and wishes it to be seen in the best possible light.

Even this, however, is not enough to achieve the transformation that leads to service excellence. So, often, the fact that a company is undercapitalized prevents it from offering a good product at a technical level. A total upgrading of all departments is related to the over all financial performance of the company. LIAT has been cash-strapped for half a century and has structural weaknesses which are only now being addressed since the recent improvement in its finances. These include the recruitment and development of good human resources and the upgrading and restructuring of its human resource department, which ultimately make the greatest difference.

## Competition versus Monopoly Status

Earlier we have gone through several situations which may be taken to make the case both in favour of and against having only one carrier serving the major intra-Caribbean routes. But the argument often expressed both inside and outside the region that the real answer to Caribbean air transportation problems is more and more competition can be shown to be simplistic. The argument is often urged by international agencies with the underlying suggestion that it would best come from foreign carriers under an open skies policy. This view is similar to that which argues that liberalization of international trade is the ideal situation and therefore the Caribbean's trading interests would be best served by pitting struggling Caribbean companies against the might of conglomerates in developed countries under systems of completely liberalized trade. The idea of special and differential treatment for unequals is simply thrown through the window.

Ideally, there are good arguments in favour of competition, and competition can produce positive results. But it is not as simple as it may seem to the uninitiated. Often in this region, the question is how much and what sort of competition. There is always a price to be paid for the loss of companies that belong to, and are under the control of, nationals. With respect to air transportation, we need to examine not only the pros and cons of competition in the abstract, but how much competition can the carriers operating in this particular region take and survive, given the economic, geographic and infrastructural realities of the region.

It has been argued that more competition on the routes will have at least three positive consequences as follows:

- It will provide more options for the travelling public – certainly true.
- It will result in lower fares – not necessarily so, but possible for some time.
- It will cause the carrier, formerly operating in the route without much competition, to operate more efficiently – rarely.

It has to be understood, however, that there certainly can be negative outcomes that flow from competition. If competition creates, as it did before in the Eastern Caribbean, a market where there are far more seats than passengers, the struggle for market share could drive fares down to the point where no carrier can operate as a viable commercial carrier. With costs and revenues out of balance, all carriers are likely to operate inefficiently. This could lead to the carrier receiving the most financial support, from whatever quarter, surviving as a monopoly operator and raising fares to the level required to continue surviving. If the surviving carrier is privately owned and indeed foreign owned, its shareholders will wish it to do more than survive, which has implications for even higher fares. Additionally, if the past is any guide to the future, Caribbean governments will, most likely, once more be approached by the foreign carriers for financial support to operate the services.

More often than not, statements are made about airline operations in this region as if they were *sui generis*. There are, however, several commuter carriers operating in the United States and Canada, for example, serving communities and geographical areas which demonstrate a lot of similarities to the situation in our region. They too are the lifeline of their communities, but they survive and serve them only by receiving federal or state subsidies; and frequently when competition is introduced, carriers are forced to close operations.

One of the examples of this was a decision by American Eagle which opened a service between a small community called Flint and New York, only to close it on 7 April 2008 after only three months of operation. As soon as American Eagle announced its intention to fly, Northwest announced similar intentions. After American Eagle pulled out of Flint, there was a fear that Northwest would pull out also. When the two services were first announced, airport officials had warned that they would be involved in a no-win, head-to-head battle in which both would lose money. They did. Competition in that particular case did not benefit the consumer.

Nearer home, in the summer of 2007, St Lucia argued the case for introducing competing services to LIAT by American Eagle, on the grounds that there was not a match between seats and rooms in St Lucia and that competition would not only increase capacity, but would bring down the price of travel. LIAT was then operating several flights a day to St Lucia, five of them from Barbados alone. In September 2006, four flights a week by American Eagle were introduced by St Lucia to carry passengers between Barbados and St Lucia; and by December 2007, it was announced that steps would be taken to increase the number of American Eagle flights to eighteen per week.

The introduction of American Eagle did not lead to any fall in the price of travel between Barbados and St Lucia. On the contrary, an article by Vina Frederick (*St Lucia Star*, 3 February 2008) quotes Jadia Jn Pierre as saying that after researching the matter she found that to leave St Lucia for Barbados between 2 February to 13 February on LIAT would cost $447.53, exclusive of departure tax, as opposed to $687.20, exclusive of departure tax on American Eagle. She added that three travel agencies had quoted American Eagle's fares as $100.00 more expensive than LIAT fares for travel on the same dates. Exactly the opposite happened to what was suggested would be the case if competition were introduced.

Further, on Thursday, 7 February 2008, American Eagle notified relevant authorities that their service between Barbados and St Lucia, BGI (AE 5040) and SLU (AE 5042) was being suspended for the period 2 March to 6 April; they were never restored – shades, I regret to say, of things to come in 2008, when massive reductions of the services of American Eagle and other foreign carriers to the region were announced.

## LIAT and Competition

The management of LIAT has gone on record to say that it has never opposed competition, but unfair competition and competition that is allowed to cherry pick only the most profitable routes across a complicated network of twenty-two destinations, where several routes are not commercially viable. That is why Air Transport Licensing Authorities remain relevant to look at routes, schedules and fares, where circumstances warrant it. The special and differential treatment, so often pleaded for by the negotiators of the developing states in international trading agreements, should also be applicable to the air transport sector of developing countries where a case can be made.

LIAT has had to battle against competition, some of it quite unfair, all its existence. One of the reasons why the elaborate Speedwing Recovery Plan fell apart from inception in 1999 was the competition introduced by BWee Express in that year and compounded by that from Caribbean Star beginning in 2000. As is well known, this competition was fierce and might easily have proven fatal to LIAT. It has already been mentioned that between 2000 and 2006, LIAT fought off a range of competing carriers, all of whom either actually stated or acted as if the demise of LIAT was their business plan.

LIAT and Caribbean Star were not seeking to merge to have market dominance. In 2007, the two airlines, of equal size, one public sector and the other private sector, operating in competition in the region, accepted that they were offering too much capacity and losing hundreds of millions of dollars. Unlike all the publicly owned CARICOM carriers, their solution for survival was to merge, which was then opposed by all the people in the region who, for most of their professional lives, had preached the virtue of Caribbean carriers merging. Throughout 2008, however, the world watched as European and US carriers began a frenzy of merger negotiations with each other, simply to survive.

The CARICOM Secretariat has spoken of the need for LIAT to come under the scrutiny of the newly formed CARICOM Competition Commission. LIAT should have no objection to a close examination of its core cost structure and revenue streams by an independent authorized body, in relation to its operations, provided the body has the knowledge of air transportation economics to carry out the exercise fairly, confidentially and free from non-professional and political interference.

LIAT also supports the idea of the CARICOM Secretariat contracting scientific studies, *in consultation with Caribbean carriers*, to provide more in-depth analysis of the causes of the inadequate regional air transportation services and participating more meaningfully in the search for realistic solutions.

The IATA airfare study which will be dealt with in the next chapter was a start. Another study might analyse the demand for airline services by the various types of travelling public in the region served by LIAT, what level and type of competition is sustainable and what is the resistance to travel at various price levels. There would then be some scientific basis for statements about the role of competition in the region's airline services.

One of the criticisms about the "merger" is that it reduced capacity and led to the demand for seats being inadequate to the need. There is inadequate evidence to support that this was the case in 2007 and 2008 except at very specific times of the year when for certain well-known reasons, for example, various festivals or public holidays, there are spikes in business.

However, without financial support, no carrier can take the financial risk of expanding its fleet beyond the proven annual demand for its own services to cover only the peaks at Christmas, Easter, July, August and festivals. That is seasonal business, with great overhead costs to bear when demand falls during much of the year.

The question whether or not the LIAT "merger" led to reduced competition in the region, to higher airfares and reduced capacity must be answered in the affirmative. But this is the right answer to the wrong questions. The questions should be: Is the market too small for the capacity on the routes? Were the fares of the carriers in the period between 2001 and 2006 too low to meet the costs of operations? If a carrier is expected to serve both commercially viable routes and social routes, that is, where there is a need, but too little business, can it be mandated to make profits and expected to operate without any form of government subsidies while offering what is in fact a public service?

## External Solutions

The idea of a well-funded, foreign, private carrier, offering very low fares, probably subsidized by other businesses, if not by Caribbean governments themselves, seems to some, at first glance, to be an attractive option for both intra-Caribbean and international transport. This is, however, likely to be a short-term fix. Low introductory fares for those entering the market, is a staple strategy in the airline business, and it inevitably leads to the competition lowering fares also.

But this cannot be sustained and will lead companies which are already in bad financial situations into bankruptcy. It is highly unlikely that any carrier operating in this region on these routes will be able for very long to sustain a regime of low fares without subsidies.

Unless such a carrier or carriers are subject to some regulation, their entry could result in a replication of the situation that existed when Caribbean Star, heavily subsidized by its owner, was introduced to compete with LIAT in 2000, and could lead to the regional carriers going out of business. This may not be considered a tragedy by those governments which have not invested in regional carriers and are, in any case, of the view that it does not matter who owns the region's airlift.

Events which unfolded in 2008 demonstrated that it matters very much who owns and controls airlift to and around the region. When things got really rough in 2008, a number of foreign carriers either pulled out or cut back service. As has happened in the past, some returned or increased service again after it was recognized that, all things being taken into consideration, more money could still be made in the Caribbean than elsewhere. It was however their call to make not the Caribbean's.

LIAT, which announced in 2005 that it was converting into an LCC, learned the hard way that this region can easily become a low-fare region, but due to high input costs, never a low-cost one *on a sustained basis*. When costs and revenues get out of balance, fares will rise, whoever is the operator; and if the foreign carrier finds itself having to subsidize its Caribbean operations, it will cease to fly. This region from time to time has heard the case argued by Caribbean businessmen for private airline operations efficiently operated by the private sector at a profit. No Caribbean private sector airline enterprise has ever been successful, to date, in the Caribbean. In fact, they have all lost phenomenal amounts of money. Air transportation is, by any standards, a very high risk business.

In 2008, oil at US$147 per barrel was clearly a deterrent to new airline entrants into the region. Although the price has since fallen below US$35.00 in March 2009 and risen again to US$70s in August 2009, new foreign entrants could very well still be attracted to the area. Then, more than ever, the Caribbean will need regionally owned and controlled air transportation services that are well capitalized, well run and supported by the people and governments of the region. They need to survive against the day when once again, because of spiralling fuel prices or for some other reason, foreign carriers take their leave and the people of the Caribbean have reason to give thanks that there are still some of their own carriers around. What is certain is that oil prices will rise again, to what level is pure speculation. Some experts suggest that US$80.00 a barrel of crude oil is a probable high for the near term.

It is being suggested that regional carriers, like LIAT, CAL, Air Jamaica, Cayman Islands Airways and Bahamasair have different roles and functions from those private international carriers that exist purely as commercial businesses, driven solely by the profit motive. The business of a government-owned Caribbean carrier is to serve the developmental interests of the people of the region and it is not kept flying to make a profit, although it should seek to operate along commercial lines and to make a profit if it can.

In conclusion, it must be admitted that there are times when, for one reason or other, industrial action or mechanical failure, LIAT has been unable to service a route satisfactorily on which it is the only carrier. It is at times like these that it wishes there were another carrier around to ease the pain of the passengers. Time will tell if the introduction of the fast ferry will assist in solving this problem. But, realistically, it has to be admitted that there is not enough business on a year long basis to support more than one carrier operating on many of the intra-regional CARICOM routes. There is therefore a huge responsibility on the shoulders of LIAT to deliver an efficient and customer friendly service every day of every year. The greatest threat to this is probably industrial action. Whether it can do so and yet make a profit, given the economic realities of the region it serves, remains an open question. Not unrelated to this question is how will it be able to meet its costs and therefore at what level must fares be set to cover operating costs. This matter will be addressed in the next chapter.

Airline fares are a constant source of controversy. One of the mysteries for the travelling public is how airline fares are set. People continue to be puzzled by how the LCCs can charge lower fares than legacy carriers and how different passengers travelling in the same cabin to the same destinations can be charged completely different fares. A great deal more will be said in chapter 9 about competition and what can result from it. Hopefully it will deal with and demystify these and other related matters.

# 9

# Deregulation, Yield Management, Fare Setting and Hedging Oil Prices

There are few topics that are discussed with more passion and controversy than the level of air fares. Airlines are often accused of price gouging and few things attract more negative publicity than fare setting in the context of a merger where the carrier is assumed to be taking advantage of a monopoly situation to overcharge the public. This chapter sets out to elucidate the dark corners of these matters by explaining the history of the regulation and deregulation of airline fares, routes and schedules across the industry, the use and role of the yield management tool, how airline fares are set, what is meant by hedging of oil prices and its value as a strategy to beat rising fuel prices. Clearly a carrier is in a better position to charge lower fares if it has access to relatively cheap fuel and if, generally speaking, it can contain certain normally fixed costs.

## Deregulation

The US Deregulation Act of 1978 passed during the presidency of Jimmy Carter is one of the most controversial pieces of legislation in the world of air transportation. It unleashed rampant competition in air transportation in the United States and, in the opinion of some, created an unstable financial situation for the legacy carriers of the United States from which they have never recovered. However, it changed the face of civil aviation in the country and in fact around the world, giving birth to completely new concepts in air transportation and to the rise of the low-cost, no-frills, low-fare carriers. Some of these have done very well and others disappeared as quickly as they came. But as a group, they offered the legacy carriers competition with which they have had difficulty in dealing.

The Civil Aeronautics Act of 1938 created the Civil Aeronautics Board through which the US government regulated airline routes, schedules and fares. The idea behind the regulation was to promote and develop the air transport industry. The board therefore determined such things as entry and exit from individual markets, route patterns, frequencies, passenger and cargo fares, safety standards, financing, subsidies to carriers flying on what may be regarded as social rather than commercial routes, mergers and acquisitions, agreements between carriers and service quality. It is important to note that airline subsidies are not a Caribbean invention.

From the very beginning, the introduction of regulation was controversial because it led to a clash of philosophies: that of seeking the greatest good for the greatest number, as opposed to the good old fashion American way of letting the market decide. The reasons advanced in support of regulation were as follows:

- It was meant to ensure that carriers did not serve only high traffic/high profit routes, neglecting low-volume/low-profit routes, thus depriving remote or underpopulated communities of air transportation services.
- Concentration on highly profitable routes by many major carriers was seen as likely to lead to cut-throat competition and therefore price wars.
- This sort of competition often leads to financial difficulties for airlines which could negatively affect maintenance and therefore safety.
- It sought to ensure that no single carrier dominated the market to the point where it could set its own level of high fares.

Others thought, however, that no government institution should decide who should make profits and who should survive, seen by some, as the very essence of what being an American is about.

Whatever its downside, regulation at least confirmed that air transportation was seen as a public service, a social good, to consult the interests and the needs of the travelling public, and from about 1940 the Civil Aeronautics Board actually picked airlines for routes. This argument about air transportation being a public service has been made several times in this book and represents the views of a democratic socialist.

So often, however, a good idea runs into difficulties because of the development of bad practices. Established carriers were involved in evaluating prospective new entrants for routes and, fearing competition, they more often than not found them unsuitable.

Furthermore, there were problems with the fare setting process; first, it often took too long time and second, problems arose because fares set between states were cheaper than fares set within states for similar distances.

In the 1970s these matters sparked a great deal of discussion about, and dissatisfaction with, aspects of regulation, and the movement for deregulation began to grow. The momentum was increased because of both international and domestic developments. Perhaps one of the major developments leading to deregulation was the entry in 1977 by Freddie Laker from Britain into the international market offering cheap transatlantic flights with Sky-Train. Second, in the United States, the Civil Aeronautics Board took two important decisions: one to free up the charter market permitting low-fare domestic charter flights and another to authorize the American Airlines low-fare "super saver" tickets.

In 1977, the US Congress deregulated cargo and in 1978, passenger traffic. From 1981 route restrictions were removed, and from 1982 airlines were free to set their own fares. By 1984 the Civil Aeronautics Board had ceased to exist.

It was an interesting phenomenon that both the major legacy carriers and the unions opposed deregulation because of common fears; the legacy carriers feared, correctly, that they would be facing competition from an exponential growth of low-cost, low-fare carriers; the unions saw that these carriers would be non-unionized.

In compensation, the major airlines were offered subsidies and workers who lost their jobs, high unemployment benefits under the deregulation act.

Deregulation of routes, schedules and fares, had a number of important consequences with advantages and disadvantages to different people and businesses, as follows:

- The creation of the hub and spoke system may be seen as one of the responses to deregulation. The legacy carriers adopted key cities as the centres of their operations where most of their flights stopped, even though those cities were not on a direct route between other end points. They ran daily round trips from their hubs, filling their seats and keeping their planes in the air. As is said often in the industry, planes do not make money sitting on the ground. Daily flights greatly increased between certain popular points.
- There was immediately a significant growth in airline passengers on major routes because of the availability of cheap fares. In 1979 around 317 million passengers flew in the United States, resulting in increased airline operating revenues.
- The downside of the aforementioned development was that many small cities were deprived of air transportation as major airlines abandoned the less profitable routes.
- The market was flooded by new entrants. New entrepreneurs came into the market offering low salaries, fewer managers, multi-tasking and often non-unionized employees who were often shareholders in the business.
- For the first time passengers were being made to pay for meals and checked-in baggage.
- The legacy carriers were now challenged both to keep a high level of service and to cut fares to be competitive. They fought back, to some extent, by taking advantage of their travel agent connections to book advance business.
- By 1981, competition and fare wars began to lead to diminishing returns and the number of passengers fell to 286 million, while operating losses grew to US$421 million.

In 1978 there had been six major legacy carriers in the United States: American, Delta, Continental, Eastern, Pan American and United. By 1991, only American, Delta, Continental and United had survived.

But not only legacy carriers suffered the fall out of deregulation. The first casualties began as early as 1982 when Braniff airline collapsed, started again in 1984 under a new owner, and went into bankruptcy again in 1989. By 1986, People's Express, the front runner in low-cost, low-fare, no-frills carriers, was in distress and had to be sold. In 1989, Continental and Eastern Airlines also went into bankruptcy. In 1991, Pan American World Airways closed down.

In summary, deregulation resulted in increased competition, lower fares, an increase in the number of smaller airlines unencumbered with union and other obligations, offering a range of new products. It also led over the long term to passenger growth through expansion of the market. But rampant competition, a lack of order in the industry and failure to protect routes also led, generally speaking, to an unsettled financial environment. As the major legacy carriers sought to compete in this new marketplace at lower ticket prices while servicing large networks, their service standards dropped and whenever the global economic climate deteriorated, their survival became threatened. Maximizing revenue became an absolute necessity. To face an uncertain future they would have to think out of the box and the management tool they devised to help them was yield and revenue management. Most airlines would later have to resort to what came to be called à la carte pricing to supplement their revenues.

In a speech to the Wings Club in New York (10 June 2008), Robert Crandall, the former legendary chairman and CEO of American Airlines, until 2008 the largest airline in the United States, was arguing in favour of "modest price regulation, slot controls at congested airports, more stringent standards for new carriers, revised labour laws, amended bankruptcy statutes and a more accommodating stance towards industry collaboration". He had been one of the greatest opponents of government intervention or control outside of airline safety issues, and a fervent supporter of deregulation, especially in route development and pricing.

Crandall expressed the view that these measures would have "a dramatic and favourable impact on the financial health of our airlines, the usefulness of our airline system service levels in the airline business and the welfare of the airline employees".

He also said, "I feel little need to argue that deregulation has worked poorly in the airline industry. Three decades of deregulation have demonstrated that airlines have special characteristics incompatible with a completely unregulated environment. To put things bluntly, experience has established that market forces cannot and will not produce a satisfactory airline industry, which clearly needs help to solve its pricing, cost and operating problems."

Crandall also called for changes to the hub-and-spoke system, of which he was the principal architect at American Airlines. He recommended alternative surface transportation to replace flights from points less than 300 miles from the hub city. Of course, this is not an option open to the Caribbean archipelago except one sees the fast ferry as an alternative.

These calls by Crandall for more regulation are being supported in some other unexpected quarters. No wonder the author frequently feels like Cassandra, the Greek prophetess, who was destined to predict the future with accuracy, but also destined never to be believed.

## Yield and Revenue Management

Another major development also seen as a response to deregulation was yield and revenue management, and it is also Robert Crandall who is quoted as saying that yield management, which dates from the mid-1980s, is the single most important technical development in transportation management since deregulation came into being.

Yield management or revenue management has been defined as the process of understanding, anticipating and influencing consumer behaviour to maximize revenue or profits from a fixed, perishable resource such as an airline seat or hotel room.

The challenge is said to be to sell the right resources to the right customer at the right time for the right price. This process can result in a situation where a firm charges customers consuming otherwise identical goods or services a different price for doing so.

An airline documentary aired by American Airlines in 2008 illustrated how and why passengers sitting next to each other in the same cabin actually paid eight different fares for their seats. The prices they paid were said to represent the value of the seat to each person, rather than to the airline. A person who simply had to travel and who booked late at the time when there were very few seats might find himself or herself paying the highest price.

Electronic commerce, greatly developed by GDSs, has made it possible for large volumes of sales to be managed without large numbers of customer service staff. It has also made it possible for management staff to have direct access both to price at the time of consumption and to the data needed for quick decision making.

Everything, however, has a downside. Airlines transact three times more business online than non-travel companies do, some 33 per cent of their revenues coming from e-commerce. They therefore have a major challenge to combat online fraud which according to a study commissioned by the CyberSource Corporation in January 2009 showed that airlines lost US$1.4 billion to online fraudsters in 2008.

The occupancy of an airline seat, like a hotel room for a night, is a perishable product. It is not like a garment in a store, which, if not sold today, remains to be stored and sold tomorrow. A seat that is not sold on Monday is lost forever. After that it becomes Tuesday's seat and so on every day. The company can never recover the loss made by not selling a seat on a particular day. Making sure that the number of seats in the cabin not sold on any one day is kept to zero or as near to that as possible, is the daily objective of any airline. It is a very complex undertaking and one to which the skill of yield management is applied.

Airline seats satisfy three conditions favourable to yield management:

1. There is a fixed amount of resources available for sale.
2. There is a time limit for selling the resources after which they cease to be of value.
3. Different customers are willing to pay the same price for using the same amount of resources.

## Industry Practices in Setting Fares

Airlines practising yield or revenue management use special software to monitor how seats are being reserved and sold and react accordingly in setting their fares. They can therefore offer discounts when they see that seats might otherwise be left unsold. All the seats in the cabin are not sold off at the discounted price. Once the break-even point is made, the rest of the seats sold represent a profit for the carrier and in certain circumstances it may be better to sell them off at discount rates depending on the strength or weakness of demand. It is in any case always better to ensure that all seats are sold.

Airlines also maximize revenue by selling different products on the same flight. This is achieved by implementing purchase restrictions, length of stay requirements and requiring fees for changing or cancelling tickets.

The airline also needs to keep a specific number of seats in reserve to cater to the probable demand for high-fare seats. The price of each seat varies inversely with the number of seats reserved, that is, the more seats that are reserved for a particular category, the lower the price of each seat. This will continue until the price of the seat in the premium class equals that of those in the concession class. Depending on this, a lower price is set for the next seat to be sold.

It is important to know that these practices are followed throughout the industry and are not peculiar to your local airline or one on which you happen to be travelling.

Companies can get yield management very badly wrong, with severe negative consequences to the carrier. Getting it right requires them to have on board analysts with detailed market knowledge and advanced computing systems who implement sophisticated, mathematical techniques to analyse market behaviour and capture market opportunities.

It is appropriate to end this section with a further quote from Robert Crandall's address to the Wings Club, but this time about pricing. He stated:

> It must now be clear to all that one of the industry's fundamental problems is the way in which it prices its product. As you all know, airlines work with a very distorted supply-demand equation. The instant perishability of empty seats, the impossibility of quickly reducing fixed and semi-variable costs when demand falters, the public's view that all airline seats are interchangeable commodities, the plethora of competitors and the desire to protect the reach of networks all create a great temptation to sustain volume by selling seats too cheaply.
>
> In addition to producing huge losses, current pricing and operating practices have produced many negative side effects. In an effort to ameliorate losses, airlines have driven load factors much higher than can comfortably be managed, have outsourced much of their labor to firms employing marginally capable personnel, have introduced hundreds of small inefficient aircraft, have eliminated amenities once considered normal and are imposing a wide range of fees to supplement revenue. The proliferation of fees irritates already unhappy customers, and some – notably baggage checking fees – slow up the check in

process and encourage passengers to carry aboard even more than they have in the past.

I have heard various proposals for solving the pricing problem. The most aggressive favour government supervised pricing discussions whose goals would be to establish minimum fares sufficient to cover full costs and produce a reasonable return. While I would fully support such an approach, the idea is deeply offensive to those who cling to the belief that the markets can solve everything.

Having dealt with deregulation and its consequences and the application of revenue management, a closer look will be now at how the deregulated environment affected LIAT and airlines like LIAT, and its battle to balance affordable fares and survive commercially.

**LIAT Fare Levels**

LIAT is a relatively small carrier that operates a hub and spoke system on a complicated intra-Caribbean network offering some one thousand flights a week to twenty-two Caribbean destinations. It services both routes that are commercially viable and ones that are socially necessary, but unprofitable. The mandate it received from its three government shareholders in 2006 was to do this without receiving any subsidies from any quarter and not to approach them in the future for any bailout support. Furthermore, only three of the twenty-two destinations it serves contribute to it financially or make any kind of capital investment in the carrier.

This is an extraordinarily difficult mandate to implement in any circumstances. But for more than six years between 2000 and 2006, LIAT struggled in a deregulated market with maximum competition that forced it to offer fares far below those needed to cover its costs. In fact the fare levels only returned to those of 2000 in 2006 (see appendix 2). What is not generally known is that the subsidies it received during that period simply went to bridge the gap between costs and revenues caused by inadequate fares. These subsidies, however, stopped at the end of 2006.

Freed from the main competition in 2007, it had no recourse but to set its fares at a level which cover its costs. This continues to receive considerable criticism both from the travelling public and other observers. They insist on comparing its fares unfavourably with those of other international carriers, without any consideration of LIAT's cost base or any analysis of the various inputs into the fare levels, the largest single one of which is probably government taxes. Please refer to appendix 8.

This chapter deals with fare setting from a broad industry perspective. An attempt is made later to make a historical analysis of LIAT's fares and of the various factors at work in determining the levels set. It will be seen that airlines around the world are facing similar challenges.

## LIAT Fare History

The figures in the table appearing below which give a sample of base fares for most frequently used fare classes, demonstrate the veracity of the claim made several times in this book that because of rampant competition and fare wars associated with deregulation, LIAT was forced for five years to cut it fares well below what it cost to operate the service. Fares in fact declined on all routes between 2001 and 2005, except for the Barbados to Guyana and the Barbados to Grenada routes. There were fare increases from 2006 onwards when both LIAT and Caribbean Star were haemorrhaging cash to an insupportable extent.

In February 2007, LIAT and Caribbean Star formed a commercial alliance and consolidated their operations. But it is remarkable that in the eight years between 2001 and 2009, LIAT's overall fares increased by less than

**Table 9.1** LIAT Fares 2001–2009

| Route | One-Way Journey (US$) | | | |
|---|---|---|---|---|
| | Fare (2001) | Fare (2005) | Fare (2009) | Change (2001–2009) (per cent) |
| ANU-BGI | 139 | 93 | 124 | 11 |
| BGI-GND | 70 | 72 | 83 | 19 |
| ANU-SLU | 132 | 91 | 109 | 17 |
| ANU-SXM | 77 | 56 | 84 | 9 |
| ANU-DOM | 85 | 56 | 76 | 11 |
| BGI-GEO | 87 | 111 | 111 | 28 |
| POS-GND | 72 | 56 | 73 | 1 |
| BGI-POS | 77 | 72 | 89 | 16 |
| BGI-SVG | 67 | 56 | 76 | 13 |
| BGI-SLU | 62 | 56 | 77 | 24 |

20 per cent and that there are even some instances in which fares are still lower in 2009 than they were in 2001. It would be difficult to give examples of any other product where over such a long period of time prices actually retreated (table 9.1).

## Oil Prices and the Fuel Surcharge

Much controversy has raged around the matter of adding fuel surcharges to the ticket price. This is an expedient which is not exclusive to airlines and certainly is practised by light and power companies. The reality is that the price of fuel has become so volatile that it is almost impossible to prepare budgets which cater adequately for an input factor that might be as large as 30 per cent or 40 per cent of your costs without any idea of what its unit cost might actually be from day to day, or month to month. It seems fair, therefore, that a model should be applied by which a base price is established and the necessary adjustments made up or down as the price of oil rises or falls.

When at the end of 2008 and beginning of 2009 the price of a barrel of oil dropped from the absurdly high price of US$147.00 in July 2008 to as low as forties and even lower in 2009, people began to demand that all fuel charges be dropped immediately. First, they ignored the fact that the price of oil had risen steadily from 2006 and throughout 2007 to the high point in July 2008 with disastrous consequences for the financial performance of all carriers. And more relevantly, that when four years before the price had jumped from US$36.00 in May 2004 to US$56.00 in June 2005, there was already a need to apply a fuel surcharge mechanism to make sense of the budgets.

Fare levels that were set between 2003 and 2006 assumed a norm of US$35.00 and had every reason to believe that US$60.00 was possible, but high. budgets were prepared accordingly. David Grossman (2005) stated "the recent news that crude oil prices topped US$60.00 a barrel is bad news for the airline industry. With load factors at an all time high some airlines that have been fighting their way back to profitability in the wake of 9/11 will get knocked flat again . . . it is difficult for any airline to be profitable at US $60.00-a-barrel costs and today's low fares." What on earth would he have written when a barrel of oil reached US$147.00 a barrel in 2008?

The price of a barrel of oil went from US$36.00 in May 2004 to US$56.00 in June 2005, a jump of US$20.00. The following increases in the price of oil followed: November 2005, US$62.00; June 2008, US$108.00; July 2008, US$147.00. Fuel charges therefore had to be adjusted upwards from US$10.00 to US$12.50, within four months, to US$18.00 within a year and to US$25.00 when the price was over US$100.00 and climbing rapidly by the day.

There are also two important additional points to make; first, there is a lag time of about two months between a change in the price on the world market and the impact on buying arrangements; second, planes are not powered by crude oil, they use aviation fuel, the price of which is different from crude oil and, in spite of the fall in the price of crude, continued to average around US$64.00 at the beginning of 2009.

In January 2009, LIAT which had already cut US$2.50 off the fuel charge, took a further US$7.00 reducing it to the level that obtained in 2006 when oil was US$60.00. Air Jamaica removed the fuel charges on Caribbean destinations but kept them on international flights, while CAL kept them in place for both regional and international flights. Some observers of international transport immediately began to compare LIAT unfavourably with other foreign carriers which had removed the fuel charge entirely by the beginning of 2009.

A survey by www.farecompare.com revealed, however, that a number of airlines which had announced the termination of their fuel charges, simply found other ways of restoring the income lost thereby. For example, in many cases the base fares were increased to cover the amount of the fuel surcharges removed and other novel means continued to be found to increase income. As the recession began to bite in the source market countries in 2009 with negative impacts on revenue, passengers were being asked to pay as much as US$7.00 for pillows and blankets in coach on certain domestic flights in what is now being called "a choose and use" or à la carte pricing policy. Ryanair even went as far as to suggest that it might introduce a policy of passengers paying for use of the toilets on board.

All airlines, both Caribbean and foreign, however, have this in common; they are challenged to cope with a growing burden of taxes and add-ons which make the ticket prices very expensive. The dilemma in the Caribbean is that the governments which themselves own the regional airlines depend very heavily on taxes raised by taxing the airlines to support the airport infrastructure.

IATA has waged a war against the practice of ever-escalating taxes on airlines, which in its opinion brings diminishing returns, but, so far, there seems little chance of stemming the tide.

In fact, as 2009 began, and the meltdown of the world economy continued, European countries were in the process of establishing new and onerous environmental taxes across the board which seem likely to impose the heaviest penalties on carriers serving places like the Caribbean.

## International Airline Taxes and Add-ons

The director of industry charges at IATA, Jeff Poole, said, "Aviation is the engine room of economic growth and development so increasing aviation taxes may raise visible revenues for national treasuries, but they are counterproductive to the broader economy and overall fiscal revenue" (quoted in Pilling 2008).

These taxes can backfire. In the Netherlands it was shown that revenues from taxes at Schiphol airport in Amsterdam fell below estimation simply because travellers shunned Amsterdam and went to airports in Belgium or Germany to avoid the taxes.

In Barbados persons who would normally travel over Barbados as a hub to other destinations began to by-pass Barbados when a one-way transit tax of US$30 was introduced. The level was later reduced.

IATA estimates that the Netherlands and United Kingdom air passenger duties in 2009 will cost around US$350 million and US$3.5 billion. Belgium and Ireland are following their example with taxes likely to cost €132 million and €150 million, respectively. By 2010 the taxes from these four European countries could amount to €3.8 billion.

These taxes are often imposed on the carriers without any consultation. In Italy the government was proposing adding a €1 fee to each ticket to help fund redundancies at Alitalia. If this were actually implemented, it would mean that other airlines and their passengers would be picking up Alitalia's costs.

In 2009, some Caribbean countries considered a proposal to add a US$3 tax to international tickets to fund a regional marketing campaign.

## UK Air Passenger Duty Tax

The tax which seems to have attracted the most attention and the most resistance is the UK government's Air Passenger Duty Tax.

The Air Passenger Duty Tax has been in place for sometime and generates around £2 billion a year. It is supposed to address in some way the impact of aviation on the environment, but there is no evidence that it has ever been used for this purpose.

It is now proposed that for economy class passengers it be increased from £40 to £50 each, from November 2009, and from £50 to £75 each, from November 2010. For premium economy and business, the percentage increases would be 25 per cent in 2009 and 94 per cent in 2010.

Countries that are between 4,001 and 6,000 miles from London would pay more than those which are less. The distance is, however, calculated as that between capitals, for example, London and Washington. There would therefore be a higher tax for those travelling to the Caribbean, than for those travelling to any part of the United States, for example, Hawaii, which clearly places Caribbean travellers in an uncompetitive position.

The finance bill which authorizes these increases was expected to come before the British Parliament in February or March 2009, but it was delayed, probably because several countries and airlines, fearful that it will have a disastrous impact on the countries affected, especially the Caribbean, have been lobbying the British government against it. See table 9.2 for a matrix of the taxes intended:

**Table 9.2** The UK Proposed Air Passenger Duty Tax

| Destination | Current (£) | Band | From 1 November 2009 (£) | From 1 November 2010 (£) |
|---|---|---|---|---|
| All EU destinations Distance London–Cyprus (LHR–PFO is 2,002 miles) | 10 | A | 11 | 12 |
| Tunisia | 40 | A | 11 | 12 |
| Morocco | 40 | A | 11 | 12 |
| Egypt (LHR–CAI is 2,197 miles) | 40 | B | 45 | 60 |
| Middle East destinations – Dubai and so on | 40 | B | 45 | 60 |

*Table 9.2 continues*

*Table 9.2 continued*

| Destination | Current (£) | Band | From 1 November 2009 (£) | From 1 November 2010 (£) |
| --- | --- | --- | --- | --- |
| Kenya, Maldives, Sri Lanka, Thailand | 40 | C | 50 | 75 |
| Australia, New Zealand | 40 | D | 55 | 85 |
| Canada | 40 | B | 45 | 60 |
| United States (LHR–Washington 3,677 miles LHR–LasVegas 5,299 miles LHR–MCO 4,336 miles LHR–SFO 5,367 miles LHR–Hawaii 7,237 miles) | 40 | B | 45 | 60 |
| Caribbean (LHR–NAS 4,342 miles LHR–BGI 4,196 miles) | 40 | C | 50 | 75 |
| Mexico | 40 | C | 50 | 75 |
| Brazil | 40 | C | 50 | 75 |
| Peru | 40 | D | 55 | 85 |
| Russia is split: West of Urals East of Urals | | A | 11 | 12 |
| (LHR–Vladivostock 5,310 miles) | 40 | B | 45 | 60 |

*Note:* LHR – London Heathrow Airport; CAI – Cairo International Airport; MCO – Orlando International Airport; SFO – San Francisco International Airport; NAS – Nassau International Airport; PFO – Paphos International Airport (Cyprus)

Individual airlines are beginning to take their own action in response to the increases in taxation. According to the *Daily Telegraph* (18 August 2009), Ryanair has decided to pull out nine of its ten routes of Manchester Airport after a dispute over landing charges. This would cost the airport forty-four flights a week, 600 passengers a year and hundreds of jobs. Only the Manchester–Dublin service will be retained. The majority of jobs were expected to be lost at Servisair, its ground handling department. It was reported that Ryanair, in making the announcement, blamed the British and Irish governments' Air Passenger Duty, and the intransigence of the airport.

In September 2009, a second airline, EasyJet, also decided to downscale its operations in the United Kingdom, blaming the increases on the airport fees and the government's Air Passenger Tax. According to the *Financial Times* (4 September 2009), EasyJet complained that airport costs had risen by 25 per cent over three years which made the Bedfordshire base no longer competitive. It planned to shut down its operations at East Midland airport and to cut its flights from Luton by 20 per cent. It was anticipated that 250 jobs would be lost.

In 2008, IATA had circulated a paper addressing the fact that increasingly governments everywhere were seeing airlines as a soft target for the imposition of taxes, which have escalated in recent years. The recommendation was that instead of imposing more and more charges on the airlines, privatized airports should create greater profits by introducing a range of commercial activities within the airports that encourage the travelling public to spend more.

In a speech at the Hilton Hotel on Jamaica Tourism Day (19 February 2008), Cyriel Kronenberg, assistant director of industry charges at IATA, called on Caribbean governments to eliminate surcharges, implement independent economic regulations and adopt a regional approach to the aviation industry. He said the airline industry was a key economic contributor, but Caribbean governments were prescribing taxes on airlines operating in the region, while the cruise lines paid little or no taxes. He was speaking of measures that must be taken to make the Caribbean competitive in the aggressive marketplace. Noting that air transportation was critical to the Caribbean and Latin America, he implored the authorities not to burden airlines flying into the region with an overdose of taxation. He added that (global) air transportation was a US$450 billion industry which supported a US$2.9 trillion economic activity, and while being responsible for providing 570,000 direct jobs and contributing more than US$20 billion to the region's GDP, yet remains an industry in crisis since 2001.

## IATA Caribbean Study

In September 2008, a study was done by IATA at the request of CARICOM and funded by the CDB on the "Costs of Air Travel in the Caribbean Region". One of its stated objectives was "to determine the justification for the level of airfares and 'add-ons' and enable informed policy decisions to be taken by CARICOM governments concerning tariff regimes and 'add-on' charges". It concluded that without access to the regional carrier budgets it was not possible to assess the appropriateness of current fare structures but, based on the analysis of the net fares, it would seem that fares are reasonable and, despite fluctuations, have remained fairly stable overall.

One of the methodologies used was to benchmark fares for routes over specific distances against fares for international services over the same distance. One of the conclusions that surprised many was that "the average net fares in the (Caribbean) routes of the analysis are 32 per cent lower than the average fares in the bench-marked routes" and "overall airport fees in the region were found to be 61 per cent higher than on the benchmark routes".[1]

Once again we face a Caribbean dilemma; the present high level of airfares in the region, however justified on commercial grounds, are being seen as a barrier to travel and injurious to the tourism industry; the taxes and add-ons currently included in the ticket price represent as much as 30 per cent of the ticket costs and exacerbate this situation. It is not easy for the governments and privatized airports to remove them, however, given the high costs of maintaining services at the airports. IATA suggests that a first step is to seek to harmonize the existing taxes and add-ons and to look at models outside of the Caribbean which other countries have introduced to assist special cases, always bearing in mind that the Caribbean region differs from other countries in many respects. (Please see appendix 3 for tables on LIAT fares and taxes.)

While we wait for a solution, some Caribbean tourism authorities and the regional carriers are operating as partners, creating joint products that attract business in difficult times; and by offering affordable promotional fares on specified conditions are motivating people to travel for leisure who might have spent their scarce resources in other ways.

## Hedging Oil Prices

It has frequently been suggested to LIAT that a possible solution to its problem of high costs and high fares would be to follow a practice of hedging oil prices, successfully done by certain carriers.

---

[1] The IATA study, funded by the CDB for CARICOM, was not published but an internal document at the CARICOM Secretariat, the CDB and LIAT.

It would be useful, therefore, to explain what is meant by hedging the price of oil.

Airlines which can afford to do so, often try to "hedge" the price of their fuel. "Hedging" in this context means buying a commodity now that one plans to use later. It may be any commodity, but, in this case, we are referring to oil or rather to aviation fuel.

"Hedging" requires that at least two assumptions be made: one is that the purchaser has enough cash to buy forward for future use and second is that the hedger, presumably with informed judgment, is betting that in future years the price of the commodity in the open market will rise, and rise considerably, above that at which it was bought. "Betting" is therefore the appropriate word since a gamble is being taken.

The airline which is famously known for successful hedging of oil prices is Southwest. As airlines watched in horror, the price of oil moved from US$35.00 a barrel in 2003 to US$60.00 in 2006 and to US$147.00 in 2008. Unable to adjust to these increased costs, a number of airlines collapsed or sought bankruptcy protection under Chapter 11.

In the meantime Southwest had locked in the costs for 65 per cent of its fuel at US$32.00 a barrel for 2006, at US$31.00 a barrel for 45 per cent of its needs for 2007, at US$33.00 a barrel for 30 per cent in 2008 and at US$35.00 for 25 per cent of its fuel needs for 2009. In 2008 it was able to report its fifty-seventh successive profitable quarter.

In contrast, every other US carrier declared losses in 2008. JetBlue, which had pre-tax income in 2007 of US$41 million, reported a pre-tax loss of US$76 million in 2008. Even Southwest had the unusual experience of losing money for the first time ever during the third quarter. The price of oil had fallen dramatically to the low forties, which was well below the price at which its total supply had been contracted.

Other carriers, got hedging very wrong. United Airlines lost some US$779 million in the third quarter of 2008, of which US$519 million was alleged to have been caused by poor hedging policies. The price had also dropped significantly below the price at which airlines like British Airways, Lufthansa and Ryanair had hedged.

They and other major European airlines decided in 2009 against entering new hedging agreements for 2010. Analysts and airlines confirm that it is far harder and more expensive to secure new hedging deals from banks in 2009 because of the credit crisis, especially since the collapse of Lehman

Brothers, which was a major player in the market. Those who were unable or unwilling to hedge before now count themselves as lucky.

LIAT has looked internally at the pros and cons of hedging the price of aviation fuel and had a briefing paper prepared by its CFO for the board's consideration.

However, given the volatility of oil prices since 2005 and the continuing uncertainty, it was decided not to entertain the idea of hedging. Instead LIAT decided to depend on the mechanism of the fuel surcharge. (The paper by LIAT's CFO, Alan Bryon, which explains some of the intricacies of hedging of oil prices, is attached as appendix 4.)

## Cutting Costs and Enhancing Revenues

The year 2008 witnessed a battle for airline survival being fought on many fronts as carriers sought both to cut costs and to introduce revenue enhancement strategies. In the face of intense competition they sought to introduce a number of efficiencies, many driven by commercial departments in an effort to create lower fares.

The year 2008 was, however, a special one. It has been described as the worst year ever experienced by air transportation and airlines since aviation began, and few doubted that well into 2009 and 2010 its fall out would be felt.

It was a year which tested all the theories and most of the practices for survival and many lessons were learned about the value of such mechanisms as application of fuel charges, mergers and acquisitions, and hedging of oil prices.

Chapter 10 will explore the many challenges faced by international carriers in 2008. It will be seen that many of the measures LIAT and Caribbean Star had taken in 2007 to survive, such as cutting capacity, addressing the costs and amount of baggage, and merging operations were used by many carriers around the world as the recipe for survival in 2008.

# 10

# 2008: The Worst Year in Civil Aviation History

No one could have believed at the beginning of 2008 that by midyear, global air transportation would be facing a crisis described as the worst in its history, even worse than the situation resulting from the terrorist attacks of 9/11. For some time there had been indicators suggesting turbulence in the world's economic environment. Economic recession loomed in the United States and threatened to spread to the rest of the world. The value of the US dollar, in which oil is priced, continued to fall against other major currencies in Europe and Asia. An escalation in the price of basic food items, not unrelated to the fact that agricultural products are now being used to supplement the supplies of fossil fuel, led to riots in a number of developing countries. The price of oil, which affects the costs of goods and services, reached levels never before anticipated. The explanations given for this were many and various; among them, surging demand for oil in the fast growing economies of China and India, instability in certain oil producing countries, including Nigeria, Iraq, Iran and Venezuela, inadequate production by the Organization of Petroleum Exporting Countries and other oil producing countries, and investor speculation.

## Escalation of Oil Prices

In April 2008, the price of a barrel of oil reached US$122 and by May 2008 it was US$126. At this point analysts began to forecast that millions of travellers who were accustomed to flying for fun and business during the previous thirty years would be grounded in the not too distant future. By July 2008 the price of oil had reached US$147 a barrel.

The rise in the price of oil now seemed likely to reverse the revolution in air travel earlier attributed in chapter 9 to deregulation. Whatever the negative financial ramification of the Deregulation Act of 1978, no one could deny that it had changed the face of air transportation and over time greatly increased the number of people travelling by air as opposed to by road. In 1979, 317 million passengers in the United States flew by air. According to www.eturbonews.com, air travel in the United States grew after deregulation at a rate five times faster than the population, to the point where 769 million passengers boarded US airlines in 2007.

## 2008 Airline Forecast

eTurboNews reported that with the jet fuel bill being 60 per cent higher in April 2008 than in April 2007, IATA had downgraded its 2008 forecast for the global airline industry for the second time in six months, reducing earlier estimates by nearly 50 per cent.

By July 2008, IATA was predicting that North American carriers would post losses of US$5.2 billion in 2008, Asia Pacific would see profits shrink from US$900 million in 2007 to US$300 million in 2008, European profits would tumble from US$2.1 billion to US$300 million, Middle Eastern profits would drop by US$100 million to US$200 million, Latin American carriers would lose US$300 million and African carriers US$700 million. In March 2009, IATA revised the total losses upwards to US$8 billion and in June 2009, yet again to US$10.4 billion.

In a speech at the IATA annual general meeting in Istanbul (2 June 2008), secretary general Bisignani (2008) had stated:

> This crisis is reshaping the industry in more severe ways than the demand shocks of SARS or 9/11. When fuel goes from 13 per cent of your costs to 40 per cent in seven years with an increased cost implication of US$183 billion, you simply cannot continue to do business in

> the same way. Fundamental change is needed. Airlines have reduced non-fuel unit costs by 18 per cent since 2001. Airports and air navigation service providers must join the effort. Efficiency gains are critical, but cannot fully absorb the impact of skyrocketing prices... [T]he crisis is highlighting the need for greater commercial freedom. Airlines are facing enormous challenges. To be successful and continue providing jobs to 32 million people and supporting US$3.5 trillion in economic activity, airlines must be able to do business like any other business.

He was referring here to the many government taxes and airport add-ons everywhere which inflate airline costs, often without any consultation of the carriers.

### Impact of 2008 Escalating Oil Prices on Leisure Travel

It was expected that resorts, hotels, cruise lines and convention destinations would be negatively affected by the escalating oil prices. In fact it was feared that the price increases would affect leisure travellers most heavily, making travel unaffordable for some would-be tourists. A *USA Today*/Gallup poll carried out in April 2008 found 45 per cent of air travellers indicating that they would be far less likely to travel in summer 2008 if fares were higher.

As 2008 progressed, the fears for tourist traffic began to be fulfilled because of the collapse of charter carriers.

In August 2008, LCC Zoom, which offered services between Europe and North America, carrying 500,000 passengers a year, suddenly went out of business leaving tourists stranded in the United States, Canada and Bermuda. The decision to ground the carrier's seven planes had come after more than twenty-four hours of frantic negotiations to save it.

On 12 September 2008, Britain's third largest package holiday group, XL, collapsed, leaving 85,000 people stranded in various countries. The group includes the Really Great Holiday Company and Kosmar Villa Holidays. XL Airways served more than fifty destinations in the Caribbean, the Mediterranean, Europe, North Africa and North America predominantly from Gatwick, Manchester and Glasglow airports. It was yet another victim to high fuel prices and a deteriorating economic climate.

In October, Icelandic-owned airline Sterling Airways which served a number of Scandinavian cities collapsed, leaving thousands of passengers stranded in England and across mainland Europe.

## US Losses and Closures

In the United States, even though airlines raised fares nineteen times between December 2007 and April 2008, increased fares in the first quarter of 2008 brought in only a 10 per cent increase in revenues. Even Southwest Airlines, which held the line on prices in the first three months of the year, was forced to raise fares twice in April 2008.

Every major US carrier, except Southwest Airlines, lost money in the first quarter of 2008. American Airlines lost US$328 million. United lost US$537 million. Delta and its potential partner, Northwest lost US$10.5 billion. Continental lost US$80 million. Southwest, which before 2008 had reported seventeen years of uninterrupted quarterly profits, was able to report a US$34 million profit due to its long-practised policy of successful fuel hedging. However, it had sustained its first quarterly loss in seventeen years during the third quarter of 2008 when load factors fell and other non-fuel costs rose.

Fuel prices forced seven small US carriers to go out of business after Christmas 2007 and Frontier Airlines, which had sought salvation in converting into an LCC, was forced into Chapter 11 bankruptcy court protection on 11 April 2008. Among those airlines closing during the first half of 2008 were ATA Airlines, Aloha, Skybus, Championair and Oasis Hong Kong; the latter leaving thousands stranded in Asia, Canada and the UK.

## Effect on Business Traffic

Rising prices were also expected to impact negatively on businessmen, especially small businessmen in cases where their business normally involves travelling. They were thought likely to explore other ways of doing business and cutting back on travel. It was even feared that small carriers operating planes with fifty or fewer passengers might be forced to reduce the number of flights, since, even when flying full, they might be unable to make enough money to cover their costs.

# Survival Strategies

In April 2008, aviation analysts argued that only extreme fare increases by airlines and dramatic cutbacks in flights on a global basis, would allow the industry to survive. Many predicted that by May 2009, there could be as many as 20 per cent fewer flights than there were in April 2008. This would translate to something like a carrier the size of American Airlines, which along with its regional carriers, operates some four thousand flights daily, going out of business. It would cause demand to increase and the price of tickets to rise. Delta CEO Richard Anderson expressed the view that it would take a rise in ticket prices of about 15–20 per cent, simply to cover the rise in the cost of fuel.

On both sides of the Atlantic, therefore, steps were taken to implement strategies such as cutting excess capacity, whether by mergers or reduction of services (both routes and schedules) of individual carriers; changes in the type of equipment used based on an assessment of fuel consumption; limiting the weight of baggage; charging heavily for overweight and even for the first piece of baggage; and raising fares as fuel costs rose. In June 2008, the US Air Transportation Association predicted that around one hundred US communities would lose regular commercial air service by the end of 2008 and that the number may well double in 2009.

## Low-Cost Carriers Forced to Raise Fares

A major development as 2008 progressed was that low-cost/low-fare carriers, which differentiate themselves in the market by charging much lower fares than the legacy carriers, were being forced to abandon these established practices and to raise fares and invent creative ways of generating additional income.

In early May 2008, Michael O'Leary, CEO of LCC Ryanair, was predicting that the high oil prices would force a number of airlines into bankruptcy and that Air Berlin, Germany's second largest airline, would be among the victims. He is reported as saying in 2008 that in five years time Ryanair and Lufthansa alone would share the German market. He went further in November 2008 to say that the recession would lead to only British Airways, Lufthansa, Air France and Ryanair surviving in Europe.

O'Leary promised to keep fares low, while grounding twenty aircraft, most at Stanstead and Dublin airports, where airport charges had increased, and seeking to absorb some of the oil costs by lowering profits. His strategy contemplated slashing costs by freezing staff pay, making job cuts at his call centre in Dublin and adding cheaper fuel-efficient aircraft to his fleet. It also included renegotiating down some of its airport maintenance and handling contracts and increasing charges for baggage and airport check-in. He reckoned that this way he would take market share from competitors as they withdrew capacity or went bust. Even so, he did not expect Ryanair to do more in 2008 than break even. These proposed measures clearly reflect the greater flexibility which the LCCs have over the major legacy carriers.

In spite of these declarations by O'Leary, doubts were raised about whether many of the LCCs, would be able to deliver on their promises to keep their fares below a certain maximum in the environment of spiralling energy costs. For years, carriers like Southwest and JetBlue which benefited from their lower operating costs due to simpler jet fleets, work rules and a less sprawling route network, promised travellers that no one-way ticket would cost more than US$299.

In June 2008 that changed when certain one-way travel costs on these carriers reached levels such as US$414 and US$599. Southwest's senior vice president for marketing and revenue management, Davis S. Ridley, was quoted as saying, "The reality is that fares must go up. The arithmetic doesn't work if we transport five people across the country at US$99 each way (Maynard 2008)."

The LCC strategy was to offer deals for passengers who book early, travel off-season and at less popular times. But, in general, LCCs were being forced to join the legacy carriers in charging higher fares, which had risen by approximately 18 per cent industry-wide in 2008. This inevitably led to a blurring of lines between LCCs and legacy carriers. Some LCCs tried to differentiate themselves from the legacy carriers by avoiding charging a variety of fees like the US$15 for checking a bag. However, LCCs JetBlue and Air Tran started charging a fee for a second bag.

In 2008, Southwest launched a major advertising campaign highlighting the differences between itself and other carriers. But it would only be a matter of time before Southwest was forced to change its model of which it had always boasted about "all flyers being equal". It introduced special boarding and special treatment for its highest paying customers, priority security lanes for premium customers at selected airports and "business select" which gives priority boarding, frequent flyer credits and free drinks for the highest-priced fares.

## Widespread Reduction in Fleets, Routes and Air Service

In 2008, as part of the survival strategy, cuts in fleets, routes and service, generally, began to be announced by almost all the carriers, posing a serious threat to all tourism destinations, including the Caribbean. This strategy was later to have positive consequences for the bottom lines of carriers when in 2009 they were in a leaner position to face the global economic meltdown that began to overwhelm the world.

But, in the second half of 2008, the prospect of major airlift disappearing from the Caribbean region caused great concern among Caribbean countries.

### American Airlines

The major threat to air service into the Caribbean came from proposed cuts in the service of American Airlines, which in 2007, provided more than 60 per cent of the passengers travelling through Puerto Rico. It announced its intention to cut domestic capacity 11 to 12 per cent during the fall of 2008 and overall, including international flights, by about 8 per cent. It therefore planned to shed about 8 per cent of its workforce or more than sixty-eight hundred jobs.

It also announced that from September 2008, there would be cuts in the number of its daily American Eagle flights out of San Juan, Puerto Rico, from ninety-three to fifty-one. Among the flights identified were those to Santo Domingo, Antigua, St Maarten, Aruba and Samana in the Dominican Republic. There were also to be fewer flights into San Juan from the US mainland, which would negatively affect the cruise ship industry, as people travel into Puerto Rico to board the ten cruise ships which are home ported in that island.

### LCC Spirit Airlines

The board of directors of LCC Spirit met on 10 June 2008 to decide how many pilots and attendants to layoff. Unions said that hundreds of jobs were at risk. San Juan, LaGuardia and Detroit were identified as airports at which employee domiciles or bases might be eliminated and Fort Lauderdale as one where the employee base might be reduced. The cuts were expected to affect as many as 242 pilots and 452 attendants or 45 per cent and 60 per cent, respectively.

**United Airlines**

In June 2008, United Airlines, then the second largest US carrier, announced plans to ground more than a fifth of its fleet, which numbered 460 planes, slash its domestic capacity by 18 per cent and cut about 1,600 jobs from its 55,000 workforce.

**Delta Airlines**

Delta spoke of cutting capacity by 11 per cent, although sensing an opportunity, it started non-stop flights on 1 June 2008, from John F. Kennedy Airport in New York to Guyana, with three weekly flights on Mondays, Wednesdays and Saturdays, and with the intention of increasing that number to five weekly flights in July. In 2009 it also increased its service to St Kitts.

**LCCs Air Tran and JetBlue**

Air Tran and JetBlue took a decision in 2008 to defer buying aircraft, although both carriers announced some flight increases to San Juan and other Caribbean destinations. In 2009, JetBlue indicated its intention to fly to Jamaica by May 2009. It later decided to fly to Barbados also by October 2009.

**US Airways**

In June, US Airways, anticipating its fuel bill to be US$1.9 billion more in 2008 than it was in 2007 (representing 39 per cent of total expenses as opposed to 14 per cent in 2000), announced that it was reducing fourth quarter domestic mainland capacity by 6 to 8 per cent, returning ten mainland aircraft in 2008 and 2009, cancelling the leases of two A330 aircraft scheduled for delivery in 2009, planning to reduce additional aircraft in 2009 and 2010 and decreasing staff levels by about 1,700 across the system. It was anticipated that about 300 pilots, 400 flight attendants, 800 airport employees and 200 staff and management would be included in that number.

By 23 July 2008, however, it was apparent that in spite of having taken in more revenue in the quarter ending June 2008, than it had done at a comparable period in 2007, it had lost some US$567 million because of soaring jet fuel costs and began talking about slashing as much as 10 per cent of its seats on domestic flights and cutting 2,000 jobs instead of 1,700.

In July 2008, it also proposed that its planes should carry less fuel to reduce the weight of the plane, since the heavier the plane, the more fuel it burns. US Airways management argued that the quantities carried would still be within the legal limit prescribed by regulators. However, the pilots, to whose discretion the quantities of fuel carried was normally left, made strenuous objections.

During the fourth quarter of 2008, US Airways lost a further US$541 million, one of the reasons being mentioned was because it had locked in fuel prices to hedge against further increases in the oil price only to see oil prices plummet.

In 2009, with 10 per cent less capacity and expecting to generate some US$160 million from new service fees such as charging for baggage and for preferred seats, US Airways expressed the view that it could be profitable in 2009. However, growing competition from Southwest and continuing industrial unrest among its pilots, who have failed to resolve the disputes arising from a merger with America West, threaten the achievement of that objective.

**Air Canada**

On 17 June 2008, Air Canada announced plans to cut 2,000 jobs and reduce its capacity by 7 per cent. It also hinted that more capacity cuts might be necessary if fuel costs remain at their then levels. The price of oil had hit a record US$142.26 a barrel in the future trading on 27 June, before settling at US$140.34. By July, it had reached US$147.00 and the much feared US$150 a barrel for oil was beginning to look like a reality.

Air Canada, citing the cause of lack of profitability of the route due to record high and rising oil prices, also announced that it would stop flying to Trinidad and Tobago at the end of August 2008, ending sixty years of uninterrupted service between Toronto and Port of Spain and would retrench thirteen local staff and transfer its customer service manager in Trinidad to another country. The slack had to be taken up by the national carrier of Trinidad and Tobago, CAL – yet another example of the foreign carrier leaving when things got really tough and the advantage of having a national carrier.

In 2009, Air Canada reported that for the full year of 2008 it had suffered a net loss of US$1,025 million, compared to a net income of US$429 million in 2007.

**Southwest Airlines**

While legacy carriers and even some LCCs were falling over themselves to park planes, close routes and cut staff, Southwest Airlines initially resisted the temptation to do so. Instead it capitalized on the fact that in 2008 fuel hedging policies, which have always been central to Southwest's policy, would gain it US$2 billion and cushion the carrier from the cruel impact of ever rising fuel prices. For the fourth quarter of 2008, it was 85 per cent hedged at US$62 a barrel; and for 2009 more than 75 per cent hedged at US$73 a barrel. This would come back to haunt the carrier when oil prices dropped dramatically in 2009 to under US$35 a barrel.

In 2008, however, CEO Gary Kelly had spoken of buying dozens of jets and expanding, rather than contracting the carrier. The plan was to grab market share from his competitors as they cut back, and to expand to Canada, Mexico, Hawaii and the Caribbean – Southwest's first expansion outside of the United States in its thirty-seven-year existence. On 26 August, however, it too announced that beginning in January 2009, it would be cutting 190 daily flights.

**Virgin Atlantic**

In September 2008, Virgin Atlantic announced that it would be cutting flights on routes with light loads, including Washington Dulles, Mumbai, New York (JFK) and the Caribbean.

**BMI**

The news of the takeover of BMI by Lufthansa was followed by an announcement on 6 November 2008 that by the end of March 2009 it would cut its services to Antigua and Barbados as well as to Las Vegas and Chicago. BMI was Britain's second largest airline after British Airways and brought more than 17,000 visitors annually from Manchester in England to Barbados. The loss of an airline service that flies directly out of the north of Britain, without having to transit London airports, would prove to be a serious loss to the region and needed to be replaced without delay. The move was, however, welcomed by Virgin Atlantic which saw the possibility of an alliance between Virgin and Lufthansa which would enable it to better compete with British Airways.

**KLM–Air France**

For the third quarter of 2008, KLM–Air France reported an operating loss of €194 million and a net loss of €505 million. It stated its intention to cut 1,000 to 1,200 jobs in 2009 through a hiring freeze and by not replacing retirees.

By February 2009, many of the predictions about cutting capacity were coming true. eTurboNews quoted London-based aviation consultant Ascend, as stating that because of the reduction of air travel due to global recession, airlines had grounded nearly 2,300 aircraft of their 20,293 planes and the percentage of idled aircraft could soon reach 13 per cent as had happened before at the end of 2001. In some cases new aircraft were replacing old ones. Emirates airline seemed to be going against the trend, however, and increasing its fleet by some 14 per cent.

# Reduction in Aircraft Size

In 2008, the major legacy carriers began to reduce the number of those full-sized jets which were known to be less fuel-efficient, and an even larger number of small regional jets. This decision has implications for small airlines that use fuel-efficient jet prop equipment like LIAT's Dash 8s, as their price will go up as demand for them increases.

Reducing capacity is a tough decision to make. It is not simply a matter of selling some planes; it involves shutting ticket counters, closing gates and laying off staff – none of which can be easily restored.

## Merger Solutions Sought

In 2007 and 2008 there were a record number of attempted airline mergers and consolidations in an effort to reduce total airline capacity as part of the survival strategy. These inevitably attract the attention of regulators and unions, the former, with a view to monitoring the competition process and the latter, out of concern for loss of jobs.

**European Mergers**

In Europe, KLM–Air France, which itself represented a merger, had sought to take over Alitalia, the struggling national carrier of Italy; but in April 2008, even though it was seen as the carrier's salvation, its bid failed due to opposition from the unions.

Alitalia continued to haemorrhage cash and it was feared that the withdrawal of KLM–Air France's offer might force it into seeking bankruptcy protection. In April, trading in Alitalia's shares was halted in Italy and the Italian Civil Aviation Authority warned that it might be forced to suspend its operating licence unless a rescue package was found quickly. The *CTO Executive Brief* (April 2008) carried a report that some wholesalers operating package tours to Italy had already put Alitalia on stop sale, thereby reducing its access to cash. Alitalia, by its own admission, had been losing between US$1.5 and US$2.9 million a day.

Italian prime minister Silvio Berlusconi, returning to office in 2008, sought to put together a rescue package for the collapsing carrier. In September 2008, a group of sixteen Italian investors offered to buy the profitable assets of Alitalia, including its newer planes and airport slots, and to invest US$1.5 billion in the company. It was planned to merge with Air One, a former rival, and to put its failed assets and debts into a separate company for liquidation. In September 2008 there were also some reports that British Airways was seeking to forge an industrial partnership with Alitalia. This came after announcements by British Airways and American Airlines in August of their intention to form a close working relationship with each other and with Iberia, a move strongly objected to by Sir Richard Branson of Virgin Atlantic, on the grounds that it would give them a monopolistic dominance over the Atlantic routes.

Prime Minister Berlusconi had issued a decree revising Italy's bankruptcy protection law to protect the group of Italian investors from Alitalia's creditors. But the European Union's regulatory authority was reviewing the Alitalia's rescue plan to see whether Italy, by changing its bankruptcy law, was providing the carrier with illegal state aid. As all this was happening, the rescue deal fell through when the unions refused to accept the conditions of the plan which involved pilots and cabin crew accepting job cuts and new contracts. The only remaining option seemed to be bankruptcy. In November 2008, there was still no clear decision on the future of Alitalia, with several airlines and other companies vying for whatever useable parts of the operations that could be acquired. It made it into 2009 losing over €2 million a day, but there were doubts that it would survive beyond March 2009. However, with Alitalia one never knows and it continued to operate in 2009.

## US Mergers

In the United States, on 14 April 2008, a merger deal was put on the table by Delta and Northwest that included retaining the name Delta Airlines. The deal faced a number of challenges: first, there was a strong lobby in the US Congress against approval and second, there was the inevitable hurdle which all airline mergers face, of sorting out how to combine the seniority pilots' lists of the two carriers.

In September 2008 the shareholders approved the deal, but there continued to be strong resistance from the unions, especially the Machinists union. Finally on 29 October 2008 the deal in which Delta paid approximately US$2.8 billion to acquire Northwest Airlines was closed, after receiving the blessing of the federal regulators and the Airline Pilots Association). The new Delta replaced KLM–Air France as the world's largest airline and American Airlines as the largest US carrier.

Several other airlines became involved in discussions about mergers since January 2008. United Airlines, which was reported to have been left at the altar by Continental Airlines, began talking to US Airways about a merger which would have made it the world's biggest airline – even larger than the Delta–Northwest deal. Combined, the two would have about 91,000 employees, 800-plus planes, and annual revenues of US$31.8 billion.

American Airlines was also reported to have been discussing a merger with US Airways and an alliance with Continental Airlines. On 19 June 2008, Continental and United Airlines announced that they would work together in an alliance they hoped would boost revenue to offset rising fuel costs.

An incentive to move quickly on these matters in 2008 was not only the likely threat from foreign carriers as trade barriers between Europe and the United States come down, but the fact that mergers of the type contemplated, especially any mergers with foreign carriers, were thought more likely to be approved under the Republican Bush administration than under a Democratic administration. In fact, there were early indications after the election of Barack Obama on 4 November 2008 that his approach to the airline industry was likely to be far more nationalistic and protectionist than it would have been under a Republican administration.

For a very long time, and certainly since 2005, the number of US carriers which have had to seek bankruptcy protection portended a reduction of the number of legacy carriers serving the routes. The rising price of fuel in 2008 strengthened the logic for consolidation of the US legacy carriers from seven to four or five. Such consolidation, which has formerly been resisted by the unions as well as by US Federal regulators, may receive a second look now that the Delta–Northwest merger has been approved and it may only be a case of delaying the inevitable. It was seen earlier that similar predictions were made for a reduction in the number of airlines in Europe.

## Baggage Allowances and Fees

Yet another survival strategy in 2008 was to reduce the weight of baggage allowed, while earning revenue by raising fees on baggage and other services.

The decision of LIAT in 2007 to limit passengers' baggage to 50 pounds per person seemed dangerously close to being an industry standard in 2008. American Airlines decided that from 12 May 2008, travellers purchasing domestic economy-class tickets would pay US$25 for checking a second bag, and contemplated charging US$15 even for the first bag. Certain classes of its passengers, for example, advantage gold, platinum and executive platinum, full fare economy, business and first-class passengers were to be exempted.

JetBlue imposed a second-bag fee of US$20. Other US carriers introduced baggage charges of various kinds. US Airways levied a first-checked-bag service fee of US$15, a new in-flight beverage purchase programme, and increased the charges associated with the airline's employee guest and parent discounted travel pass programme.

In 2009, British Airways decided that from 7 October it would join several US carriers in reducing the baggage allowance for economy passengers. It will now permit economy passengers to have only one bag of 23 kg carried free. Additional bags would be charged £35 a piece at the check-in counter. If the passenger is travelling with skis or a snowboard, the charge will be £70 for check-in at the counter and £50 for check-in online. Virgin Atlantic, one of British Airways' major competitors, has rushed to reverse its intended £90 for a second suitcase. These additional baggage charges are standard on the no-frills carriers.

## Cutting Travel Agent Commissions

In 2008 in an effort to cut costs, airlines were forced, reluctantly, to cut commissions to one of the oldest classes of their travel partners, the travel agent. This has long been seen as an inevitable development, which now places the responsibility on travel agents to re-invent themselves and to rework their revenue streams.

## Indian Airlines

Indian airlines, Jet Airways, Kingfisher Airlines and Air India decided to scrap their 5 per cent commissions for travel agents from 1 October 2008. The Indian aviation industry considered this action because of prospects of a loss of US$1.86 billion in 2008 due to fuel price hikes and inflation. Foreign carriers serving India, like Lufthansa, Singapore Airlines and British Airways, among others, did the same. Indian airlines were said to be no longer chasing growth and market share, but focusing on cost savings and increasing per passenger revenue. In 2008 they were suspending routes with less load factors and between April 2008 and August 2008 daily flights had gone down by some 12 per cent. Airlines have also been bargaining with GDSs to lower the fees for putting their inventory on the terminals of travel agents. This ultimately could lead to airlines having the payment of GDS fees transferred to being paid by agents.

This move by the Indian airlines was expected to hit more than four thousand travel agents across the country whose annual turnover is nearly US$8.38 billion. Additionally, agents were being negatively affected by the fact that there has been a fall in base fares (that is, the airline fare, minus the taxes) on which agents calculate their commissions. The fare was normally broken out into 65 per cent fare and 35 per cent taxes. Currently in India, the base fare proportion has dropped to 40 per cent and the tax proportion to 60 per cent.

However, three associations, the Travel Agent Association of India, the Travel Association Federation of India and the Indian Association of Tour Operators, representing over forty-five hundred IATA-accredited international and domestic agents and more than 85 per cent of the total air ticketing business, met in Mumbai on the 21 July 2008 and threatened to stop selling tickets until the Indian airlines reversed their decision to cancel all commissions from the 1 October 2008. It was agreed that the agents and the leading airlines were to meet again in Delhi to discuss a solution to the problem. The proposed action by the agents sought to leave passengers with no option for booking or cancelling tickets except through company-owned ticketing counters or the Internet. However, it was hoped that by 1 November 2008 some solution would be found. It is to be noted that airlines in Pakistan had also introduced the zero commission policy, but reversed it after one week.

Indian travel agents have no doubt seen the writing on the wall and are reported to be looking to lucrative hotel deals as add-ons to air packages to keep afloat and retain their client base, and making the customer pay for the special add-on services. Realistically passengers go to travel agents mainly to purchase airline tickets and somehow travel agents may have to make the transition from being paid commissions by airlines to charging passengers for their services.

## No Airline Business Model for US$200-a-Barrel Oil

In 2006, airlines were speaking about the challenges they would face if the price of a barrel of oil broke the US$70-a-barrel barrier. When in July 2008 it reached US$147 and the head of the Organization of Petroleum Exporting

Countries, Algerian oil minister Chakib Khelil, spoke to reporters of the possibility of oil reaching US$200 a barrel, airlines made it clear that there is no airline business model which could support such costs.

Tom Horton, American Airlines' CFO, commented, "Air travel has been one of the incredible bargains for US consumers. We're now in a world where airfares are going to have to reflect the cost of the product" (Adams and Reed 2008). My fear is that the travelling public will not be able to afford such costs.

As the price of oil escalated, a number of air transportation initiatives taken by visionaries soon became victim of this development; one of these was the launch of all-business executive jet services focused largely on top executives making transatlantic trips. These were not being marketed on price, but on a belief that there was a demand by executives for high-quality travel.

EOS Airlines flew four times a day from Stanstead Airport in London to New York, JFK. It offered flat beds, free helicopter rides from helipads in Manhattan to JFK, champagne and use of the Emirates Airlines lavish lounges for a return fare of US$2,981. In 2008, EOS declared bankruptcy and suspended all services.

Silver-Jet, less up-market than EOS Airlines, flew twice daily from Luton, England, to Newark for a return fare of US$2,207. Launched in May 2006, its shares plunged from a high of 209 pence to 19 pence before it went out of business.

MaxJet, a US-based carrier, serving this niche market, went bust in December 2007, two years after its launch, because of spiralling costs, competition pressure and weakening market confidence.

It remained to see if the fourth carrier, L'Avion of France, would join MaxJet, EOS and Silver-Jet in the air transportation graveyard, as aircraft lease costs, maintenance problems and oil prices soared.

A report published by *Business Travel Coalition and Airline Forecast* (13 June 2008) stated:

> The impact of sky-high oil prices at US$130 to US$140 levels could result in the loss of 75,000 to 85,000 direct airline industry jobs, many of which are high paying, including 11,500 pilot positions. To cover oil prices at these levels, fares would have to go up 21 per cent to 24 per cent and airline seat capacity reduced by 18 per cent to

20 per cent. Were oil to climb towards US$200, as some analysts predict, the damage escalates and the airline industry could be forced to shrink 35 per cent or more.

The airlines are on pace to spend US$30 billion more on jet fuel in 2008 versus 2007. At best, and based upon the past four-year top-line revenue increases, the airline industry will be able to generate only US$3 billion in fare increases to offset the higher cost. What's more, all the extra-bag charges and other fees implemented by airlines recently, will only yield US$1 billion to US$1.5 billion at the industry level. Airlines can attempt to radically shrink capacity, but given the competitive situation they face, it's highly unlikely that they will have the ability to reduce capacity to levels that will allow them to earn a normal, risk-adjusted rate of return. Instead, absent direct policy intervention, the likelihood is that there will be more bankruptcies, including some liquidations.

As the price of fuel skyrockets, the US airline industry stands on a ledge, staring into an abyss. Before time runs out on the nation's air carriers, policy makers must adopt new energy policy priorities with great purpose and haste.

A catastrophic result for US airlines can be averted if policy makers, particularly in the White House and Congress, step up purposefully to address this monumental challenge. There is still time to make a difference. This is important not only for airlines and their passengers, but also for every business that uses oil products.

By the end of 2008, as the entire world stood looking into that abyss, the price of a barrel of oil dropped as dramatically as it had risen, at one point to below US$40 a barrel. In 2009, it fell further to below US$35 a barrel, proving that the best explanation for its meteoric rise in 2008 in the first place was the greed of speculators.

The one positive of the crisis was that it has demonstrated the necessity for conservation of energy resources and escalation of the search for alternative sources of energy nationally and internationally across the globe. These initiatives found a leader in President Obama whose energy plan for the United States promised to create an energy revolution in that country. The proposed plan seeks to support greater use of ethanol and higher efficiency standards in cars, aimed at cutting US oil consumption by about four million barrels a day. He promised that the United States would seek to save more oil within ten years than it currently imports from the Middle East and Venezuela combined. This would have serious repercussions for oil producing countries and refineries everywhere.

In the short term, however, assuming that the cause of the rise in prices in 2008 was in fact speculation and the greed of mankind, the chances of it happening again in 2009 and 2010 cannot be ruled out, except there is state intervention to outlaw some of the current practices of speculators. We should not, however, believe that the volatility of oil prices seen in 2008 is necessarily a thing of the past. By mid-2009 it had again risen above US$70, and where it will ultimately go is anyone's guess.

As 2008 progressed, it seemed reasonable to believe that the events of that year which had caused such disruption in international air transportation services would place Caribbean tourism in some danger. Public and private sector leaders therefore decided to give travel and tourism elevated importance in their counsels as will be discussed in chapter 11.

# 11

# The Caribbean Reacts to the 2008 Crisis

It is always important to remind people in the Caribbean that this region depends four times more than any region of the world on tourism for its socio-economic development. There are those who think this is a bad thing and who wish it were otherwise, but this changes nothing. It is also worth repeating that more than 90 per cent of the foreign exchange spent in the region by tourists comes from the stay-over visitors who travel to the region by air. Air transportation is therefore a critical link in the tourism chain and events in 2008 seemed to threaten the very existence of the air transportation industry on a global scale. The region faced the prospect of either loss of or reduction of the services provided by foreign carriers and even the worst critics of Caribbean carriers were grateful for their existence, even if not so grateful as to say so explicitly.

## Action by Caribbean Tourism Leaders

In anticipation of the proposed downsizing by airlines serving the Caribbean and its impact on Caribbean tourism, a series of crisis meetings were held from as early as May 2008 at both public and private sector tourism levels in the region to strategize about what alternative airline services were available, or to discover if some means could be found to persuade or motivate the foreign airlines serving the region to amend their plans for reduction of capacity or withdrawal of service altogether.

### Meeting of Caribbean Tourism Organization Ministers of Tourism

The first initiative was a meeting of ministers of tourism of the CTO held in Antigua on 28 May 2008 to discuss the following issues:

- Cooperation over the regional hubs
- Promoting the region
- Providing revenue guarantees to airlines
- Providing a more efficient intra-Caribbean air transportation service

Four committees were established for each area and they reported to the First Annual Caribbean Tourism Summit organized by the CTO, which took place from 21 to 24 June 2008, in Washington, DC.

### Meeting of LIAT Shareholder Prime Ministers

A second initative was a meeting of the three LIAT shareholder prime ministers, the Hon. Baldwin Spencer of Antigua and Barbuda, the Hon. David Thompson of Barbados (replacing the Rt. Hon. Owen Arthur), and Dr the Hon. Ralph Gonsalves of St Vincent and the Grenadines held on 8 June in Barbados to review the carrier's performance, the likely fallout from the proposed reduction of airline services to the region, and LIAT's future role in addressing the anticipated crisis.

At the meeting, LIAT's CEO Mark Darby restated the need for governments to assist by taking immediate action in the following areas:

- A reduction of government taxes and airport add-ons on airline fares which were pushing up air ticket costs. These had grown even higher because travel agents were often adding their own service charges to

replace revenue lost or reduced by commission cuts by the carriers (see appendix 3).
- More effective regulation of airports, air traffic control, civil aviation authorities and fuel suppliers. The emphasis was on the need for some regulation in setting airport user charges and a greater focus on airports developing non-aviation sources of revenue, a matter which had been raised independently by IATA.
- The need for a single Caribbean sky with a unified air traffic control environment. The issue of a single Caribbean sky is often confused with the issue of open skies. There is therefore a detailed note explaining what a single Caribbean sky is about at appendix 5.
- The need to subsidize social routes which are not commercially viable.
- The need for improved infrastructure–airport terminals, navigation aids, improved runways and safety factors.
- Improved facilitation and support from customs and immigration authorities.

In July 2008, the Government of Barbados responded positively to calls for a reduction in its US$30 one-way airport intransit tax. It was reduced by 75 per cent for intra-Caribbean travellers and 50 per cent for international travellers. However, the Government of Antigua and Barbuda, which was in the middle of financing significant airport improvements, increased its airport passenger charges by EC$40.00(US$1.00 = EC$2.70). Most of the issues raised by the LIAT CEO, however, remain as work in progress to be addressed.

## Meeting of CARICOM Heads in July 2008

A third initiative may be said to be the tourism and air transportation components of the agenda of CARICOM heads of government who met in Antigua from 1 to 4 July 2008. This included receiving reports from the previous meetings referred to earlier. Quite a comprehensive number of important decisions were made, suggesting an appreciation of the crisis facing regional tourism and air transportation in 2008–9.

## CARICOM Summit Agreements on Tourism and Air Transportation

A list of tourism and air transportation issues was presented to the heads of government by a tourism task force and the following agreements were announced:

- That the heads supported the proposal for establishment of a US$60 million marketing fund to promote the Caribbean as a single destination.
- That CARICOM countries would contribute US$21 million towards the fund, while the remainder would come from the Caribbean Hotel Association, the CTO and other stakeholders.
- That a Caribbean regional tourism brand should be adopted and a timely and comprehensive information gathering system established which would adequately reflect the contribution of tourism to the national economies.
- That a special meeting of the CARICOM Council for Trade and Economic Development would be convened with a tourism and air transportation agenda to examine the regional marketing fund and related modalities and report to a meeting of the Bureau of Heads of Government within sixty days.
- That tourism ministers would in future be permitted to participate in meetings of the Council for Trade and Economic Development, the second highest decision-making body of CARICOM.
- That other discussions about fund contributions would be held with the Dutch Antilles, the French Antilles, US territories, the Spanish-speaking countries and the cruise industry.
- That the heads recognized the need for improvement in the inter-regional airline system and for hubs operating in Barbados, Antigua and Montego Bay, Jamaica, to function more effectively.
- That they had also recognized the need for the inter-regional carriers to be able to interline with other carriers to provide cost-effective connections, to have the intransit taxes now imposed by some governments eliminated, and to have passengers able to check-in to other

flights, without having to go through customs and immigration and re-check at airline counters.
- That the heads supported stronger collaboration and functional cooperation among the regional airlines and the establishment of regional hubs. They mandated CAL, the carrier of Trinidad and Tobago and LIAT to hold discussions about inter-carrier cooperation.
- That further steps should be taken to increase and improve safety and security with respect to the region's air transportation, which is a most welcomed development and one that will enhance the prospects for further cooperation between regional and foreign carriers.
- That regional governments should work closer with the United States government to achieve a number of objectives, such as exempting people travelling to the Caribbean from having to pay the US$40 departure tax imposed by the US authorities, to open US pre-clearance facilities in the Caribbean and to secure an increase in duty-free allowances for Americans travelling back from the Caribbean to their country.
- That the CARICOM Transport Committee, headed by the prime minister of St Vincent and the Grenadines, would review the preceding recommendations with a view to early action.

## Safety in Air Transportation

During the meeting of heads, the Caribbean Safety and Security Oversight System (CASSOS) was established on the signing by the governments of Barbados, Guyana, St Lucia, Suriname, and Trinidad and Tobago of the Agreement Establishing the Caribbean Aviation and Security Oversight System. It was also designated an institution of CARICOM by the conference, pursuant to Article 21 of the Revised Treaty of Chagueramas.

CASSOS succeeds the Regional Aviation Safety Oversight System with expanded functions. It formalizes, in a cost-effective manner, the sharing of the technical aviation expertise of the region, the harmonization of training, licensing, certification and inspection procedures and providing technical support to the participating states to enable them to achieve and maintain full compliance with international safety and security standards in keeping with their obligations as contracting states to the Convention on International Civil Aviation (the Chicago Convention 1944).

The regional approach is consistent with the global strategy promoted by the International Civil Aviation Organization and the US FAA to address safety and security oversight issues in contracting states, and CARICOM joins other regions in establishing its own entity, membership of which is open to non-CARICOM Caribbean states and territories.

This agreement marks a very important step forward in civil aviation in the region and is yet another example of what the regional integration movement can achieve for the Caribbean.

The new governing body for air traffic control in the region held its first meeting on Friday 14 February 2009 under its new chairman, Mr Anthony Archer, director of civil aviation of Barbados, and made plans to begin its work by March 2009. Its stated primary objectives are as follows:

- To assist states parties in meeting their obligations as contracting states to the Chicago Convention by achieving and maintaining full compliance with the standards and recommended practices of the International Civil Aviation Organization.
- To facilitate and promote the development and harmonization of civil aviation regulations, standards, practices and procedures among its states parties consistent with the annexes to the Chicago Convention.

CASSOS, which will report annually to the CARICOM Council for Trade and Economic Development will be the main forum through which its states parties will harmonize and update their civil aviation safety and security regulations. It will also promote the interest of the states parties in regional and international aviation fora.

## Functional Cooperation between CAL and LIAT

The frequency with which CARICOM leaders return to the subject of cooperation among Caribbean carriers reflects both the importance given to the subject and the difficulty of making something significant happen. At the 2008 conference of heads of government, LIAT's CEO, Mark Darby, outlined a number of areas where functional cooperation between CAL and LIAT could begin almost immediately. This list included

- Schedule coordination
- Maintenance
- Quality assurance
- Purchasing of fuel, aircraft spares, advertising, ground services, simulator training
- HQ functions: revenue accounts
- Frequent flyer programmes
- Call centres
- City ticket offices
- Training: in customer service and so on

## Follow-up to the Heads of Government Meeting

Caribbean governments and tourism leaders concentrated on the deterioration in the health of the global air transportation industry during the first seven months of 2008 and the threat this posed to Caribbean tourism and it was hoped that there would be urgent follow-up action to certain key agreements reached by heads of government in July 2008.

A year later, however, while some things were done, there was little progress made in those areas. For example, many hurdles still lay in the path of the creation of the regional marketing fund and there was no significant advance in the area of inter-carrier cooperation, beyond what was already happening between CAL and LIAT, before the injunction of the heads of government.

Caribbean countries tend to respond to crises and it may very well be that the general improvement in the two carriers' financial status in 2008 was one of the factors that reduced the motivation for greater cooperation and coordination of their functions.

With respect to the creation of a significant regional marketing fund, the region had struggled to make this happen since the early 1990s. In July 2008, at the Heads of Government meeting, it seemed that for the first time the region would break through the barrier of resistance to the idea of creating such a regional fund to promote and market the thirty-three member states of the CTO region as a single tourism destination. When Council for Trade and Economic Development met in Port of Spain in September 2008, however, once again the countries failed to agree on a formula for raising the funds but agreed to continue talking.

However, there were some individual responses to the crisis created by events in 2008 both from individual countries and by individual Caribbean carriers of which two examples follow.

The Puerto Rico Tourism Company mounted an aggressive campaign to entice airlines to retain and increase their services. It created a co-op marketing programme under which the company promised to match every dollar up to US$3 million that the airline industry spent in the promotion of travel to Puerto Rico.

## LIAT: One of the Regional Solutions

The steps taken by LIAT towards reconstruction in 2007, which had been very unpopular, in fact placed it in a position to better assist the region when matters seriously deteriorated in 2008 and 2009. These included reduced head count, capacity reduction, fuel saving, increased fuel surcharge, reduction of travel agent commissions, negotiations regarding sales tax and so on with other possible options such as sale or wet-leasing of equipment. The consequence of this was that while airlines everywhere were either suffering considerable losses or actually closing down, LIAT was able to keep its head above water and achieve a small operating profit in 2008.

When American Eagle actually began to implement its promised cuts, LIAT was able to respond to the requests of the Caribbean governments to expand, rather than to reduce, its services as it had intended. In particular it responded to the initiatives of the Government of Puerto Rico and increased services between Puerto Rico and a number of Eastern Caribbean destinations towards the end of 2008. During the last quarter of that year, LIAT's critics once more faced the reality, which they would have preferred to ignore, that the carrier is currently the only company in the Eastern Caribbean without which the social and business life of the sub-region and its intra-Caribbean tourism specifically would be somewhat paralysed. It should be noted that American Eagle, after some consideration, decided to reinstate some of those flights that had been cancelled as shown in the following table:

**Comparison of Increase in American Airlines' Frequency to Each Destination**

| Destination | Current | Proposed |
|---|---|---|
| St Marten | two flights daily | three flights daily |
| Tortola | three flights daily | six flights daily |
| St Thomas | five flights daily | six flights daily |
| St Croix | six flights daily | no change |
| Guadeloupe | four flights per week | one flight daily |
| Martinique | five flights per week | one flight daily |
| Trinidad | four flights per week | one flight daily |
| Grenada | four flights per week | no change |
| St Lucia | one flight daily | no change |

In mid-2008 the region had been sufficiently concerned about the future of its tourism sector to bring together decision makers at the highest public and private sector level to explore new approaches to protect Caribbean tourism and the all-important air transportation services on which it depends. It would be useful, therefore, to review how Caribbean tourism actually performed in 2008, how that performance was impacted by economic factors which themselves were affecting the state of regional and international air transportation services and what were the region's tourism prospects going forward in 2009 and beyond. That is done in chapter 12 that follows.

# 12

# Caribbean Tourism Performance, 2008

Tourism's growth and decline are influenced by a number of factors; one obvious positive factor is economic prosperity and people having the disposable income to spend on leisure products. It has been observed, however, that there is a certain resistance to abandoning the holiday, even in difficult times. Instead, most people first seek to shorten the holiday or to choose destinations either nearer home or at home. They feel that they have earned a break from the challenges and stress of daily work and the holiday is both their reward for hard work and a source of revitalization of their energies. For those who are rich enough to be recession proof, it is a part of the good life.

## The Economic Factor in Source Markets

Any analysis of the performance of Caribbean tourism has to begin by examining the state of economic well being of the major markets from which it draws its main business. These are the United States, Canada, Western Europe, the United Kingdom and the Caribbean. The rest of the business comes from secondary markets such as South America, Russia, Eastern Europe and Asia among others, but not so far in sufficient quantities to be regarded as significant. These latter are regarded as having the potential to produce business but, inevitably, marketing priorities have to be established in the context of foreign exchange constraints and other demands on both the public and private purse.

## The Safety and Security Factor

Another important factor driving the extent and direction of tourism flows in today's world, where terrorism is common, is perception by the potential visitor that a destination is safe and secure. When this is added to proximity or accessibility, a destination receives an added advantage.

## The Caribbean Advantage

### Stay-over Visitors

A review of international tourism flows following 9/11 revealed that after the first week when no planes were permitted to fly into the United States, there was a dramatic drop in business. But as soon as air traffic recommenced, stay-over tourist arrivals to the Caribbean recovered quickly and grew at the expense of business to other parts of the world. The same happened after disasters such as SARS, tsunamis and mad cow disease. In short, the Caribbean has tended to benefit from disasters that befall people in other regions. After 9/11 many Americans who had been planning to go to Europe on holiday in 2002 chose the Caribbean instead as it was safe and nearer home. Europeans, who would normally have travelled to the United States, also saw it as unsafe after the attack on the towers in New York and on the Pentagon in Washington and, given the then strength of the pound versus the US dollar to which many Caribbean currencies are tied, continued to see the Caribbean both as a bargain and safe.

This sense of security had to do with a low expectation of acts of terrorism and a healthy environment. They knew about natural disasters in the Caribbean like hurricanes, but knew that they could plan around the hurricane season. Many parts of the world experience natural disasters, but a factor that assists the Caribbean is that it is easy to predict when hurricanes are coming and systems are in place to give advanced warnings so that steps can be taken to protect life and property. Moreover, some countries in the region have had no experience of hurricanes for several decades.

## Speedy Cruise Tourism Recovery

After 9/11 there had been an equally speedy recovery in cruise passenger traffic in the Caribbean. The cruise lines made adjustments to their routes and schedules so as to reduce the number of ports to which people had to fly to board ships but, by and large, the Caribbean remained their main area of operation. The chief beneficiaries of the changes in itineraries were the northern and western Caribbean.

A survey conducted by the Cruise Line International Association in 2008 confirmed once again that the Caribbean remains the preferred destination of cruise visitors. It was a random survey of 2,426 persons, with an average age of twenty-five years and a minimum household income of US$40,000. Cruise industry officials reported that the Caribbean was growing at the expense of the Mediterranean mainly due to the rising fuel costs in 2008, among other factors. Once again it was proven that the geographical location of the Caribbean territories (a night's sailing from each other), the proximity to major markets, the year round climate and tranquil seas (except when disturbed by hurricanes during a specific period of the year), and the good reputation of the region, to date, for safety and security, make the Caribbean a natural first choice for those wishing to take a cruise vacation. It was also shown to be increasingly the choice of those wishing to take a family holiday.

The region is not so naïve as to believe that with so many international visitors, especially Americans, it could not be a possible target for terrorism and therefore its vigilance in matters of security has sharpened. Until now, however, it does not appear as if the region is seen by tourists as a likely place for terrorist activity. Nevertheless, the concern about general safety of the person and possessions is growing due to extensive coverage in the media of the marketplace of the deaths of a few visitors and repeated reports of homicides in a few countries, even though visitors are seldom involved.

These developments, however, point to the need for the Caribbean to develop strategies to combat crime as a major plank of tourism planning, especially as the worsening economic situation in the world seems to be leading to increased robberies in both developed and developing countries by people desperate for money to buy essentials.

In the marketplace, reports about crime involving a tourist in any one Caribbean country, especially a homicide, nearly always make reference at some point to the Caribbean region as a whole. There is, of course, a decided risk in mounting an aggressive campaign about any Caribbean country being a safe destination, since that will last only as long as the next incident in the region. When some tragedy happens in a Caribbean destination involving tourists, however, as will be the case from time to time, there must be professional crisis management systems already in place to deal with it, with clear allocation of responsibilities of who does what, especially in handling the press.

## The Air Transportation Factor

Economic prosperity and safety are necessary, but not sufficient conditions for successful tourism. At least one other factor is absolutely critical for the success and even the existence of Caribbean tourism, and that is, air access to and between Caribbean countries from tourism markets. In 2008 the escalating price of oil and therefore aviation fuel, threatened the very existence of air transportation. The Caribbean's reality, comprising as it does largely an archipelago, a group of islands separated from the rest of the world and from each other by sea, makes air transportation its lifeline. It was the fear of losing air access that caused Caribbean governments a great deal of concern and led to the crisis meetings in 2008. They would have had even greater reason for concern if none of the carriers serving the region were under their ownership and control.

## Source Market Performance

The year 2008 had begun badly for the economies of the Caribbean's source markets and continued to deteriorate as the year progressed.

### US Economy

At the start of 2008 unemployment in the United States stood at 4 per cent but increased at an accelerated rate as the year progressed until it stood at 7.2 per cent by year end. Inflation was 4 per cent on average but dropped as low as 1.1 per cent in November.

The US dollar to which the value of the currency of a number of Caribbean countries is tied, gained in strength against most currencies. By the end of 2008 it had risen to some 29 per cent against the pound sterling which was itself in decline. For those Caribbean countries whose currencies are tied to the US dollar, this literally devalued the currencies of those other countries. It certainly devalued the pound sterling and therefore the spending power of the British, who are the main customers for countries like Antigua and Barbuda and Barbados.

Real GDP was forecast to remain in the realm of –0.4 per cent to –0.6 per cent.

## Canadian Economy

Average unemployment in Canada over a period of two years before 2008 had been about 6 per cent and moved slowly up to 6.6 per cent by year end of 2008.

Inflation was about 2.1 per cent in 2007 but averaged 2.5 per cent overall in 2008 after peaking at 3.5 per cent between June and November and falling back to 2 per cent. The Canadian dollar gained strength against most major currencies, although remaining on par with the US dollar and declining slightly against the pound. Real GDP growth was small with personal spending slowing after the third consecutive quarter of deceleration.

## United Kingdom

Unemployment stood at 2.7 per cent but crept up after mid-2008. Inflation went up from 2.3 per cent in 2007 to 3.7 per cent early in 2008. It peaked at 5.2 per cent in April but dropped back to 4.1 per cent in November.

As was stated earlier, the pound sterling weakened against most major currencies with significant declines against the US and Canadian dollars. Real GDP growth was small but positive.

## Other Region

With respect to other regions it is worth noting that according to International Labour Organization estimates, North Africa and the Middle East had unemployment rates of 10.3 per cent and 9.4 per cent at the end of 2008. Central and South East Europe, as well as the former Soviet Union countries ended 2008 with unemployment at 8.8 per cent. It was 7.9 per cent in sub-Saharan Africa and 7.3 per cent in Latin America.

## Overall Tourism Performance in 2008

Given the preceding data on source markets' economic performance, Caribbean tourism could have been expected to perform a great deal worse. According to the statistics published by CTO 2008, however, there was a mixed individual country tourism performance among the thirty-three CTO member states in 2008, but stay-over arrivals to the Caribbean in 2008 were about 23,181,000, representing a 2.2 per cent increase over arrivals in 2007 which were 22,683,000 (see appendix 6 – CTO 2008 Caribbean tourism statistics).

There were gains in every market ranging from 1.1 per cent in the US market, 14.0 per cent in the Canadian market, 2.9 per cent in the European market and 5.4 per cent in other markets. With respect to other markets, the intra-Caribbean market which had fallen by −7.3 per cent in 2007 declined by a further −1.3 per cent in 2008.

There were strong individual performances by Cuba +11 per cent, Curaçao +30 per cent, Cancun +6 per cent, Jamaica +4 per cent, St Lucia +4 per cent, Antigua and Barbuda +3 per cent, St Maarten +4 per cent, and the increase in the Dominican Republic was modest with +0.7 per cent. There were, however, steep fall offs in the Bahamas and Puerto Rico.

In 2008, 14 of the 27 countries reporting to CTO suffered declines. The declines in stay-over visitors did not begin until April and were heaviest in the second half of the year.

Cruise tourism fell from 16,927,000 in 2007 by some −6.0 per cent to 15,914,000 in 2008. In 2008, the declines in cruise tourism began in May and were particularly steep in every month until the end of the year.

The overall performance suggests a high correlation with increasing fuel prices and fares for all airlines, diminishing air services for some and increasing services for others. There can be no doubt that the Dominican Republic and Puerto Rico suffered because of diminishing air service. Growth in the Canadian market not only reflected the strength of the Canadian dollar but new air services out of Canada. Equally it is certain that in spite of the considerable financial difficulties of Air Jamaica, its presence operating in the marketplace and its role as the major carrier to Jamaica helped to keep Jamaica in the positive category of arrivals in 2008 with increases of +4 per cent.

What would have been also an important factor in 2008 is that the booking window for Caribbean tourism from international markets is long and several passengers would have booked their 2008 holiday in 2007 before the economic meltdown and the escalation of fuel prices really began in 2008. There were increases in January 2008 of 7.3 per cent, in February of 9.3 per cent, and in March of 5.8 per cent. The first decrease of −1.3 per cent came in April 2008.

## Performance of Caribbean Carriers in 2008

The Caribbean's positive tourism growth in 2008 was truly commendable, given that 2008 has been described as the world's worst year for air transportation. The director general of European Regional Airlines expressed the view in October 2008 that thirty-five airlines had gone into bankruptcy in 2008 and he thought that the number might double by the winter of 2009.

In the United States the story was similar. With the exception of Southwest Airlines, all US carriers had lost money in 2008. However, we have seen that even Southwest lost money for the first time in seventeen years during the third quarter of 2008.

In contrast to many US and European carriers, both CAL and LIAT did reasonably well in 2008. Air Jamaica, in spite of its high losses, continued to demonstrate its importance to the country by carrying some 50 per cent of passengers to Jamaica. The difference in financial performance between CAL and LIAT on the one hand and Air Jamaica on the other was possibly due to the different abilities of the first two to get rid of the accumulated debt of LIAT and CAL's predecessor BWIA. In the case of LIAT, it had been EC$311 million.

### LIAT Performance in 2008

During the first half of 2008, LIAT experienced a reduction in demand and lower yields as rising oil prices and various other costs affected the disposable income of the travelling public. But because of its marketing campaigns, it did particularly well in July, August and October 2008; and by year end, like CAL, had made a small operating profit.

Freedom from debt made it possible for CAL and LIAT to concentrate on their restructuring plans. LIAT was able, for example, to put improvements in place, like its major programme of IT system renewal and a new safety management system. In addition it met a number of important deadlines; IATA had set 31 May 2008 as the date by which the world's airlines must move to electronic ticketing (e-ticketing). From that date unless the airlines were e-ticket compliant or bilateral arrangements had been put in place, all interline agreements lapsed. Becoming compliant involved a considerable amount of work and planning in the IT area – with the tie up between each interline partner taking several weeks. LIAT met the deadline with respect to a number of important carriers such as British Airways, Virgin Atlantic, BMI, Hahn Air and Air France. In September it completed arrangements with CAL and US Airways and was on track to do so with Air Jamaica.

Most of LIAT's interlining arrangements with American carriers had lapsed as some of its former interlining partners like American Airlines, Delta, Continental and Air Canada stated that they were unable to complete the necessary IT links with LIAT within the deadline. As the pressure to meet the deadline ended, LIAT began approaching these carriers afresh, in an effort to establish whether they wished to interline with it and within what timeframe. Doing so was important as LIAT moved to expand its flights to take up some of the slack created by the reduction in the services of certain US carriers and to make seamless connections with other US carriers out of San Juan, Puerto Rico. It increased its flights from the Eastern Caribbean to San Juan, Puerto Rico, so that it has services to that country from Antigua, St Lucia, St Vincent and the Grenadines, Dominica, and the British Virgin Islands. It next held discussions with St Kitts–Nevis and Anguilla about similar services.

In March 2009 LIAT entered, of its own free will, the IATA Operational Safety Audit Programme, which covers examining a range of processes involved in flight operations, dispatch, ground handling, aircraft maintenance, cabin operations and operational safety. It is expected that on completion of the exercise, LIAT will be placed on the IATA Operational Safety Audit Programme register.

**Caribbean Airlines in 2008**

When CAL began operations on 1 January 2007, BWIA, its predecessor had already closed its services to Manchester, London, its New York and Toronto routes (with stops at Barbados or Antigua), its services to St Lucia, cut its fleet to six Boeing 737-800 aircraft, and reduced its staff to 800. CAL was launched as an entirely new carrier which was not only free of debt, but free of the industrial disputes which had hobbled BWIA for many years. Having made a profit of US$6.9 million before formation, structuring and transition costs in 2007, it actually achieved a net profit at the end of 2008.

## Air Jamaica Performance in 2008

At the end of 2008 the situation of Air Jamaica, with an accumulated debt estimated at US$1.3 billion, remained uncertain. Senator Don Wehby, who had responsibility for air transportation matters in Jamaica, announced early in 2009 that the Air Jamaica Privatisation Committee was in serious discussions with three potential buyers from three different geographic regions and that the March 2009 sale deadline was still doable. He gave the objectives of the deal as management and operational control, recapitalization of the airline with its enormous debt and retention of the Air Jamaica brand. However, the government seemed to face the reality that if no suitable investor were found, it would be left with no option but to liquidate the carrier.

## Other Caribbean Carriers

In 2008 the Caribbean carriers continued to supply critical services to the region. The Bahamas Government continued to encounter arguments to close its carrier, but started exploring possibilities of finding an investor who would purchase a less than 50 per cent stake in Bahamasair. The Cayman Islands government continued its policy of subsidizing the losses of Cayman Airways with the firm conviction that the carrier's contribution to its tourism industry and to the society as a whole, far outweigh the annual losses suffered.

Most tourism-dependent countries and airlines will remember the year 2008 for its many trials and tribulations. They looked forward to 2009 with hope, but little conviction, that things would be better in 2009. Chapter 13 looks at how 2009 did turn out and seeks to propose a vision for Caribbean carriers into the future.

# 13

# Air Transportation in the CSME: Beyond 2009

As 2008 gave way to 2009, the price of crude oil fell as dramatically as it had risen in 2008. It continued to fall in 2009 to the point where in mid-February 2009 the price of light sweet crude for delivery in March fell to US$37.55 a barrel.

Euphoria among airlines soon gave way to concern when it was realized what was the cause of the decrease in oil prices; a global economic meltdown was reducing the demand for goods and services on an international scale, leading also to a reduction in the demand for oil and energy products generally. Unfortunately this also meant a reduction in the demand for air transportation services which was as likely to reduce airline revenues as the escalation in the price of oil had done.

As 2009 began, economic recession in Europe and North America began to take hold in a manner that was second in its severity only to that of the Great Depression of the 1930s. Regions like the Caribbean which are heavily dependent on tourism, feared, not unreasonably, that it was only a matter of time before the meltdown reached the developing world and in particular that tourist flows and tourism investment would dwindle in 2009 and beyond. By the month of February 2009 the fall out was already visible to the naked eye (see appendix 7 – CTO 2009 Caribbean tourism statistics).

There was good reason to fear that in 2009 airline companies in Europe and the United States would not escape the serious problems facing automobile companies in those same countries. The concern was that if millions of people were losing their jobs and businesses closing their doors every day in the Caribbean's source markets, it would not be long before the airlines that currently serve the region from those same countries, began to feel the draught and to cut their services deeper than in 2008.

## Economic Situation in 2009

Early in 2009 these fears were being reinforced by the fact that a number of important and credible voices were suggesting that the deterioration in the global economy would continue in 2009 and that there was no clarity with respect to when the recovery would begin.

Director-general of the International Labour Organization Juan Somavia, writing in the ILO Global Employment Trends 2009 report, painted a bleak picture. In February 2009, he was quoted as saying "We are now facing a global jobs crisis. Many governments are aware and acting, but more decisive and coordinated international action is needed to avert a global social recession. Progress in poverty reduction is unravelling and middle classes worldwide are weakening." This was concerning for tourism-dependent countries since the middle classes make up the vast majority of their tourism clientele.

In February 2009, US President Barack Obama described the delay in getting his economic recovery bill passed in Congress as "inexcusable and irresponsible" "when 3.6 million Americans had lost their jobs since the recession began" (*Barbados Advocate*, 7 February 2009). By February 2009 the rate of unemployment in the United States had reached 7.6 per cent and every day more and more companies were laying off people in thousands. By March 2009, the US employment rate was given as 8.1 per cent and in four states it was as high as 10 per cent. By September 2009, in spite of recovery in the stock market, US unemployment has passed 9.5 percent.

In early 2009, this scenario was being replicated around the world and financial analysts were speaking of the implosion of the banking and credit markets. Householders were losing their homes to foreclosures and it became very difficult either to buy or sell homes in a situation where banks were not extending credit. There could be no greater disincentive to taking a holiday than losing jobs, together with the family home.

The impacts of deteriorating economies in North America and Europe began to be seen in the Caribbean as 2009 progressed. In Caribbean countries where remittances comprise a significant proportion of the foreign exchange inflows, there was a noticeable fall off from this quarter.

Caribbean financial centres were being threatened by the renewed efforts of the governments of the European Union and the United States to clamp down on offshore financial centres generally, regarded by them as one of the causes of the present global financial crisis.

Since the Caribbean has no voice in the forums where these matters are discussed, it was seen as critical that the opportunity be taken by Caribbean governments attending the Summit of the Americas in Port of Spain in April 2009, to acquaint US President Barack Obama, who was a delegate at the meeting, of the threat posed to their economies by such anti–offshore financial centre activities. Moreover, he had also been particularly critical of the widespread practices by major US companies of hosting incentive and group tourism business for the purpose of motivating staff, without seeming to be as aware as he needed to be of the economic contribution of these tourism activities both to the United States and our economies. Some of the Caribbean countries are heavily dependent on the US market, one example being the Bahamas, which receives as much as 85 per cent of its visitors from that market.

Every US president needs to know that if Caribbean tourism and financial industries are destroyed, failing economies in a region often referred to as the "soft underbelly" of the United States will not only pose a serious threat to US security, but will also directly hurt business in the United States. States like Florida supply a great deal of the goods and services that are consumed by tourists in the Caribbean. When Caribbean tourism slumps, sales in Florida drop and American companies there start laying off staff. Manchester Trade reported in March 2009 that the business of one company in Florida was down by 15 per cent and shipments from Food Distributor, Cheney Bros, were down by 50 per cent to some island hotels, as Caribbean tourism contracted.

## Official Reports Confirm Downturn in Caribbean Tourism in 2009

Early reports in 2009 from individual countries and from the CTO suggested that while there were isolated reports of growth, for example, in Cuba and Jamaica, there was, generally speaking, a slide in tourist numbers in several Caribbean countries in the first quarter of 2009. This would normally be unheard of in what is the height of the tourist season in the region (see appendix 7 – CTO 2009 tourism statistics).

In a number of countries there were either stoppages or a slow down in construction, as foreign investment in hotel plant, second homes and rental villas declined. This confirmed, if there was any doubt, that a great deal of foreign investment in the Caribbean, especially in construction, is driven by tourism.

In several countries, hotels experiencing cancellations or reductions in stay, advised labour unions about possible layoffs and suggested that the focus of industrial negotiations in the hotel sector be switched from demands for more pay to saving the maximum number of jobs. Hoteliers in a number of countries approached their governments for some kind of stimulus package and tax relief to cushion the negative impacts of the expected decrease in business. There was closure of a number of restaurants in the region.

A report from the *Economist* intelligence unit entitled "Lonely Beaches" (13 June 2008) stated that the normally full hotels and packed beaches in the Caribbean were experiencing a significant decline as a result of reduced travel by cash strapped North Americans and Europeans. The report also quoted the CTO as predicting that visitor numbers in 2009 could fall by as much as a third.

Puerto Rico's Governor, Luis Fortuno, announced on 3 March 2009 that more than 30,000 employees, about 14 per cent of the workforce in a population of 3.9 million, could soon lose their jobs and that taxes would be increased to shore up the country's ailing economy. The government of this country, normally one of the most prosperous in the Caribbean, and a member of the CTO, was said by its governor to be bankrupt.

As business from foreign tourism markets decreased, several Caribbean countries began to promote the idea of "Staycations", which means local Caribbean people taking vacations in their country of residence, thus patronizing hotel rooms and other local tourism services that were now not being fully used by foreign tourists.

This idea is good in some ways, but it is a two-edged sword. People who vacation in their country of residence do not use airplanes or ships, thus reducing the business of carriers and others engaged in the many aspects of outward-bound tourism, whether international or intra-Caribbean. More importantly, in 2009 the idea of staycations was being promoted also in those foreign markets from which the Caribbean gets its business.

According to a YouGov poll for the *Sunday Times* carried in its newspaper of 16 August 2009, 54 per cent of the British holiday makers stated that they are planning to take their vacation at home in 2010, which is more than double the 26 per cent who said they were going to do so in 2009. Only 11 per cent said they were going overseas in 2010. Official British figures showed that 4.87 million people travelled overseas in June 2009 as opposed to 5.98 million in June 2008, the lowest figure for seven years.

Since the British staycationers are reported to have given this response, in spite of having endured lashing rain and over-priced hotels in Britain in 2009, it is clear that the Caribbean has a lot of work to do reversing this practice before it becomes a trend. A lot of time and money has been spent in the past by several warm weather countries, persuading the British that it is "cool" and worth the extra costs, to distinguish oneself from the masses by holidaying overseas in a genuine warm weather country.

## Impact on International Air Transportation

Early in 2008, IATA had forecast that the losses of international carriers would be about US$5.2 billion. It has been already stated that during the first quarter of 2009 the amount of the 2008 losses were revised upwards to US$8 billion. It had also been predicted that the amount of losses would continue in 2009, but at a lower level of about US$2.5 billion, in the expectation that the amount of potential damage would be mitigated by the severe cut back in equipment, routes and services by airlines in 2008, in the face of rising oil prices.

The reality is, however, that since September 2008, airline load factors fell more sharply than the carriers were able to match by cutting capacity, and the losses in 2009 were seriously underestimated by IATA. In April 2009, analysts were projecting that the nine largest US airlines might report losses of as much as US$2.3 billion in the first quarter of 2009. Airline capacity cuts were just not enough to staunch the haemorrhaging of cash due to passenger traffic declines of about 8 per cent each month for the first quarter.

Giovanni Bisignani, IATA's director general and CEO, while giving his state of the industry address to five hundred of the industry's top leaders attending the sixty-fifth IATA annual general meeting in Kuala Lumpur, Malaysia (8 June 2009), revised the 2008 global airline losses upwards to US$10.4 billion and forecast losses for 2009 of US$9 billion.

Some of the world's normally most successful airlines suffered record losses or greatly reduced profits in 2008–9. For its financial year ending March 2009, British Airways announced its biggest ever full year loss of £401 million since the former national carrier had been privatized in 1987. This contrasted with a profit of £712 million in the previous year. Total passenger numbers for the year were down by 4.3 per cent to 33.1 million, as its fuel bill increased by 44.5 per cent to £3 billion. Further, the number of premium-fare passengers – those travelling first or business class – declined by 17.7 per cent in April 2009. In June 2009 CEO of British Airways Willie Walsh asked 30,000 staff to work without pay for between one and four weeks, in what he called a fight for the company's survival. He offered not to draw his own salary of £61,000 for the month of July 2009.

In July 2009, *Travel Agent Magazine* reported that negotiations between British Airways and the two unions, Unite, and GMB, had ended without resolution, over disagreement about the airline's proposal to cut up to 3,700 jobs, introduce a two-year pay freeze and other radical changes to terms and conditions. Apparently the unions had themselves proposed some cost saving measures: Unite agreeing to a cut in pay for cabin crew; and Balpa, the pilots union, agreeing to accept a pay cut in return for shares.

As 2009 progressed, airlines were having to choose between a number of unpopular options which include pay cuts and short time work, as opposed to cutting jobs outright. To supplement revenue, legacy carriers began to introduce an ever increasing number of à la carte fees and prices, normally more associated with the LCCs.

Singapore Airlines' profit for the January–March 2009 period, plunged 92 per cent from SG$528 million to SG$41.9 million (US$28.7 million) as travellers cut back on trips and, according to the *Financial Times* of 20

August 2009, the airline announced in July that it could make a full year loss for the first time since it was founded in 1972.

In Australia, Quantas announced in April 2009 a revision downwards of its 2008–9 forecast by several hundreds of millions of dollars due to the deteriorating market conditions, especially in its international business. It was experiencing decreased demand in its premium classes and was feeling pressure from competition which was prepared to cut fares by as much as 50 per cent. In August 2009, as Quantas announced an 87 per cent slide in full year profits, CEO Alan Joyce stated: "There has never been a more volatile or challenging time for the world's aviation history"(Joyce 2009).

In August the Irish flag carrier, Aer Lingus, having seen its first half year losses quadrupled to €93 million(£82 million) with revenues down to 12.2 per cent, was facing a third attempt at a takeover by LCC Ryanair which already has a 30 per cent shareholding in that airline. It blamed 10 per cent higher fuel costs and having to cut fares by an average of 17.1 per cent in a bid to counter falling demand. Throughout its existence Aer Lingus has worked closely with the Irish Tourist Board as an instrument of national tourism development and the wider implications of it disappearing would be great.

The losses of 2009, added to those of 2008, spell considerable difficulty for the global air transportation industry. Declining load factors and declining revenues will make it difficult for carriers to take advantage of lower energy costs to cut fares. There may therefore be intermittent fare sales, but, generally speaking, airlines will be forced to keep fares high, in addition to seeking every opportunity of earning extra income through such passenger irritations as charging for pillows and blankets and possibly, as Ryanair has mused, even for going to the bathroom.

The problem will be further compounded by the prospect of escalating ticket taxes unless the various lobbies being mounted in 2009 against increased taxation can persuade European governments to drop them. Some economic gurus were already predicting in 2009 that it will take until 2011 for the various economic stimuli in Europe and North America to work and for the economies to turn around. Others saw a sudden rocketing in the price of shares in late August 2009 as evidence that on both sides of the Atlantic the recession was on its way out.

However, serious damage was already done in the first three quarters of 2009. Cuts in services by many carriers in 2008 certainly deepened in 2009. Even if there is an economic recovery in Europe and North America in 2010, airline companies can be expected to take much longer to recover their financial health. Some may never do so.

This situation posed serious challenges for the chronically tourism-dependent Caribbean countries and led to aggressive activity by individual Caribbean countries to maintain air services to their own destinations. These efforts, however, needed more than ever, to be supported, at both national and regional levels, by marketing activity to sell the Caribbean as a refuge from the storms of life.

## Marketing the Region

Earlier we discussed the "Caribbean advantage" – situations in which the Caribbean actually did well after natural or man-made disasters like terrorism, when other regions suffered. There is also another advantage which some Caribbean countries have: while there are many countries whose business comes mainly from the middle classes, there are some Caribbean countries where a significant proportion of their clientele is super rich and in the past have proven to be somewhat recession-proof.

The situation in 2009, however, probably differed somewhat from what occurred in the past. A combination of inadequate regulation of financial institutions in the developed countries, unbridled greed by some CEOs, and either alleged or real Ponzi schemes, put at risk the fortunes of some of the world's wealthiest people. This situation was exacerbated by the dramatic fall in the value of shares on the various stock exchanges around the world.

The Caribbean region knows from long experience, that however bleak the economic landscape, some people will travel on holiday and every effort must be made to persuade those who do to choose the Caribbean over other destinations. What the developments in 2009 therefore called for, was a double pronged approach in which each country needed to treat its marketing efforts as a priority for the allocation of its scarce resources, but the region also needed to come together and put the strongest possible regional marketing campaign into those markets most likely to yield business. The slogan "Life Needs the Caribbean" that was used by the Caribbean Hotel Association and the CTO in 2003–4 has never been truer or more relevant.

It is against this challenging background of global economic distress, diminishing tourism flows and uncertain times for airlines everywhere, that CARICOM countries are being requested to review the present situation of their own air transportation services and be prepared to make major decisions about the best way to retain control over their own destinies.

## The Lessons for Airlines of the Events of 2008 and 2009

The events of 2008 and 2009 discussed in chapter 10 and the following chapters were shown to have caused bankruptcies and the closure of a number of airlines. Perhaps even more significant is that airlines which had never lost money before, like Southwest in the United States and Singapore Airlines in Asia, either did so or were on track to do so for the first time. Stalwarts and household names, like British Airways, were forced to take extraordinary action to ensure their survival. The entire industry was repeating in 2009 the billion dollar losses made in 2008.

During an investor conference in New York in June 2009, executives from several airlines, including Delta, Southwest, US Airways, Continental and American suggested that the outlook for business remained bleak. None of this was helped by another upward trend in fuel prices since June 2009 and the advent of influenza A (H1N1), also known as swine flu. In June, Delta again spoke of cutting capacity by 10 per cent and American by 7.5 per cent in September 2009 after the summer peak.

The harsh lessons of 2008 and 2009 seem therefore to be that the survival of no individual airline can be taken for granted in circumstances where factors like the present come together and persists for any length of time. Those who find this hard to believe should reflect that in comparatively recent times, a number of prominent airlines like Swissair and Sabena have disappeared; before them, Eastern Airlines and Pan American World Airways, major carriers to the Caribbean, which were both as prominent and dominant as British Airways, American Airlines and Virgin Airways are today, also disappeared. They did so suddenly and without either trace or notice as a result of board room decisions that had nothing to do with the Caribbean. Consequently, they did not have to consult with this region as to the impact of their closure on its economies.

Of course, taking an optimistic view, this economic cycle could be followed by a recovery in which a period of prosperity wipes out the bad airline memories of 2008 and 2009. However, such dramatic recoveries can sometimes prevent persons and countries from giving serious thought to what action they need to take in addressing their long-term interests. The best time to plan one's future is often during a period of severe hardship.

The bad news in 2008 and 2009 could be taken as supporting either of two opposing conclusions for the Caribbean about air transportation; one is that the airline business is not one in which a poor region and struggling governments should be involved, and the other is that in really bad times, the only helping hand you can guarantee counting on is the one at the end of your own wrist. Of course, the region should expect this latter view to be opposed by such institutions as the World Bank and the International Monetary Fund, almost inextricably linked to privatization and policies of no subsidies from governments.

It is, however, possible to hedge one's bets and, while accepting that the CARICOM region can never provide for itself all the air transportation services necessary for its socio-economic needs, it is worth repeating that the nature of the region's geography and its core business of tourism demand that it retains ownership over certain key aspects of its air access.

If one accepts this perspective, the questions to revisit and answer first, therefore, should be as follows:

- What are the advantages and disadvantages of ownership of Caribbean carriers?
- Are the existing national and sub-regional carriers viable?
- Should some other form of Caribbean ownership be considered other than that which currently exists?

## Advantages of Ownership

The arguments in favour of ownership are restated in the following text.

### Determining National Policy

The first and foremost advantage of local ownership of airlines is the ability it gives to countries to make decisions in key areas of national social, commercial and economic policy. Underscoring this fact is that locally owned carriers have nowhere else to go and will not be reassigned by their owners to other regions when the going gets tough.

It has been said earlier, and bears repeating, that whatever promises are made and however good the intentions expressed by foreign commercial carriers, when they begin to lose money or see a prospect of losing money, they have little option but to cut back or cease operations, unless they are subsidized by Caribbean destinations to continue flying. As is well known from past experience, even an offer of government subsidies is no guarantee of operations continuing. The options to stay or go will always be in their hands.

It is not being argued here that major foreign carriers will act irresponsibly, or lightly take a decision to leave the region. In fact, there have been good and proper commercial reasons why certain foreign-owned air transportation services have continued over the years to serve the Caribbean, which is a major tourist destination and received over 23 million stay-over visitors in 2008. The routes to Europe and North America have proven profitable for those individual carriers which have dominated the business. There are therefore times when they have diverted equipment from other places in the world to serve the Caribbean.

It is further recognized that even in the difficult circumstances that existed globally in 2009, a number of carriers saw opportunities for expanded service to the Caribbean. Among them were Spirit Airline, which decided to expand its Caribbean network into the Dominican Republic from Fort Lauderdale; JetBlue, which started service between New York and Montego Bay in May 2009 with an US$89 fare and also decided to fly to Barbados, Kingston (Jamaica) and St Lucia in October 2009 with an introductory fare sale of US$99 one way; and Delta, which agreed to add a second weekly non-stop flight during the peak winter season from Atlanta to St Kitts.

Chris Floistad, Delta's network general manager for Latin America and the Caribbean, in fact announced that their schedules called for a 24 per cent increase in Caribbean frequencies for the winter of 2009–10. Fortunately in 2009 there is a great deal of spare capacity available, as airlines have cut services and parked planes. Some seventy-three older aircraft had been parked in 2008, as capacity was cut to deal with falling demand. A note of caution, however, is that there is a fine line between diversifying airline services and diluting traffic to the point where no single carrier can operate profitably. More carriers on a route do not necessarily mean more passengers. As far as possible, additional air services should be out of new gateways with a view to developing new markets.

Some Caribbean governments and carriers are already aware of the advantages and privileges of ownership.

## CAL/BWIA

The Government of Trinidad and Tobago has been shown to use its national carrier as an effective instrument of its ethnic and business travel. And even though several Eastern Caribbean states depended on those services for delivering tourists to their countries, it had no obligation to get their agreement about reducing its services or closing it down. It made decisions in what it considered to be in its own best national interest.

## Air Jamaica

Air Jamaica, in spite of its heavy losses, is reported to carry some 50 per cent of all passengers to Jamaica, while also providing some services to a number of other Caribbean countries as well. But the Government of Jamaica has used it effectively as an instrument of the business, social and tourism policy of the country. Its marketing value to Jamaica has been powerful. Jamaica, therefore, may announce to other CARICOM member states when it is about to change its schedules or cut services, and even to sell the carrier, but this in no sense constitutes a consultation which would determine the ultimate decision.

## LIAT

LIAT, the Caribbean airline, is owned 91 per cent by Antigua and Barbuda, Barbados, and St Vincent and the Grenadines. (The total shareholding is shown in appendix 7.) These shareholders have been able to take tough decisions about the carrier even when they did not have the support of other members of CARICOM. These include various rescue packages and buying out the assets of Texan billionaire Sir Allen Stanford, owner of Caribbean Star. Their ability to make these decisions as owners arguably resulted in saving intra-Caribbean air transportation services from destruction in 2008. Part ownership of LIAT also guarantees that the Government of St Vincent and the Grenadines which, to date, has no international airport has within its own hands both the ability to maintain intra-Caribbean services and connections with the hubs to which international carriers fly.

**Serving Social Routes**

Another argument in favour of ownership is the ability to meet social needs in transportation services. Caribbean countries have found in the past, and will find again, that a number of the services needed by small Caribbean communities must be classified as social rather than commercial, and foreign carriers cannot be expected to provide such services to and around the Caribbean at their own costs.

The writer of an editorial in the *Cayman News* (11 January 2009) stated emphatically: "An airline is not, and cannot be a social service." The writer could not be more wrong. It is important to recognize that these Caribbean carriers are performing a critical social service and should be treated as such.

**Human Resources**

There is another social consideration that too often is ignored when people speak of closing down the regional carriers. They employ a significant number of people and as importantly, many of them like pilots, engineers, IT personnel, analysts, HR and IR specialists, legal advisers, to name a few, are highly skilled. All these jobs and skills, honed over half a century, could in a moment disappear from this region or be transferred overseas. Clearly an airline is not an employment agency. But in 2009, in the midst of rampant unemployment, there could have been few more important considerations for the Caribbean countries than to preserve jobs and skills.

**Economic Linkages**

Airlines have extensive economic links with other companies in the society from which they buy supplies. These create employment beyond the airline and produce revenues for governments. The extent of these linkages would not be fully realized unless the airline company closes.

## The Disadvantages of Ownership

There is clearly a downside to national or sub-regional ownership of airlines in the Caribbean region; they are expensive enterprises and most Caribbean countries already carry a burden of debt, the relation of which to GDP is already far too high. The burden of rescuing the airline when it is in deep financial or other trouble falls on a limited number of shoulders, and this can reach unsustainable levels, as is now being argued by many with respect to Air Jamaica in 2009. This sort of situation has political consequences with which the Government of Jamaica continues to wrestle. Moreover, keeping the carriers afloat with government financial subsidies have been said to lead to what is called "moral hazard", a concept which will be dealt with later as we discuss its alternative, "too big to fail".

### Too Big to Fail

The arguments in favour of Caribbean governments bailing-out their own carriers, which have been supported consistently in this book, have encountered serious opposition from many important quarters. Even within national cabinets, ministers of tourism and civil aviation have often not been supported by their own colleagues when proposing financial support for the national carrier. It has been easier to win support for subsidizing foreign airlines to provide air services into the destination. It was therefore timely when the subject was addressed by Andrew Downes, professor of economics and director of the Sir Arthur Lewis Institute of Social and Economic Studies, University of the West Indies at the Cave Hill campus, Barbados.

The concept of "too big to fail" was explored by Downes (2009). While the paper seemed largely concerned with banks and financial institutions, there were many aspects applicable to other types of companies, including airlines.

He argued that an insolvent business has three options:

- Liquidation/closure (bankruptcy laws apply)
- Purchase and assumption (turn around management)
- Bail-out/public assistance

He also argued that the main rationale for a "too big to fail" policy is *systemic risk* which involves "potential spill-over effects leading to widespread depositor runs, impairment of public confidence in the broader financial system or serious disruptions in the domestic and international payment and settlement system".

He then presented arguments for and against it, as it relates to a number of types of companies, especially those dealing with finance or insurance.

The arguments presented as in favour of "too big to fail" are as follows:

1. The prevention of systemic risk which can overwhelm the financial sector or any other key sector
2. The preservation of the integrity and confidence in the financial sector (where relevant)
3. Related to point 2, the avoidance of depositor runs in banks or insurers cashing in their policies in insurance companies
4. The reduction of the adverse impact of the payment system which can stymie economic activity in the real sector
5. Limiting the spill-over which a large institution has on the overall economy
6. The long legal process associated with liquidating or selling a bank
7. The difficulty in identifying viable and non-viable financial institutions once a run on deposits/policies begin
8. The desire to avoid social dislocation through unemployment
9. The desire to maintain competition in a particular industry
10. The institution's status as a large, important and complex/interconnected entity.

The arguments given against the "too big to fail" principle is when a bail-out creates what is known as "Moral Hazard" defined as "a lack of an incentive to guard against risky activities, protection against the consequences of such activities and preventing inefficient institutions from exiting the scene".

On the negative side, therefore, according to Downes (2009), bail-outs could potentially lead to the following:

1. Unfair competition distortions
2. Large institutions being favoured at the expense of efficient smaller institutions which have the potential to grow

3. Encouragement of poor risk management procedures by large institutions
4. Reduction of healthy market discipline and creative destruction

In the end Downes concludes that the deciding factor is economic reality which derives from the interconnectivity of the particular business with other critical sectors of the economy.

In the case of many of the large companies of the United States and Europe, because they are connected nationally and globally with many large companies, their collapse would have many negative global implications.

In the Commonwealth Caribbean, CAL, LIAT and Air Jamaica are relatively large employers and play a critical role in the socio-economic development of the region. Downes therefore included them among those companies "too big and important" to fail.

The regional airline shareholder prime ministers now know what US President Barack Obama and several leaders in Europe have learned the hard way – that there are financial and economic crises so deep that the "let-the-market-decide" philosophies need to be thrown through the window and only state intervention can save the day. It is an era in which people dare to suggest that the US government should nationalize its banks.

## Future Scenarios

Caribbean people need to pause for a moment, therefore, and focus on what it would have been like to see LIAT closed, Caribbean Star survive and then grounded, when all the assets of Sir Allen Stanford, Caribbean Star's owner, were seized by US authorities in 2009.

They need to peep over the edge of the abyss and imagine what it would be like to wake up one morning and find major foreign carriers gone and Air Jamaica, Bahamasair, CAL, Cayman Airways and LIAT closed. Arguably, that scenario will never present itself. It is, however, worth a thought.

Having argued in favour of ownership of the Caribbean carriers, the second controversial question we pose to ourselves is, are the existing locally owned carriers viable and, in the context of the costs involved, is there a compelling case for the governments that own them to continue supporting them as national carriers?

These are two different and separate questions. It needs to be stated at the outset that "viability" in this context is not to be defined as making an operating or a net profit every year. It means delivering an acceptable level of service, operating within the financial capacity of the shareholders, and making a valuable overall contribution to the greater socio-economic good of the society.

How viable, therefore, are the existing Caribbean carriers?

**Air Jamaica**

Given the preceding definition of viability, it could be argued that Air Jamaica does not pass the test of being operational within the financial capacity of its owners. However, a new business plan unveiled in January 2009 was aimed at achieving viability. It sought to eliminate cash losses by exiting loss-making markets and revising capacity in others, improving aircraft utilization by more than 25 per cent, and executing an efficiency plan and productivity improvements aimed at bringing unit costs in line with international standards.

Air Jamaica president and CEO Bruce Nobles announced that, effective 26 February 2009, it would exit the Atlanta, Los Angeles, Miami, Grand Cayman routes as well as discontinue service between Jamaica and Barbados and Jamaica and Grenada. He expressed the intention to maintain flights between Jamaica and the following cities: Toronto, New York, Chicago, Baltimore, Philadelphia, Orlando, Fort Lauderdale, Curaçao, Nassau and Havana, and between New York and Barbados and New York and Grenada. The plan further involved, cutting about six hundred jobs, reducing the fleet from fifteen to nine aircraft, returning aircraft and restructuring existing leases.

Senator Don Wehby, at the time minister without portfolio in the Jamaica Ministry of Finance and the Public Service, stated that the action being taken was designed to save the country an average of US$150 million a year (approximately J$12.8 billion) and help to turn a loss-making situation into a break-even one. It was stressed that the key to success was cost control.

It has to be assumed that the plan involved the Government of Jamaica making arrangements for handling the airline's accumulated debt. The idea behind the business plan seemed, however, to be focused on facilitating the privatization process rather than stabilizing the carrier to operate under continued Jamaican government ownership. In fact, it was expected that after private divestment, the government would cease to be involved in its day-to-day management or financing.

In July 2009, there was a strong rumour that LCC Spirit Airlines, which competed with Air Jamaica out of Fort Lauderdale and which had lost market share to American Airlines in that market, was a front-runner for the purchase of Air Jamaica. The sale would have made Spirit Airlines the largest carrier flying to Jamaica from the United States, with 28 per cent of the market as opposed to American Airlines with 25 per cent. It was, however, denied at the highest level that there was any intention to sell Air Jamaica to Spirit Airlines.

In September 2009, it seemed that the plan was still to sell the carrier with the government retaining a minority equity stake. Press reports, however, suggested that even this plan was likely to be frustrated through delays in reaching agreement caused by internal disagreements about the way forward. There was a danger, therefore, that that time could run out to strike a deal, leaving the government with no choice but to shut down the carrier altogether.

**Bahamasair**

Is Bahamasair viable? Bahamasair makes an important contribution to the all important tourism sector of the Bahamas, which is arguably the most tourism-dependent country in the world's most tourism-dependent region. It earns more than US$2 billion a year from that industry which employs 50 per cent of its workforce and contributes 40 per cent of its GDP. Being itself an archipelago of some seven hundred islands, it is critically dependent on air transportation. It is also the country's bus service to and among its many islands.

An annual loss in the region of US$20 million does not seem excessive, given, first of all, that it competes on the international routes with carriers like US Airways, Continental, American Airlines, Spirit Airlines and Air Tran, and within the Bahamas, with small carriers like Pineapple Air, Cat Airways, Western Air and Southern Air, as it provides a major social service between the islands. Common sense suggests that there is a strong case for ensuring that at least one of the airlines that connect this tourism-dependent country of seven hundred islands to the external world, and parts of it to each other, be owned by the country itself.

Finally, those who argue that it should be closed down because it does not make a profit and has to be subsidized should remember why it was created in the first place – it came into being in the Bahamas because British Airways and Pan American Airways closed their services to that country in the 1970s.

It is understood that the search continues to find a private investor willing to come to the table with an investment of less than 50 per cent of the shares, which would still leave control in the hands of the Bahamas government.

Given, therefore, that for more than thirty years Bahamasair has played a major role in the commercial and social life of the Bahamas, the decision of the Bahamas government in 2009 to continue an annual government subsidy of about US$28 million to keep it operating is sound. The Bahamas is better off with, than without, Bahamasair.

**Caribbean Airlines**

Launched by Trinidad and Tobago in 2007, with its fleet of eight Boeing 737-800s of fairly recent vintage (7.8 years) and five Dash 8s, CAL seems in 2009, from a financial perspective, the Caribbean airline most capable of surviving on its own. It is well capitalized, has no debt, currently has no industrial problems, a staff cut to 800, a reduced itinerary and is owned by the richest government among the CARICOM states.

It currently serves Toronto, Fort Lauderdale, New York and Miami, and in the Caribbean, Antigua, Barbados, Jamaica, St Maarten, Guyana, Suriname and Venezuela. It also has a code share arrangement with British Airways to London Gatwick, but it is possible that it could return to operating this route on its own. In fact, it is rumoured that CAL has ambitions to extend its present international routes. It was reported in September 2009 to be one of the carriers tendering for buying Air Jamaica. There is no reason to expect that it will not continue to receive the support of its government and be able to survive on its own.

**Cayman Airways**

Nothing has changed in recent times with Cayman Airways. The Government of the Cayman Islands sees it as playing a central role in its economy which is based largely on travel and tourism and financial services. There are more than six hundred banks in the territory and banking assets exceed US$500 billion. The World Travel and Tourism Council, in a 2008 study of the Cayman Islands estimated that the contribution of the travel and tourism economy to employment would rise to 9,000 jobs in 2008, some 32.9 per cent of total employment, and to 10,000 jobs or 37.6 per cent of total employment (1 in every 2.7 jobs) by 2018. Export earnings from international visitors and tourism goods were expected to generate 42.3 per cent of total exports, some US$453.9 million in 2008.

The population enjoys a high standard of living and stands at only 47,862. A note of caution, however, is that the financial sector of the Cayman Islands has become a major target of the OECD countries and in 2009 concerns began to be aired about falling revenue. However, at this stage, an annual subsidy to the airline of US$20 million to support an industry of this magnitude remains defensible.

It is therefore unlikely, in spite of the strident voices of those who would wish to see the carrier privatized or even closed down and replaced by foreign carriers, that government policy with respect to the carrier will change in the near future. This is because every Cayman Islands government has had, from the beginning, a clear idea of the role which it wishes its carrier to play in the country's socio-economic development. It is judged simply in terms of its contribution to GDP and its ability to perform a critical social service.

## LIAT

Is LIAT viable? LIAT is now in its fifty-third year and it would be fair to say that its viability has often been in doubt. Its history and the causes of its problems have been detailed at great length already in the previous chapters, but it can be summarized here as follows: by 2004 it had accumulated a debt of EC$311 million, was losing a great deal of money every year, and was an insolvent company; by 2007 a series of fortuitous events, some good negotiations, hard work by the staff and board, the intervention of the CDB, and the continuing financial support of its three major shareholders had transformed its situation. The financial support it received was applied largely to paying off its various debts and not for operations. Once it had removed the incubus of Caribbean Star's unfair competition from off its back, early in 2007, it was able to operate successfully on a commercial basis. The year 2007 was therefore one of recovery and 2008, a year of profitability.

Its critical role is to do the following:

- Facilitate intra-Caribbean business travel
- Promote intra-Caribbean leisure travel
- Provide connectivity between the destination countries and interline connections to all the major carriers
- Provide mail, air freight and courier services to the countries it serves
- By the end of 2009/early 2010, to provide an intra-Caribbean cargo service

In view of the improved financials, one might be tempted to conclude that LIAT is now a viable company.

However, taking a more hard nosed and realistic view, its ability to execute its defined role efficiently and indeed its future viability depends on its meeting and overcoming a number of challenges some of which are as follows:

- First, having to operate both commercial and social routes, without receiving any further financial support from its three shareholder governments or from the other governments it serves requires it to maintain a high-fare regime to cover its costs.
- High fares, made up of base fares, taxes and other add-ons are unpopular and clearly will, in the not too distant future, meet customer resistance. This could have a negative impact on the volume of its business.
- To lower fares, while flying on a purely commercial basis, would force LIAT to drop completely a number of routes, thereby depriving a number of small Eastern Caribbean communities of daily air service. The carrier has no desire to do this. Instead it has introduced other means of stretching its resources, such as route adjustments.
- Given the crisis in 2008 and the continuing challenges in 2009, LIAT had to make adjustments to its operating plan, effective from 15 January 2009. It examined its schedules and saw that some flights had good

loads and others were weak as a result of a softening of business that was unusual for the beginning of the year. This has not led to an across the board reduction in capacity. Rather, the plan is to add capacity as demand grows and cut it, as loads fall. Special arrangements are also being made to increase capacity to cope with spikes in business, such as those that arise as a result of well-known scheduled regional festivals and the activities that normally take place on the Easter weekend.

- LIAT is a high-cost operation with other major and escalating costs in addition to fuel. It employs nine hundred persons based in several offices in twenty-two different destinations, incidentally, speaking four different languages, and organized industrially by some ten labour unions. Payroll in 2008 accounted for some 27 per cent of operating costs but LIAT has striven to save jobs even in difficult times. It has faced many increases in costs in such areas as aircraft engines, spare parts, ground handling contracts and airport fees and charges (see appendix 9 for a pie chart showing LIAT's cost distribution).
- Its route structure and network as it seeks to serve twenty-two destinations daily is complex and makes considerable demands on its equipment and personnel. This, together with an aging fleet, leads to costly maintenance and some service disruption.
- In view of the aforementioned, the need for fleet renewal is urgent which has implications for capital investment. In its existing financial circumstances, such capital expenditure would have to come either from the three major shareholders, all of which in 2009 are under some financial stress, from aid sources, from commercial loans, or a combination of all the preceding. All the options are, however, very challenging in the present regional and global economic environment.
- Its near monopoly status, which has been shown to have both minuses and pluses, helps it to survive in what is a difficult economic climate. But the governments it serves are under considerable pressure to introduce competition on routes which cannot really support it. The introduction of the fast ferry service is one such initiative, but it could prove a blessing to LIAT in sharing some of the load of regional transportation. When and if it gets off the ground, it might be useful for LIAT to enter into discussions with its owners about some areas of cooperation.

- LIAT has had excellent relations with nine of its ten unions, but it has been unfortunate so far in its industrial relations with its pilots union. This has led to disruptions in service and a poor public service image. Positive change is necessary and, hopefully, is just around the corner.
- Over the years, LIAT's weak financial situation has left its mark on its systems and structure. The problems are currently being identified and recommendations for solutions made in an institutional study being executed by Price Waterhouse Cooper and funded by the CDB. Implementing these improvements will also have some financial implications.

In view of all that has been said, LIAT's future viability depends on a number of factors about which no one can pronounce at this time with certainty. Given, however, the significant role which it plays in the life of twenty-two different Caribbean territories, and having been identified as a Caribbean company which is too big and important to be allowed to fail, its board and management are constantly in search of solutions to the aforementioned challenges which must be found. Hopefully, these will not, at any time, include selling the carrier to a foreign country or company.

## Short-term Approaches

Unless we are thinking way out of the box, the outlook for the short and probably the medium term, would seem to be for very little change with respect to the region's locally owned air transportation services. This would mean Air Jamaica being sold, hopefully not to a foreign entity or closed altogether; CAL continuing to operate, but hopefully not on a comparatively modest level; Bahamasair, Cayman Airways and LIAT carrying on very much as they are today, with moments of disquiet and ever so often, talk about their being sold to foreigners or put out of business by foreign competition.

If, however, we are prepared to think out of the proverbial box, perhaps we may dream of a Caribbean air transportation future that rises above struggling national carriers. What is the alternative?

# A Vision for the Future

### Commitment to the Concept of Regionalism

The great Barbadian trade union leader and national hero of Barbados, Sir Frank Walcott, often said that Caribbean people are crisis people, which means that action which should have been taken early and could have transformed situations positively is delayed until matters reach a state of crisis. It is only then that they are moved to take remedial action which is either too late or a great deal more difficult and more costly than needed to be the case.

The time to be thinking out of the box about how to provide the region with reliable, adequate and efficient air services is not when, or because, our individual carriers have ceased to be viable, or to operate at all, but when they are still offering an acceptable service which could be built upon by creative initiatives.

In chapter 4, several forms of cooperation between Caribbean carriers were reviewed and the conclusion reached was that, for a number of reasons, no serious attempt has ever been made at a policy level to implement them. The CIAH proposal between BWIA and LIAT in 2003 came closest, but was brought to an abrupt end by the withdrawal from the process of Trinidad and Tobago.

Further, it is certainly reasonable to argue that before 2007, nothing in the global external economic and business environment was driving the government-owned carriers, with one exception, to look for solutions in any kind of closer association between themselves. There are stories of consultations between Air Jamaica under private ownership and BWIA over the years. But these were exploratory and never reached any serious level, largely as was said earlier, because they had little in common except being Caribbean owned.

The exception was LIAT, which came to the conclusion in 2006, that its survival lay either in its major competitor, Caribbean Star, leaving the field altogether or in some kind of alliance, even to the extent of a merger, with that carrier. It is now a matter of history that LIAT took over Caribbean Star's assets in 2007 and eliminated competition from that source.

In 2009, it is clear that much has changed for the worst about the landscape of air transportation. The struggles encountered by major carriers around the world in 2008 and 2009 involving billions of dollars in losses have led to many new developments. "Airline Information" reported in September 2009 that many airlines have now been forced to rely on ancillary revenue, also known as à la carte pricing, to make the difference between profit and loss. This has now grown to a figure of some US$10.25 billion and US carriers alone hope to raise US$4 billion from à la carte pricing in 2009.

It was shown in chapter 10 that a number of large airlines around the world either merged, are seeking to merge, or to form some kind of alliance during the past few years simply to survive. The latest example that has surfaced in September 2009 is discussion about a possible link up between American Airlines or Delta with Japan Airlines, which after suffering serious losses in 2009 talked about laying off seven thousand employees.

It is against this background that the question arises whether it is feasible and desirable at this time, to bring back to the table the idea of giving serious consideration once again to creating a single CARICOM carrier. Perhaps it is truer now, than ever before, that one should not be seeking to cross a chasm by taking many small steps.

To raise this matter now would be to do so at a time when there seems to be growing resistance to the idea of deepening regional integration. In fact, it could be argued that since the signing on 5 July 2001 of the Revised Treaty of Chaguaramas with a view to establishing the Caribbean Single Market and Economy, there has been no period when the commitment of CARICOM states to deepen the integration process has been so often and so seriously questioned, as it has been in 2007 and the immediate following years.

This may be explained by the fact that it was in 2007 that the impending gloom of global economic meltdown first cast its shadow and, as matters worsened in 2008 and 2009, a "circling the wagons" mentality began to take hold and national interests began to be seen as pre-eminent over regional ones. There was definitely increased focus in 2009 on the problems caused by intra-Caribbean migration and freedom of movement which are simply symptoms of the larger problems of growing unemployment, reduced earnings and negative economic growth at national levels.

In such circumstances, when, logically, regional cooperation should recommend itself, it becomes increasingly difficult to sell the concept that we are all better off working together than alone. It is also politically attractive to tell local audiences, for example, that the national tourism brand is stronger than that of the Caribbean, and ownership of a national carrier too useful an instrument of national policy and objectives to share even with our brothers and sisters in the region.

But while we may pause for a moment to bask in the reflected glory of Jamaica's Usain Bolt or even Barbados's Ryan Brathwaite's national athletic successes, it is useful to return to reality and contemplate how small, weak and vulnerable the Caribbean states really are, facing a hostile world as the separate so-called sovereign mini states.

At such times it is suggested that we should stop and reflect on what successes, at a level of excellence, the region has achieved in the past through regional institutions such as the West Indies cricket team, the University of the West Indies, the CDB, CARICOM, the Caribbean Examinations Council, the OECS, the Eastern Caribbean Central Bank and the much underrated organization, the CTO, which over a period of fifty-eight years has managed to unify thirty-four countries of the entire Caribbean region, speaking four different languages, in a single purpose, that of developing and marketing the region's most powerful economic activity-tourism.

Suggestions that because the West Indies cricket team is undergoing a period of difficulty, the solution is to dissolve into several national entities are simply absurd and reflect the level of despair and disappointment flowing from a string of defeats. What major team would wish to play the individual West Indies territories which currently struggle collectively to field a competitive regional team of eleven players? Given that international sport is also a major and costly business, what gate receipts would such games attract?

It should be remembered that Sir Frank Worrell's chief contribution to West Indies cricket may very well be that, on becoming captain of the West Indies cricket team, he brought a vision that its future strength would result from involving all the Windward and Leeward islands, in addition to Barbados, Guyana, Jamaica, and Trinidad and Tobago, as formerly obtained. This widened and developed the pool of skills available for selection. Were it not for Sir Frank, a Barbadian, the world might never have heard of the great Sir Vivian Richards or Curtly Ambrose of Antigua and Barbuda.

The institutions mentioned earlier have been able to unify island entities which by their very nature are given to fragmentation and fractious behaviour. In looking for successful models for integration of Caribbean carriers, there may well be lessons to be learned from the experiences of some of those successful regional institutions mentioned earlier, which, given their longevity, must have discovered systems and structures which have allowed them to withstand the many shocks, cries of alarm and forces of disintegration over the years.

Those who are familiar with the details of the financial situation of individual Caribbean companies and Caribbean treasuries are aware of the realities that daily confront the countries and their leadership. A number of countries are challenged even to meet their recurrent financial responsibilities to their public servants and are having recourse to the mechanisms of the International Monetary Fund for support. Their individual treasuries are not currently a likely source of major investment capital for grandiose national projects. The option where a course of action is desirable is to seek salvation in cooperative action and pooling of resources.

At this time and stage of Caribbean development, we must assume, therefore, that whatever the recent doubts that assail the region about certain aspects of Caribbean integration, Caribbean leaders and Caribbean societies remain committed to the process and to the realization of the Caribbean Single Market and Economy as our best hope of socio-economic survival in the future. If that is so, it is suggested that CARICOM members begin to give serious consideration, from a total community perspective, to its air transportation needs.

The reasons for this are many. Air transportation that moves people and goods both to and between the territories is probably the single most important element in facilitating and strengthening the regional integration movement. Like any bridge, its true value will not be realized until it no longer exists.

A CARICOM carrier, under the ownership and control of its members, is not aiming to be the only link with the outside world, but it certainly should be one of the effective means of guaranteeing this communication. In a vibrant, working, single market and economy, therefore, where there is greater harmonization of regional and international policies than currently exist, the political directorate of the CARICOM member states must know for certain that it is not a hostage to external forces, for either political or economic reasons. It should not be possible for it to be cut off from the rest of the world and the member states from each other, simply because it offends some other country or some other person outside the community.

One of the results of community ownership would hopefully be the transfer to all the members of the group, the same emotions about the carrier and commitment to its welfare, which are now manifested by the governments of Antigua and Barbuda, Bahamas, Barbados, Cayman Islands, Jamaica, and Trinidad and Tobago to their national carriers because of their ownership and financial investment. A logical conclusion is that we would see the same passion at a regional level for finding solutions for the CARICOM carrier and a willingness to take responsibility for its management, performance and survival. Standing on one side and levelling criticisms at the owners or taking a totally hands-off posture and recommending bringing in competing foreign carriers as a first option as soon as difficulties appear should be a thing of the past.

The community would be able to use its own carrier as an instrument of planning and policy, especially, but not exclusively, with respect to tourism, for the Caribbean Single Market and Economy as a whole; and, in doing so, would have to take into consideration the interests and concerns of all members states. One of the problems that currently exists in the region is that any foreign company or country which owns an airline or an aviation company can approach any of the tiny states in the Caribbean and seek to sell them on a solution to their individual air transportation problems. This can lead to a chaotic situation. What should be happening is that some CARICOM air transportation authority should be the entity to be approached about solutions for the group as a whole, thus avoiding individual state decisions that have too narrow a focus. CASSOS, with its expanded role, should also play a part in such discussions.

## The Role of the Community Carrier

What should a CARICOM carrier do?

### International Routes

One view being expressed here is that at a minimum, the first priority of such a service should be to retake control over core European and North American tourist markets lost in the downsizing of Air Jamaica and BWIA/CAL. It would, however, have the resources to compete with foreign carriers on a level playing field.

**Intra-regional Routes**

It would be largely responsible for operating connecting services and serving the intra-Caribbean routes of all fourteen CARICOM member states in a seamless manner. Within the Eastern Caribbean, the islands of the Bahamas and the Cayman Islands, where it has been demonstrated that there is not enough business for several carriers of the same size to operate parallel services on certain routes, it is folly to encourage rampant competition just for the sake of it. It makes more sense for smaller private carriers to fill in the gaps in the schedules.

Given the realities of air transportation economics, foreign carriers permitted to operate on these routes at commercially unjustifiably low fares, will either soon go out of business themselves or destroy the locally owned carriers before raising fares and demanding subsidies from Caribbean governments.

*The Caribbean is not a low-cost area and is therefore unlikely for any period of time, to sustain unreasonably low fares unless they are subsidized.*

**Other Services**

It would forge links with the international freighting carriers currently serving the region to upgrade the moving of cargo by air around the Caribbean territories.

*Preferred Partner*

It would be the preferred partner with governments and the private sector in exploring the possibilities of new markets which foreign carriers are unlikely to attempt without themselves receiving substantial subsidies or guarantees.

*Costs Containment*

As an integrated regional service, it would take advantage of lower overheads, achieved by various consolidations of the activities of the individual carriers with respect to management, operations and finance, with a view to cutting costs. No efficient employee of such a carrier with its expanded mandate should need fear lost of employment.

## Need for a Feasibility Study

None of this should, however, be taken on anyone's say so. The creation of a single CARICOM carrier is not something to be rushed into blindly without scientific study. It would be advisable to have an independent feasibility study done, looking at the role of this carrier, what markets it should serve, what equipment it should use and on what terms, the related capital and operating costs, how funds would be raised and share-ownership allocated, governance and management structure, staffing and conditions of service, including union arrangements, how the assets of existing carriers would be integrated into the single carrier and other relevant issues.

### Financing

The CDB should be approached to assist in finding the money for the study and should a regional carrier be recommended, the bank should be asked to assist in raising the funds in the capital markets or from development banks to launch, as was done with the Caribbean Court of Justice. This is the sort of major life-changing developmental project that regional development banks should be prepared to support.

### Next Steps

If, however, such a concept is to make progress, CARICOM heads need, first of all, to treat the single airline concept with all the seriousness which was applied to the establishment of the CDB and even the Caribbean Court of Justice which makes sense and will eventually do what it was intended to do. Second, process is very important. Fifty years of experience in the Caribbean of how Caribbean states are prepared to work together suggest that "takeover bids" do not work. Whatever the project, it must belong to all of them, each participating according to his ability to pay, if it is to be acceptable to all.

## Government Ownership

Without prejudice to the findings of any scientific study, a few observations are made below which may be permitted to the author of the book:

Much has been said both regionally and internationally in condemnation of government ownership of airlines based on theories that governments are incapable of managing businesses. There seems, however, to be some confusion between governments owning and governments managing businesses. Governments do not need to interfere in the day-to-day affairs of a company simply because they are its shareholders. But there is a further point. Public transport services are different from other commercial operations. Even Robert Crandall admitted that airlines have special characteristics incompatible with a completely unregulated environment. In the area of public transport services, it is difficult for a private company to balance making profits with providing social services which cater to the needs of all communities. Small communities tend to get neglected. There is nothing wrong with having a mix of public and private operators as happens so often with ground transport services. But ultimately if public transport is not government owned, some element of it has to be subsidized. These arguments are further supported by the fact that no privately owned Caribbean carrier has so far been shown to operate as a financial success in the Caribbean. It is assumed that the CARICOM carrier would be operating in competition with privately owned foreign carriers on the international routes. Only a government-owned carrier can, however, be guaranteed to operate as an instrument of the policy of the country.

The chances of success, however, depend on governments following strict observance of what their roles should be. Political interference, as opposed to intervention, should be off limits and hopefully it would be easier to avoid this in a regional than in a national entity. It is highly desirable for CARICOM governments to appoint a competent board of directors for a regional carrier, with a mixture of public and private sector skills, and leave it to get on with the management of the carrier. Where social considerations determine the need for subsidies, government ownership will make this easier to achieve.

*The suggested name for a CARICOM carrier is Caribbean Airways.*

## Conclusion

The overarching theme of this book has been that no group of countries, comprising largely an archipelago and dependent largely on tourism, can risk alienating ownership of all its air transport services. Local ownership of some carriers therefore is necessary. However, in view of the major costs involved and the multiplicity of scarce skill sets needed, these small territories would seem to have a better chance of coping if they created and supported a single CARICOM community carrier that seeks to serve the collective interests of all the member states.

Along the way, the book has looked at the history of the Caribbean carriers and examined their operational and financial performance. It has also looked closely at the operational and financial performance of many of the major international carriers, both legacy and low cost. It came to the conclusion that many of the critics of Caribbean carriers are unaware of how complex and difficult an air transportation industry is, how the industry as a whole performs, and that, by comparison, Caribbean carriers do no worse than carriers across the world.

It has looked at some of the challenges and models of inter-carrier cooperation, examined what is involved in mergers, explained some of the mysteries of deregulation, yield management, fare setting and oil hedging, and discussed the pros and cons of an airline monopoly.

It has reviewed some of the most harrowing experiences of airlines in some of the worst years for airline operations and discussed the impact on the region's most important industry – tourism. In the end, the author returns to the theme expounded in chapter 1 and remains committed to the proposition that our regional airlines have, between them, served as bridges between ourselves, and between us and the external world for a total of more than two hundred years. His preference is that the region continues to support them in playing this role until we can establish a single efficient CARICOM community carrier.

While we wait for such a vision and dream to attain reality, this book remains an exhortation to Caribbean governments and people not to burn whatever bridges continue to exist between them.

# Appendix 1

## LIAT Shareholders, Board and Management, 2009

## Major Shareholder Prime Ministers

Antigua and Barbuda – Hon. Baldwin Spencer
Barbados – Hon. David Thompson replacing out-going prime minister shareholder in 2008, the Rt. Hon. Owen Arthur.
St Vincent and the Grenadines – Dr the Hon. Ralph Gonsalves

## Board of Directors

Chairman and Barbados director – Dr the Hon. Jean S. Holder

## Directors (at September 2009)

### Antigua and Barbuda

Mr Brian Challenger
Mr George Goodwin
Mr Miguel Southwell

### Barbados

Mr Grantley Smith (alternate – Mrs Juanita Thorington-Powlett)
Mrs Gabrielle Springer-Taylor (alternate – Ms Valerie Brown)
Mr Trevor Mayers

### St Lucia

Mr Mario Reyes

### St Vincent and the Grenadines

Mr Isaac Solomon (alternate – Mr Godfred Pompey)

**LIAT Provident Fund**

Mr Lesroy Brown

**Caribbean Development Bank**

Mrs Tessa Williams-Robertson (alternate – Mr Alexander Augustine)

**Senior Executive Management**

Mr Brian Challenger, acting CEO, replacing outgoing CEO, Mr Mark Darby in May 2009.
Mrs Julie Reifer-Jones, CFO
Mrs Leesa Parris Rudder, CCO
Ms Diane Shurland, company secretary and legal counsel
Mr Alan Alexander, director of maintenance
Mr George Arthurton, director of flight operations
Mr Lesroy Browne, director of schedules and special projects
Mr Wilbur Edwards, director of ground operations, cargo and Quikpak
Mrs Sonja John, director of customer service
Mr William Tomlinson, director of human resources and security

# Appendix 2

## LIAT Average Fares, 1998–2007

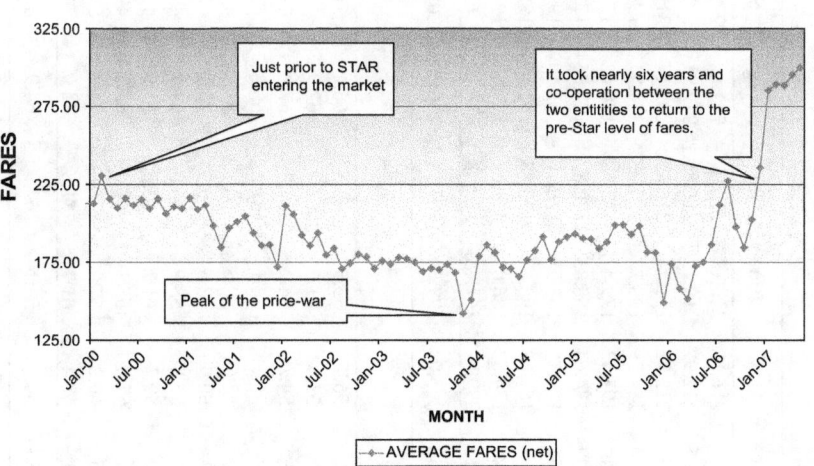

LIAT (1974) Limited Graph Support – Average Fares Load Factors 1998–2007

**Average Fares**

|  | Jan | Feb | Mar | Apr | May | Jun | Jul | Aug | Sep | Oct | Nov | Dec | Average |
|---|---|---|---|---|---|---|---|---|---|---|---|---|---|
| 1998 | 211.08 | 206.39 | 214.41 | 209.37 | 216.18 | 216.18 | 214.92 | 211.82 | 222.02 | 219.94 | 217.78 | 209.48 | 214.13 |
| 1999 | 216.16 | 221.59 | 208.54 | 212.95 | 212.97 | 210.12 | 216.81 | 217.91 | 202.89 | 216.66 | 213.15 | 212.63 | 213.53 |
| 2000 | 212.56 | 230.34 | 215.58 | 209.53 | 215.73 | 211.44 | 215.03 | 209.17 | 215.68 | 206.02 | 210.40 | 209.17 | 213.39 |
| 2001 | 216.22 | 208.63 | 211.49 | 198.20 | 184.29 | 196.72 | 200.75 | 204.21 | 193.57 | 185.54 | 185.99 | 171.79 | 196.45 |
| 2002 | 211.12 | 205.41 | 192.22 | 185.40 | 193.43 | 179.41 | 183.73 | 170.62 | 174.22 | 179.78 | 178.12 | 170.71 | 185.35 |
| 2003 | 175.51 | 173.65 | 177.78 | 176.99 | 174.64 | 168.83 | 170.87 | 170.05 | 173.52 | 168.06 | 141.99 | 150.68 | 168.55 |
| 2004 | 178.58 | 185.94 | 181.05 | 171.52 | 170.75 | 165.58 | 176.18 | 182.19 | 191.04 | 176.37 | 187.92 | 191.09 | 179.85 |
| 2005 | 193.02 | 190.20 | 189.63 | 183.68 | 187.68 | 198.63 | 198.88 | 192.59 | 198.07 | 181.20 | 180.76 | 149.04 | 186.95 |
| 2006 | 173.65 | 157.86 | 151.39 | 172.20 | 174.82 | 186.03 | 211.64 | 227.08 | 197.35 | 184.12 | 202.12 | 235.59 | 189.49 |
| 2007 | 285.00 | 289.09 | 288.30 | 295.13 | 299.87 | 262.43 | 270.58 | 278.12 | 265.02 | 256.02 | 261.22 | 267.26 | 276.50 |
| Average | 207.29 | 206.91 | 203.04 | 201.50 | 203.04 | 199.54 | 205.94 | 206.38 | 203.34 | 197.37 | 197.95 | 196.74 | 202.42 |

**Average Load Factors**

|  | Jan | Feb | Mar | Apr | May | Jun | Jul | Aug | Sep | Oct | Nov | Dec | Average |
|---|---|---|---|---|---|---|---|---|---|---|---|---|---|
| 1998 | 54.4 | 54.6 | 55.3 | 54.4 | 56.7 | 53.5 | 62.5 | 66.4 | 51.4 | 50.7 | 56.5 | 59.1 | 56.3 |
| 1999 | 56.7 | 56.9 | 52.9 | 59.6 | 53.3 | 51.6 | 62.0 | 62.9 | 47.5 | 47.4 | 58.1 | 54.8 | 55.3 |
| 2000 | 41.2 | 58.0 | 57.7 | 60.1 | 54.7 | 54.2 | 62.8 | 67.0 | 49.1 | 50.0 | 50.8 | 55.2 | 55.1 |
| 2001 | 49.3 | 50.9 | 48.6 | 54.9 | 55.1 | 54.1 | 61.2 | 65.3 | 49.3 | 51.5 | 52.5 | 55.1 | 54.0 |
| 2002 | 48.1 | 48.6 | 53.3 | 52.5 | 48.6 | 50.5 | 60.1 | 62.5 | 43.3 | 51.6 | 51.6 | 58.4 | 52.4 |
| 2003 | 52.1 | 49.0 | 52.2 | 56.3 | 50.9 | 48.6 | 60.5 | 70.1 | 47.6 | 51.1 | 56.0 | 56.9 | 54.3 |
| 2004 | 61.5 | 55.6 | 53.6 | 60.6 | 56.8 | 58.0 | 66.5 | 64.4 | 49.3 | 54.9 | 57.7 | 58.7 | 58.1 |
| 2005 | 58.2 | 59.5 | 60.6 | 60.9 | 59.2 | 61.2 | 63.9 | 61.9 | 46.4 | 59.7 | 59.8 | 50.4 | 58.5 |
| 2006 | 58.4 | 50.4 | 49.8 | 70.4 | 57.4 | 55.1 | 67.0 | 63.2 | 49.5 | 53.0 | 47.2 | 52.8 | 56.2 |
| 2007 | 53.3 | 57.1 | 54.8 | 64.6 | 60.2 | 57.7 | 71.8 | 74.0 | 54.9 | 59.6 | 62.1 | 67.6 | 61.5 |
| 2008 | 60.8 | 61.3 | 61.3 | 67.1 | 62.4 | 61.7 | 71.8 | 74.0 | 54.9 | 59.6 | 62.1 | 63.6 | 63.4 |
| Average | 53.3 | 53.7 | 53.8 | 58.8 | 54.7 | 54.1 | 62.9 | 64.9 | 48.1 | 52.2 | 54.5 | 55.7 | 55.6 |

Represents projected values
Represents estimated (historic) values

# Appendix 3

Fares and Taxes:
Year-on-Year Comparison
for 2007–2008

## ANTIGUA (ANU)

| Origin | Fare 2007 | Fare 2008 | Taxes 2007 | Taxes 2008 | LIAT Fuel and S/Charge | Total 2007 | Total 2008 | Taxes as a per cent of Total Fares/2007 | Tax as a per cent of Total Fare/2008 | Increase/ Decrease per cent 2008 Over 2007 |
|---|---|---|---|---|---|---|---|---|---|---|
| ANU | | | | | | | | | | |
| AXA | 156.00 | 156.00 | 65.00 | 65.00 | | 221.00 | 221.00 | 29.41 | 29.41 | 0.00 |
| BGI | 248.00 | 248.00 | 99.20 | 106.20 | | 347.20 | 354.20 | 28.57 | 29.98 | 1.41 |
| CUR | 456.00 | 456.00 | 50.00 | 80.00 | | 456.00 | 536.00 | 10.96 | 14.93 | 3.96 |
| DOM | 152.00 | 152.00 | 61.40 | 61.40 | | 213.40 | 213.40 | 28.77 | 28.77 | 0.00 |
| EIS | 192.00 | 192.00 | 57.00 | 57.00 | | 249.00 | 249.00 | 22.89 | 22.89 | 0.00 |
| FDF | 230.00 | 230.00 | 80.28 | 80.28 | | 310.28 | 310.28 | 25.87 | 25.87 | 0.00 |
| GEO | 456.00 | 456.00 | 118.40 | 118.40 | | 574.40 | 574.40 | 20.61 | 20.61 | 0.00 |
| GND | 316.00 | 316.00 | 98.71 | 98.71 | | 414.71 | 414.71 | 23.80 | 23.80 | 0.00 |
| NEV | 128.00 | 128.00 | 62.80 | 62.80 | | 190.80 | 190.80 | 32.91 | 32.91 | 0.00 |
| POS | 316.00 | 316.00 | 104.90 | 104.90 | | 420.90 | 420.90 | 24.92 | 24.92 | 0.00 |
| PTP | 214.00 | 214.00 | 81.91 | 81.91 | | 295.91 | 295.91 | 27.68 | 27.68 | 0.00 |
| SDQ | 340.00 | 340.00 | 169.30 | 175.65 | | 509.30 | 515.65 | 33.24 | 34.06 | 0.82 |
| SJU | 190.00 | 190.00 | 77.45 | 78.95 | | 267.45 | 268.95 | 28.96 | 29.35 | 0.40 |
| SKB | 128.00 | 128.00 | 67.80 | 67.80 | | 195.80 | 195.80 | 34.63 | 34.63 | 0.00 |
| SLU | 218.00 | 218.00 | 76.55 | 101.55 | | 294.55 | 319.55 | 25.99 | 31.78 | 5.79 |
| STT | 204.00 | 204.00 | 69.50 | 69.50 | | 273.50 | 273.50 | 25.41 | 25.41 | 0.00 |
| STX | 204.00 | 204.00 | 69.50 | 69.50 | | 273.50 | 273.50 | 25.41 | 25.41 | 0.00 |
| SVD | 240.00 | 240.00 | 62.00 | 62.00 | | 302.00 | 302.00 | 20.53 | 20.53 | 0.00 |
| SXM | 168.00 | 168.00 | 50.00 | 94.35 | | 218.00 | 262.35 | 22.94 | 35.96 | 13.03 |
| TAB | 316.00 | 316.00 | 99.90 | 159.90 | | 415.90 | 475.90 | 24.02 | 33.60 | 9.58 |

Means same city pairs

Means that fare exist only in one direction or not all

227

## ANGUILLA (AXA)

| Origin | Fare 2007 | Fare 2008 | Taxes 2007 | Taxes 2008 | LIAT Fuel and S/Charge | Total 2007 | Total 2008 | Taxes as a per cent of Total Fares/2007 | Tax as a per cent of Total Fare/2008 | Increase/Decrease per cent 2008 Over 2007 |
|---|---|---|---|---|---|---|---|---|---|---|
| ANU | 156.00 | 156.00 | 80.60 | 80.60 | | 236.60 | 236.60 | 34.07 | 34.07 | 0.00 |
| AXA | | | | | | | | | | |
| BGI | 382.00 | 382.00 | 124.30 | 122.65 | | 506.30 | 504.65 | 24.55 | 24.30 | −0.25 |
| CUR | 0.00 | 456.00 | 0.00 | 80.00 | | 0.00 | 536.00 | 0.00 | 14.93 | 14.93 |
| DOM | 240.00 | 240.00 | 73.00 | 93.00 | | 313.00 | 333.00 | 23.32 | 27.93 | 4.61 |
| EIS | 140.00 | 140.00 | 62.00 | 82.00 | | 202.00 | 222.00 | 30.69 | 36.94 | 6.24 |
| FDF | | | | | | | | | | |
| GEO | 620.00 | 620.00 | 148.00 | 228.00 | | 768.00 | 848.00 | 19.27 | 26.89 | 7.62 |
| GND | 404.00 | 404.00 | 112.51 | 132.51 | | 516.51 | 536.51 | 21.78 | 24.70 | 2.92 |
| NEV | 160.00 | 160.00 | 71.00 | 71.00 | | 231.00 | 231.00 | 30.74 | 30.74 | 0.00 |
| POS | 404.00 | 404.00 | 123.10 | 143.10 | | 527.10 | 547.10 | 23.35 | 26.16 | 2.80 |
| PTP | | | | | | | | | | |
| SDQ | | | | | | | | | | |
| SJU | | | | | | | | | | |
| SKB | 160.00 | 160.00 | 76.00 | 76.00 | | 236.00 | 236.00 | 32.20 | 32.20 | 0.00 |
| SLU | 308.00 | 308.00 | 89.79 | 133.29 | | 397.79 | 441.29 | 22.57 | 30.20 | 7.63 |
| STT | 160.00 | 160.00 | 74.50 | 74.50 | | 234.50 | 234.50 | 31.77 | 31.77 | 0.00 |
| STX | | | | | | | | | | |
| SVD | 404.00 | 404.00 | 75.20 | 95.20 | | 479.20 | 499.20 | 15.69 | 19.07 | 3.38 |
| SXM | | | | | | | | | | |
| TAB | | | | | | | | | | |

Means same city pairs

Means that fare exist only in one direction or not all

## BARBADOS (BGI)

| Origin | Fare 2007 | Fare 2008 | Taxes 2007 | Taxes 2008 | LIAT Fuel and S/Charge | Total 2007 | Total 2008 | Taxes As a per cent of Total Fares/2007 | Tax as a per cent of Total Fare/2008 | Increase/ Decrease per cent 2008 Over 2007 |
|---|---|---|---|---|---|---|---|---|---|---|
| ANU | 248.00 | 248.00 | 86.80 | 93.80 | | 334.80 | 341.80 | 25.93 | 27.44 | 1.52 |
| AXA | 382.00 | 382.00 | 67.00 | 94.00 | | 449.00 | 476.00 | 14.92 | 19.75 | 4.83 |
| BGI | | | | | | | | | | |
| CUR | 222.00 | 222.00 | 85.30 | 59.00 | | 307.30 | 281.00 | 27.76 | 21.00 | -6.76 |
| DOM | 172.00 | 172.00 | 64.90 | 71.90 | | 236.90 | 243.90 | 27.40 | 29.48 | 2.08 |
| EIS | 355.00 | 355.00 | 59.00 | 66.00 | | 414.00 | 421.00 | 14.25 | 15.68 | 1.43 |
| FDF | 210.00 | 210.00 | 82.28 | 89.28 | | 292.28 | 299.28 | 28.15 | 29.83 | 1.68 |
| GEO | 222.00 | 222.00 | 85.30 | 92.30 | | 307.30 | 314.30 | 27.76 | 29.37 | 1.61 |
| GND | 178.00 | 178.00 | 96.65 | 93.90 | | 274.65 | 271.90 | 35.19 | 34.53 | -0.66 |
| NEV | 326.00 | 326.00 | 84.60 | 111.60 | | 410.60 | 437.60 | 20.60 | 25.50 | 4.90 |
| POS | 178.00 | 178.00 | 86.20 | 93.20 | | 264.20 | 271.20 | 32.63 | 34.37 | 1.74 |
| PTP | 340.00 | 340.00 | 83.91 | 90.91 | | 423.91 | 430.91 | 19.79 | 21.10 | 1.30 |
| SDQ | 578.00 | 578.00 | 209.38 | 242.73 | | 787.38 | 820.73 | 26.59 | 29.57 | 2.98 |
| SJU | 428.00 | 428.00 | 69.45 | 77.95 | | 497.45 | 505.95 | 13.96 | 15.41 | 1.45 |
| SKB | 300.00 | 300.00 | 87.00 | 109.00 | | 387.00 | 409.00 | 22.48 | 26.65 | 4.17 |
| SLU | 154.00 | 154.00 | 73.75 | 105.75 | | 227.75 | 259.75 | 32.38 | 40.71 | 8.33 |
| STT | 414.00 | 414.00 | 61.50 | 88.50 | | 475.50 | 502.50 | 12.93 | 17.61 | 4.68 |
| STX | 414.00 | 414.00 | 61.50 | 88.50 | | 475.50 | 502.50 | 12.93 | 17.61 | 4.68 |
| SVD | 152.00 | 152.00 | 59.60 | 66.60 | | 211.60 | 218.60 | 28.17 | 30.47 | 2.30 |
| SXM | 345.00 | 345.00 | 52.00 | 103.35 | | 397.00 | 448.35 | 13.10 | 23.05 | 9.95 |
| TAB | 183.00 | 183.00 | 86.95 | 93.95 | | 269.95 | 276.95 | 32.21 | 33.92 | 1.71 |

Means same city pairs

Means that fare exist only in one direction or not all

## CURAÇAO (CUR)

| Origin | Fare 2007 | Fare 2008 | Taxes 2007 | Taxes 2008 | LIAT Fuel and S/Charge | Total 2007 | Total 2008 | Taxes as a per cent of Total Fares/2007 | Tax as a per cent of Total Fare/2008 | Increase/Decrease per cent 2008 Over 2007 |
|---|---|---|---|---|---|---|---|---|---|---|
| ANU | 456.00 | 456.00 | 95.60 | 102.80 | | 551.60 | 558.80 | 17.33 | 18.40 | 1.07 |
| AXA | | | | | | | | | | |
| BGI | 220.00 | 220.00 | 87.30 | 76.65 | | 307.30 | 296.65 | 28.41 | 25.84 | -2.57 |
| CUR | | | | | | | | | | |
| DOM | | | | | | | | | | |
| EIS | | | | | | | | | | |
| FDF | | | | | | | | | | |
| GEO | | | | | | | | | | |
| GND | 314.00 | 314.00 | 88.50 | 126.00 | | 402.50 | 440.00 | 21.99 | 28.64 | 6.65 |
| NEV | | | | | | | | | | |
| POS | 306.00 | 306.00 | 93.40 | 93.40 | | 399.40 | 399.40 | 23.39 | 23.39 | 0.00 |
| PTP | | | | | | | | | | |
| SDQ | | | | | | | | | | |
| SJU | | | | | | | | | | |
| SKB | | | | | | | | | | |
| SLU | 300.00 | 300.00 | 72.69 | 127.69 | | 372.69 | 427.69 | 19.50 | 29.86 | 10.35 |
| STT | | | | | | | | | | |
| STX | | | | | | | | | | |
| SVD | 300.00 | 300.00 | 55.00 | 115.00 | | 355.00 | 415.00 | 15.49 | 27.71 | 12.22 |
| SXM | | | | | | | | | | |
| TAB | | | | | | | | | | |

Means same city pairs

Means that fare exist only in one direction or not all

## DOMINICA (DOM)

| Origin | Fare 2007 | Fare 2008 | Taxes 2007 | Taxes 2008 | LIAT Fuel and S/Charge | Total 2007 | Total 2008 | Taxes as a per cent of Total Fares/2007 | Tax as a per cent of Total Fare/2008 | Increase/Decrease per cent 2008 Over 2007 |
|---|---|---|---|---|---|---|---|---|---|---|
| ANU | 152.00 | 152.00 | 65.50 | 65.50 | | 217.50 | 217.50 | 30.11 | 30.11 | 0.00 |
| AXA | 240.00 | 240.00 | 55.00 | 75.00 | | 295.00 | 315.00 | 18.64 | 23.81 | 5.17 |
| BGI | 172.00 | 172.00 | 77.80 | 84.80 | | 249.80 | 256.80 | 31.14 | 33.02 | 1.88 |
| CUR | | | | | | | | | | |
| DOM | | | | | | | | | | |
| EIS | 258.00 | 258.00 | 47.00 | 67.00 | | 305.00 | 325.00 | 15.41 | 20.62 | 5.21 |
| FDF | 0.00 | 204.00 | 0.00 | 80.28 | | 0.00 | 284.28 | 0.00 | 28.24 | 28.24 |
| GEO | 456.00 | 456.00 | 108.40 | 168.40 | | 564.40 | 624.40 | 19.21 | 26.97 | 7.76 |
| GND | 258.00 | 258.00 | 82.91 | 102.91 | | 340.91 | 360.91 | 24.32 | 28.51 | 4.19 |
| NEV | 176.00 | 176.00 | 57.60 | 77.60 | | 233.60 | 253.60 | 24.66 | 30.60 | 5.94 |
| POS | 272.00 | 272.00 | 88.30 | 98.30 | | 360.30 | 370.30 | 24.51 | 26.55 | 2.04 |
| PTP | 224.00 | 214.00 | 66.91 | 81.91 | | 290.91 | 295.91 | 23.00 | 27.68 | 4.68 |
| SDQ | 460.00 | 460.00 | 178.50 | 204.85 | | 638.50 | 664.85 | 27.96 | 30.81 | 2.86 |
| SJU | 320.00 | 320.00 | 67.45 | 78.95 | | 387.45 | 398.95 | 17.41 | 19.79 | 2.38 |
| SKB | 176.00 | 176.00 | 62.60 | 82.60 | | 238.60 | 258.60 | 26.24 | 31.94 | 5.70 |
| SLU | 152.00 | 152.00 | 61.59 | 86.59 | | 213.59 | 238.59 | 28.84 | 36.29 | 7.46 |
| STT | 274.00 | 274.00 | 59.50 | 79.50 | | 333.50 | 353.50 | 17.84 | 22.49 | 4.65 |
| STX | 274.00 | 274.00 | 59.50 | 79.50 | | 333.50 | 353.50 | 17.84 | 22.49 | 4.65 |
| SVD | 178.00 | 178.00 | 48.90 | 88.90 | | 226.90 | 266.90 | 21.55 | 33.31 | 11.76 |
| SXM | 202.00 | 202.00 | 40.00 | 104.35 | | 242.00 | 306.35 | 16.53 | 34.06 | 17.53 |
| TAB | | | | | | | | | | |

Means same city pairs

Means that fare exist only in one direction or not all

231

## TORTOLA (EIS)

| Origin | Fare 2007 | Fare 2008 | Taxes 2007 | Taxes 2008 | LIAT Fuel and S/Charge | Total 2007 | Total 2008 | Taxes as a per cent of Total Fares/2007 | Tax as a per cent of Total Fare/2008 | Increase/Decrease per cent 2008 Over 2007 |
|---|---|---|---|---|---|---|---|---|---|---|
| ANU | 192.00 | 192.00 | 76.20 | 76.20 | | 268.20 | 268.20 | 28.41 | 28.41 | 0.00 |
| AXA | 140.00 | 140.00 | 62.00 | 82.00 | | 202.00 | 222.00 | 30.69 | 36.94 | 6.24 |
| BGI | 355.00 | 355.00 | 112.25 | 112.25 | | 467.25 | 467.25 | 24.02 | 24.02 | 0.00 |
| CUR | 0.00 | 258.00 | 0.00 | 86.36 | | 0.00 | 344.36 | 0.00 | 25.08 | 25.08 |
| DOM | 258.00 | 258.00 | 66.36 | 66.36 | | 324.36 | 324.36 | 20.46 | 20.46 | 0.00 |
| EIS | | | | | | | | | | |
| FDF | 0.00 | 304.00 | 0.00 | 97.28 | | 0.00 | 401.28 | 0.00 | 24.24 | 24.24 |
| GEO | 628.00 | 628.00 | 141.20 | 141.20 | | 769.20 | 769.20 | 18.36 | 18.36 | 0.00 |
| GND | 378.00 | 378.00 | 101.90 | 121.90 | | 479.90 | 499.90 | 21.23 | 24.38 | 3.15 |
| NEV | 156.00 | 156.00 | 62.60 | 82.60 | | 218.60 | 238.60 | 28.64 | 34.62 | 5.98 |
| POS | 436.00 | 436.00 | 119.90 | 139.90 | | 555.90 | 575.90 | 21.57 | 24.29 | 2.72 |
| PTP | 296.00 | 296.00 | 78.91 | 98.91 | | 374.91 | 394.91 | 21.05 | 25.05 | 4.00 |
| SDQ | 400.00 | 400.00 | 175.90 | 170.25 | | 575.90 | 570.25 | 30.54 | 29.86 | -0.69 |
| SJU | | | | | | | | | | |
| SKB | 172.00 | 172.00 | 69.20 | 69.20 | | 241.20 | 241.20 | 28.69 | 28.69 | 0.00 |
| SLU | 312.00 | 312.00 | 80.59 | 125.59 | | 392.59 | 437.59 | 20.53 | 28.70 | 8.17 |
| STT | | | | | | | | | | |
| STX | 0.00 | 180.00 | 0.00 | 76.50 | | 0.00 | 256.50 | 0.00 | 29.82 | 29.82 |
| SVD | 330.00 | 330.00 | 63.50 | 103.50 | | 393.50 | 433.50 | 16.14 | 23.88 | 7.74 |
| SXM | 136.00 | 136.00 | 47.00 | 91.35 | | 183.00 | 227.35 | 25.68 | 40.18 | 14.50 |
| TAB | | 436.00 | | 184.90 | | | 620.90 | | 29.78 | 29.78 |

Means same city pairs

Means that fare exist only in one direction or not all

## MARTINIQUE (FDF)

| Origin | Fare 2007 | Fare 2008 | Taxes 2007 | Taxes 2008 | LIAT Fuel and S/Charge | Total 2007 | Total 2008 | Taxes as a per cent of Total Fares/2007 | Tax as a per cent of Total Fare/2008 | Increase/Decrease per cent 2008 Over 2007 |
|---|---|---|---|---|---|---|---|---|---|---|
| ANU | 230.00 | 230.00 | 103.28 | 103.28 | | 333.28 | 333.28 | 30.99 | 30.99 | 0.00 |
| AXA | | | | | | | | | | |
| BGI | 210.00 | 210.00 | 113.78 | 105.03 | | 323.78 | 315.03 | 35.14 | 33.34 | -1.80 |
| CUR | 0.00 | 204.00 | 0.00 | 115.58 | | 0.00 | 319.58 | 0.00 | 36.17 | 36.17 |
| DOM | | | | | | | | | | |
| EIS | 0.00 | 362.00 | 0.00 | 97.28 | | 0.00 | 459.28 | 0.00 | 21.18 | 21.18 |
| FDF | | | | | | | | | | |
| GEO | 0.00 | 296.00 | 0.00 | 144.68 | | 0.00 | 440.68 | 0.00 | 32.83 | 32.83 |
| GND | 290.00 | 290.00 | 116.38 | 146.38 | | 406.38 | 436.38 | 28.64 | 33.54 | 4.91 |
| NEV | | | | | | | | | | |
| POS | 296.00 | 296.00 | 122.18 | 152.18 | | 418.18 | 448.18 | 29.22 | 33.96 | 4.74 |
| PTP | | | | | | | | | | |
| SDQ | | | | | | | | | | |
| SJU | | | | | | | | | | |
| SKB | 0.00 | 254.00 | 0.00 | 120.68 | | 0.00 | 374.68 | 0.00 | 32.21 | 32.21 |
| SLU | 182.00 | 182.00 | 94.13 | 119.13 | | 276.13 | 301.13 | 34.09 | 39.56 | 5.47 |
| STT | | | | | | | | | | |
| STX | | | | | | | | | | |
| SVD | 290.00 | 290.00 | 84.78 | 114.78 | | 374.78 | 404.78 | 22.62 | 28.36 | 5.73 |
| SXM | 0.00 | 340.00 | 0.00 | 134.63 | | 0.00 | 474.63 | 0.00 | 28.37 | 28.37 |
| TAB | | | | | | | | | | |

Means same city pairs

Means that fare exist only in one direction or not all

## GUYANA (GEO)

| Origin | Fare 2007 | Fare 2008 | Taxes 2007 | Taxes 2008 | LIAT Fuel and S/Charge | Total 2007 | Total 2008 | Taxes as a per cent of Total Fares/2007 | Tax as a per cent of Total Fare/2008 | Increase/ Decrease per cent 2008 Over 2007 |
|---|---|---|---|---|---|---|---|---|---|---|
| ANU | 456.00 | 456.00 | 95.60 | 95.60 | | 551.60 | 551.60 | 17.33 | 17.33 | 0.00 |
| AXA | 620.00 | 620.00 | 55.00 | 135.00 | | 675.00 | 755.00 | 8.15 | 17.88 | 9.73 |
| BGI | 222.00 | 222.00 | 85.30 | 92.30 | | 307.30 | 314.30 | 27.76 | 29.37 | 1.61 |
| CUR | 0.00 | 456.00 | 0.00 | 134.20 | | 0.00 | 590.20 | 0.00 | 22.74 | 22.74 |
| DOM | 456.00 | 456.00 | 74.20 | 74.20 | | 530.20 | 530.20 | 13.99 | 13.99 | 0.00 |
| EIS | 628.00 | 628.00 | 47.00 | 47.00 | | 675.00 | 675.00 | 6.96 | 6.96 | 0.00 |
| FDF | 0.00 | 296.00 | 0.00 | 100.28 | | 0.00 | 396.28 | 0.00 | 25.31 | 25.31 |
| GEO | | | | | | | | | | |
| GND | 314.00 | 314.00 | 88.50 | 148.50 | | 402.50 | 462.50 | 21.99 | 32.11 | 10.12 |
| NEV | 0.00 | 530.00 | 0.00 | 143.00 | | 0.00 | 673.00 | 0.00 | 21.25 | 21.25 |
| POS | 230.00 | 306.00 | 82.00 | 93.40 | | 312.00 | 399.40 | 26.28 | 23.39 | -2.90 |
| PTP | | | | | | | | | | |
| SDQ | | | | | | | | | | |
| SJU | | | | | | | | | | |
| SKB | 480.00 | 480.00 | 93.00 | 113.00 | | 573.00 | 593.00 | 16.23 | 19.06 | 2.83 |
| SLU | 322.00 | 300.00 | 74.34 | 127.69 | | 396.34 | 427.69 | 18.76 | 29.86 | 11.10 |
| STT | 600.00 | 600.00 | 59.50 | 139.50 | | 659.50 | 739.50 | 9.02 | 18.86 | 9.84 |
| STX | | | | | | | | | | |
| SVD | 300.00 | 300.00 | 55.00 | 115.00 | | 355.00 | 415.00 | 15.49 | 27.71 | 12.22 |
| SXM | 560.00 | 560.00 | 40.00 | 84.35 | | 600.00 | 644.35 | 6.67 | 13.09 | 6.42 |
| TAB | 306.00 | 306.00 | 88.40 | 148.40 | | 394.40 | 454.40 | 22.41 | 32.66 | 10.24 |

Means same city pairs

Means that fare exist only in one direction or not at all

## GRENADA (GND)

| Origin | Fare 2007 | Fare 2008 | Taxes 2007 | Taxes 2008 | LIAT Fuel and S/Charge | Total 2007 | Total 2008 | Taxes as a per cent of Total Fares/2007 | Tax as a per cent of Total Fare/2008 | Increase/ Decrease per cent 2008 Over 2007 |
|---|---|---|---|---|---|---|---|---|---|---|
| ANU | 316.00 | 316.00 | 98.71 | 98.71 | | 414.71 | 414.71 | 23.80 | 23.80 | 0.00 |
| AXA | 404.00 | 404.00 | 72.11 | 92.11 | | 476.11 | 496.11 | 15.15 | 18.57 | 3.42 |
| BGI | 178.00 | 178.00 | 105.00 | 102.80 | | 283.00 | 280.80 | 37.10 | 36.61 | -0.49 |
| CUR | 314.00 | 314.00 | 57.10 | 94.60 | | 371.10 | 408.60 | 15.39 | 23.15 | 7.77 |
| DOM | 258.00 | 258.00 | 76.47 | 96.47 | | 334.47 | 354.47 | 22.86 | 27.22 | 4.35 |
| EIS | 378.00 | 378.00 | 64.10 | 104.10 | | 442.10 | 482.10 | 14.50 | 21.59 | 7.09 |
| FDF | 290.00 | 290.00 | 87.38 | 117.38 | | 377.38 | 407.38 | 23.15 | 28.81 | 5.66 |
| GEO | 314.00 | 314.00 | 104.20 | 164.20 | | 418.20 | 478.20 | 24.92 | 34.34 | 9.42 |
| GND | | | | | | | | | | |
| NEV | 328.00 | 328.00 | 89.90 | 109.90 | | 417.90 | 437.90 | 21.51 | 25.10 | 3.58 |
| POS | 146.00 | 146.00 | 86.50 | 86.50 | | 232.50 | 232.50 | 37.20 | 37.20 | 0.00 |
| PTP | 296.00 | 296.00 | 89.01 | 109.01 | | 385.01 | 405.01 | 23.12 | 26.92 | 3.80 |
| SDQ | 536.00 | 536.00 | 207.76 | 227.76 | | 743.76 | 763.76 | 27.93 | 29.82 | 1.89 |
| SJU | 344.00 | 344.00 | 84.55 | 86.05 | | 428.55 | 430.05 | 19.73 | 20.01 | 0.28 |
| SKB | 330.00 | 330.00 | 95.10 | 115.10 | | 425.10 | 445.10 | 22.37 | 25.86 | 3.49 |
| SLU | 142.00 | 142.00 | 77.59 | 132.96 | | 219.59 | 274.96 | 35.33 | 48.36 | 13.02 |
| STT | 344.00 | 344.00 | 76.60 | 96.60 | | 420.60 | 440.60 | 18.21 | 21.92 | 3.71 |
| STX | 344.00 | 344.00 | 76.60 | 96.60 | | 420.60 | 440.60 | 18.21 | 21.92 | 3.71 |
| SVD | 136.00 | 136.00 | 63.90 | 63.90 | | 199.90 | 199.90 | 31.97 | 31.97 | 0.00 |
| SXM | 324.00 | 324.00 | 57.10 | 141.45 | | 381.10 | 465.45 | 14.98 | 30.39 | 15.41 |
| TAB | 146.00 | 146.00 | 81.50 | 81.50 | | 227.50 | 227.50 | 35.82 | 35.82 | 0.00 |

Means same city pairs    Means that fare exist only in one direction or not all

## NEVIS (NEV)

| Origin | Fare 2007 | Fare 2008 | Taxes 2007 | Taxes 2008 | LIAT Fuel and S/Charge | Total 2007 | Total 2008 | Taxes as a per cent of Total Fares/2007 | Tax as a per cent of Total Fare/2008 | Increase/ Decrease per cent 2008 Over 2007 |
|---|---|---|---|---|---|---|---|---|---|---|
| ANU | 128.00 | 128.00 | 62.80 | 62.80 | | 190.80 | 190.80 | 32.91 | 32.91 | 0.00 |
| AXA | 160.00 | 160.00 | 55.00 | 65.00 | | 215.00 | 225.00 | 25.58 | 28.89 | 3.31 |
| BGI | 326.00 | 326.00 | 100.90 | 127.90 | | 426.90 | 453.90 | 23.64 | 28.18 | 4.54 |
| CUR | | | | | | | | | | |
| DOM | 176.00 | 176.00 | 53.20 | 73.20 | | 229.20 | 249.20 | 23.21 | 29.37 | 6.16 |
| EIS | 156.00 | 156.00 | 47.00 | 67.00 | | 203.00 | 223.00 | 23.15 | 30.04 | 6.89 |
| FDF | | | | | | | | | | |
| GEO | 530.00 | 530.00 | 119.50 | 169.50 | | 649.50 | 699.50 | 18.40 | 24.23 | 5.83 |
| GND | 328.00 | 328.00 | 88.90 | 109.90 | | 416.90 | 437.90 | 21.32 | 25.10 | 3.77 |
| NEV | | | | | | | | | | |
| POS | 336.00 | 336.00 | 97.90 | 117.90 | | 433.90 | 453.90 | 22.56 | 25.97 | 3.41 |
| PTP | 0.00 | 328.00 | 0.00 | 109.90 | | 0.00 | 437.90 | 0.00 | 25.10 | 25.10 |
| SDQ | | | | | | | | | | |
| SJU | | | | | | | | | | |
| SKB | 0.00 | 212.00 | 0.00 | 61.20 | | 0.00 | 273.20 | 0.00 | 22.40 | 22.40 |
| SLU | 0.00 | 252.00 | 0.00 | 114.09 | | 0.00 | 366.09 | 0.00 | 31.16 | 31.16 |
| STT | 0.00 | 216.00 | 0.00 | 79.50 | | 0.00 | 295.50 | 0.00 | 26.90 | 26.90 |
| STX | | | | | | | | | | |
| SVD | 306.00 | 306.00 | 55.30 | 75.30 | | 361.30 | 381.30 | 15.31 | 19.75 | 4.44 |
| SXM | 192.00 | 192.00 | 70.00 | 104.35 | | 262.00 | 296.35 | 26.72 | 35.21 | 8.49 |
| TAB | | | | | | | | | | |

Means same city pairs

Means that fare exist only in one direction or not all

## TRINIDAD (POS)

| Origin | Fare 2007 | Fare 2008 | Taxes 2007 | Taxes 2008 | LIAT Fuel and S/Charge | Total 2007 | Total 2008 | Taxes as a per cent of Total Fares/2007 | Tax as a per cent of Total Fare/2008 | Increase/ Decrease per cent 2008 Over 2007 |
|---|---|---|---|---|---|---|---|---|---|---|
| ANU | 316.00 | 316.00 | 89.10 | 89.10 | | 405.10 | 405.10 | 21.99 | 21.99 | 0.00 |
| AXA | 404.00 | 404.00 | 62.50 | 82.50 | | 466.50 | 486.50 | 13.40 | 16.96 | 3.56 |
| BGI | 178.00 | 178.00 | 86.20 | 93.20 | | 264.20 | 271.20 | 32.63 | 34.37 | 1.74 |
| CUR | 306.00 | 306.00 | 47.50 | 47.50 | | 353.50 | 353.50 | 13.44 | 13.44 | 0.00 |
| DOM | 272.00 | 272.00 | 67.90 | 77.90 | | 339.90 | 349.90 | 19.98 | 22.26 | 2.29 |
| EIS | 436.00 | 436.00 | 54.50 | 94.50 | | 490.50 | 530.50 | 11.11 | 17.81 | 6.70 |
| FDF | 296.00 | 296.00 | 77.78 | 77.78 | | 373.78 | 373.78 | 20.81 | 20.81 | 0.00 |
| GEO | 230.00 | 230.00 | 82.00 | 93.40 | | 312.00 | 323.40 | 26.28 | 28.88 | 2.60 |
| GND | 146.00 | 146.00 | 79.20 | 79.20 | | 225.20 | 225.20 | 35.17 | 35.17 | 0.00 |
| NEV | 336.00 | 336.00 | 97.90 | 101.10 | | 433.90 | 437.10 | 22.56 | 23.13 | 0.57 |
| POS | | | | | | | | | | |
| PTP | 362.00 | 362.00 | 79.41 | 99.41 | | 441.41 | 461.41 | 17.99 | 21.54 | 3.55 |
| SDQ | 614.00 | 614.00 | 210.64 | 230.64 | | 824.64 | 844.64 | 25.54 | 27.31 | 1.76 |
| SJU | 422.00 | 422.00 | 74.95 | 76.45 | | 496.95 | 498.45 | 15.08 | 15.34 | 0.26 |
| SKB | 352.00 | 352.00 | 87.70 | 107.70 | | 439.70 | 459.70 | 19.95 | 23.43 | 3.48 |
| SLU | 208.00 | 208.00 | 73.29 | 98.29 | | 281.29 | 306.29 | 26.05 | 32.09 | 6.04 |
| STT | 380.00 | 380.00 | 67.00 | 87.00 | | 447.00 | 467.00 | 14.99 | 18.63 | 3.64 |
| STX | 380.00 | 380.00 | 67.00 | 87.00 | | 447.00 | 467.00 | 14.99 | 18.63 | 3.64 |
| SVD | 170.00 | 170.00 | 56.00 | 56.00 | | 226.00 | 226.00 | 24.78 | 24.78 | 0.00 |
| SXM | 378.00 | 378.00 | 47.50 | 111.85 | | 425.50 | 489.85 | 11.16 | 22.83 | 11.67 |
| TAB | | | | | | | | | | |

Means same city pairs

Means that fare exist only in one direction or not all

## GUADELOUPE (PTP)

| Origin | Fare 2007 | Fare 2008 | Taxes 2007 | Taxes 2008 | LIAT Fuel and S/Charge | Total 2007 | Total 2008 | Taxes as a per cent of Total Fares/2007 | Tax as a per cent of Total Fare/2008 | Increase/ Decrease per cent 2008 Over 2007 |
|---|---|---|---|---|---|---|---|---|---|---|
| ANU | 214.00 | 214.00 | 103.31 | 103.31 | | 317.31 | 317.31 | 32.56 | 32.56 | 0.00 |
| AXA | | | | | | | | | | |
| BGI | 340.00 | 340.00 | 134.91 | 126.41 | | 474.91 | 466.41 | 28.41 | 27.10 | -1.30 |
| CUR | | | | | | | | | | |
| DOM | 224.00 | 214.00 | 83.71 | 97.97 | | 307.71 | 311.97 | 27.20 | 31.40 | 4.20 |
| EIS | 296.00 | 296.00 | 78.91 | 98.91 | | 374.91 | 394.91 | 21.05 | 25.05 | 4.00 |
| FDF | | | | | | | | | | |
| GEO | | | | | | | | | | |
| GND | 296.00 | 296.00 | 118.61 | 138.61 | | 414.61 | 434.61 | 28.61 | 31.89 | 3.29 |
| NEV | 224.00 | 0.00 | 94.31 | 0.00 | | 318.31 | 0.00 | 29.63 | 0.00 | -29.63 |
| POS | 362.00 | 362.00 | 133.71 | 143.71 | | 495.71 | 505.71 | 26.97 | 28.42 | 1.44 |
| PTP | | | | | | | | | | |
| SDQ | | | | | | | | | | |
| SJU | | | | | | | | | | |
| SKB | 224.00 | 224.00 | 99.31 | 119.31 | | 323.31 | 343.31 | 30.72 | 34.75 | 4.04 |
| SLU | 282.00 | 282.00 | 103.77 | 128.77 | | 385.77 | 410.77 | 26.90 | 31.35 | 4.45 |
| STT | 0.00 | 296.00 | 0.00 | 116.41 | | 0.00 | 412.41 | 0.00 | 28.23 | 28.23 |
| STX | | | | | | | | | | |
| SVD | 258.00 | 258.00 | 84.91 | 104.81 | | 342.91 | 362.81 | 24.76 | 28.89 | 4.13 |
| SXM | 236.00 | 236.00 | 71.91 | 136.26 | | 307.91 | 372.26 | 23.35 | 36.60 | 13.25 |
| TAB | | | | | | | | | | |

Means same city pairs

Means that fare exist only in one direction or not all

## SANTO DOMINGO (SDQ)

| Origin | Fare 2007 | Fare 2008 | Taxes 2007 | Taxes 2008 | LIAT Fuel and S/Charge | Total 2007 | Total 2008 | Taxes as a per cent of Total Fares/2007 | Tax as a per cent of Total Fare/2008 | Increase/Decrease per cent 2008 Over 2007 |
|---|---|---|---|---|---|---|---|---|---|---|
| ANU | 340.00 | 340.00 | 148.90 | 155.25 | | 488.90 | 495.25 | 30.46 | 31.35 | 0.89 |
| AXA | | | | | | | | | | |
| BGI | 578.00 | 578.00 | 203.60 | 236.95 | | 781.60 | 814.95 | 26.05 | 29.08 | 3.03 |
| CUR | | | | | | | | | | |
| DOM | 460.00 | 460.00 | 139.40 | 165.75 | | 599.40 | 625.75 | 23.26 | 26.49 | 3.23 |
| EIS | 400.00 | 400.00 | 111.90 | 138.25 | | 511.90 | 538.25 | 21.86 | 25.69 | 3.83 |
| FDF | | | | | | | | | | |
| GEO | | | | | | | | | | |
| GND | 536.00 | 536.00 | 175.60 | 195.60 | | 711.60 | 731.60 | 24.68 | 26.74 | 2.06 |
| NEV | | | | | | | | | | |
| POS | 614.00 | 614.00 | 204.50 | 224.50 | | 818.50 | 838.50 | 24.98 | 26.77 | 1.79 |
| PTP | | | | | | | | | | |
| SDQ | | | | | | | | | | |
| SJU | | | | | | | | | | |
| SKB | 424.00 | 424.00 | 152.30 | 183.65 | | 576.30 | 607.65 | 26.43 | 30.22 | 3.80 |
| SLU | 470.00 | 470.00 | 150.35 | 201.70 | | 620.35 | 671.70 | 24.24 | 30.03 | 5.79 |
| STT | | | | | | | | | | |
| STX | | | | | | | | | | |
| SVD | 506.00 | 506.00 | 130.26 | 150.20 | | 636.26 | 656.20 | 20.47 | 22.89 | 2.42 |
| SXM | 460.00 | 460.00 | 104.90 | 169.25 | | 564.90 | 629.25 | 18.57 | 26.90 | 8.33 |
| TAB | | | | | | | | | | |

■ Means same city pairs

■ Means that fare exist only in one direction or not all

## PUERTO RICO (SJU)

| Origin | Fare 2007 | Fare 2008 | Taxes 2007 | Taxes 2008 | LIAT Fuel and S/Charge | Total 2007 | Total 2008 | Taxes as a per cent of Total Fares/2007 | Tax as a per cent of Total Fare/2008 | Increase/Decrease per cent 2008 Over 2007 |
|---|---|---|---|---|---|---|---|---|---|---|
| ANU | 190.00 | 190.00 | 96.45 | 97.75 | | 286.45 | 287.75 | 33.67 | 33.97 | 0.30 |
| AXA | | | | | | | | | | |
| BGI | 428.00 | 428.00 | 133.65 | 142.15 | | 561.65 | 570.15 | 23.80 | 24.93 | 1.14 |
| CUR | | | | | | | | | | |
| DOM | 320.00 | 320.00 | 91.45 | 90.95 | | 411.45 | 410.95 | 22.23 | 22.13 | −0.09 |
| EIS | | | | | | | | | | |
| FDF | | | | | | | | | | |
| GEO | | | | | | | | | | |
| GND | 344.00 | 344.00 | 118.95 | 123.25 | | 462.95 | 467.25 | 25.69 | 26.38 | 0.68 |
| NEV | | | | | | | | | | |
| POS | 422.00 | 422.00 | 138.25 | 108.10 | | 560.25 | 530.10 | 24.68 | 20.39 | −4.28 |
| PTP | | | | | | | | | | |
| SDQ | | | | | | | | | | |
| SJU | | | | | | | | | | |
| SKB | 208.00 | 208.00 | 93.25 | 104.35 | | 301.25 | 312.35 | 30.95 | 33.41 | 2.45 |
| SLU | 336.00 | 336.00 | 102.84 | 136.74 | | 438.84 | 472.74 | 23.43 | 28.92 | 5.49 |
| STT | | | | | | | | | | |
| STX | | | | | | | | | | |
| SVD | 360.00 | 360.00 | 85.45 | 86.95 | | 445.45 | 446.95 | 19.18 | 19.45 | 0.27 |
| SXM | 196.00 | 196.00 | 67.45 | 133.30 | | 263.45 | 329.30 | 25.60 | 40.48 | 14.88 |
| TAB | | | | | | | | | | |

Means same city pairs

Means that fare exist only in one direction or not all

## ST THOMAS (STT)

| Origin | Fare 2007 | Fare 2008 | Taxes 2007 | Taxes 2008 | LIAT Fuel and S/Charge | Total 2007 | Total 2008 | Taxes as a per cent of Total Fares/2007 | Tax as a per cent of Total Fare/2008 | Increase/ Decrease per cent 2008 Over 2007 |
|---|---|---|---|---|---|---|---|---|---|---|
| ANU | 204.00 | 204.00 | 89.90 | 89.90 | | 293.90 | 293.90 | 30.59 | 30.59 | 0.00 |
| AXA | 160.00 | 160.00 | 74.50 | 74.50 | | 234.50 | 234.50 | 31.77 | 31.77 | 0.00 |
| BGI | 414.00 | 414.00 | 123.60 | 150.60 | | 537.60 | 564.60 | 22.99 | 26.67 | 3.68 |
| CUR | | | | | | | | | | |
| DOM | 274.00 | 274.00 | 80.06 | 100.06 | | 354.06 | 374.06 | 22.61 | 26.75 | 4.14 |
| EIS | | | | | | | | | | |
| FDF | | | | | | | | | | |
| GEO | 600.00 | 600.00 | 149.50 | 229.50 | | 749.50 | 829.50 | 19.95 | 27.67 | 7.72 |
| GND | 344.00 | 344.00 | 111.00 | 131.00 | | 455.00 | 475.00 | 24.40 | 27.58 | 3.18 |
| NEV | 216.00 | 216.00 | 81.10 | 101.10 | | 297.10 | 317.10 | 27.30 | 31.88 | 4.59 |
| POS | 380.00 | 380.00 | 124.00 | 144.00 | | 504.00 | 524.00 | 24.60 | 27.48 | 2.88 |
| PTP | 296.00 | 296.00 | 91.41 | 116.41 | | 387.41 | 412.41 | 23.60 | 28.23 | 4.63 |
| SDQ | | | | | | | | | | |
| SJU | | | | | | | | | | |
| SKB | 180.00 | 180.00 | 82.50 | 82.50 | | 262.50 | 262.50 | 31.43 | 31.43 | 0.00 |
| SIU | 334.00 | 334.00 | 94.75 | 139.75 | | 428.75 | 473.75 | 22.10 | 29.50 | 7.40 |
| STT | | | | | | | | | | |
| STX | | | | | | | | | | |
| SVD | 344.00 | 344.00 | 76.70 | 96.70 | | 420.70 | 440.70 | 18.23 | 21.94 | 3.71 |
| SXM | 188.00 | 188.00 | 59.50 | 103.85 | | 247.50 | 291.85 | 24.04 | 35.58 | 11.54 |
| TAB | | | | | | | | | | |

Means same city pairs

Means that fare exist only in one direction or not all

241

## ST CROIX (STX)

| Origin | Fare 2007 | Fare 2008 | Taxes 2007 | Taxes 2008 | LIAT Fuel and S/Charge | Total 2007 | Total 2008 | Taxes as a per cent of Total Fares/2007 | Tax as a per cent of Total Fare/2008 | Increase/ Decrease per cent 2008 Over 2007 |
|---|---|---|---|---|---|---|---|---|---|---|
| ANU | 204.00 | 204.00 | 89.90 | 89.90 | | 293.90 | 293.90 | 30.59 | 30.59 | 0.00 |
| AXA | | | | | | | | | | |
| BGI | 152.00 | 152.00 | 74.80 | 150.60 | | 226.80 | 302.60 | 32.98 | 49.77 | 16.79 |
| CUR | | | | | | | | | | |
| DOM | 274.00 | 274.00 | 80.06 | 100.06 | | 354.06 | 374.06 | 22.61 | 26.75 | 4.14 |
| EIS | | | | | | | | | | |
| FDF | | | | | | | | | | |
| GEO | | | | | | | | | | |
| GND | 344.00 | 344.00 | 111.00 | 131.00 | | 455.00 | 475.00 | 24.40 | 27.58 | 3.18 |
| NEV | | | | | | | | | | |
| POS | 380.00 | 380.00 | 124.00 | 144.00 | | 504.00 | 524.00 | 24.60 | 27.48 | 2.88 |
| PTP | | | | | | | | | | |
| SDQ | | | | | | | | | | |
| SJU | | | | | | | | | | |
| SKB | 180.00 | 0.00 | 82.50 | 0.00 | | 262.50 | 0.00 | 31.43 | 0.00 | -31.43 |
| SLU | 334.00 | 334.00 | 94.75 | 139.75 | | 428.75 | 473.75 | 22.10 | 29.50 | 7.40 |
| STT | | | | | | | | | | |
| STX | | | | | | | | | | |
| SVD | 344.00 | 344.00 | 76.70 | 96.40 | | 420.70 | 440.40 | 18.23 | 21.89 | 3.66 |
| SXM | 180.00 | 180.00 | 59.50 | 103.85 | | 239.50 | 283.85 | 24.84 | 36.59 | 11.74 |
| TAB | | | | | | | | | | |

Means same city pairs

Means that fare exist only in one direction or not all

## ST VINCENT (SVD)

| Origin | Fare 2007 | Fare 2008 | Taxes 2007 | Taxes 2008 | LIAT Fuel and S/Charge | Total 2007 | Total 2008 | Taxes as a per cent of Total Fares/2007 | Tax as a per cent of Total Fare/2008 | Increase/Decrease per cent 2008 Over 2007 |
|---|---|---|---|---|---|---|---|---|---|---|
| ANU | 240.00 | 240.00 | 74.00 | 74.00 | | 314.00 | 314.00 | 23.57 | 23.57 | 0.00 |
| AXA | 404.00 | 404.00 | 55.00 | 75.00 | | 459.00 | 479.00 | 11.98 | 15.66 | 3.68 |
| BGI | 152.00 | 152.00 | 74.80 | 81.80 | | 226.80 | 233.80 | 32.98 | 34.99 | 2.01 |
| CUR | 300.00 | 300.00 | 40.00 | 100.00 | | 340.00 | 400.00 | 11.76 | 25.00 | 13.24 |
| DOM | 178.00 | 178.00 | 53.36 | 73.36 | | 231.36 | 251.36 | 23.06 | 29.19 | 6.12 |
| EIS | 330.00 | 330.00 | 47.00 | 87.00 | | 377.00 | 417.00 | 12.47 | 20.86 | 8.40 |
| FDF | 290.00 | 290.00 | 70.28 | 70.28 | | 360.28 | 360.28 | 19.51 | 19.51 | 0.00 |
| GEO | 300.00 | 300.00 | 85.00 | 145.00 | | 385.00 | 445.00 | 22.08 | 32.58 | 10.51 |
| GND | 136.00 | 136.00 | 70.70 | 70.70 | | 206.70 | 206.70 | 34.20 | 34.20 | 0.00 |
| NEV | 306.00 | 306.00 | 70.60 | 90.60 | | 376.60 | 396.60 | 18.75 | 22.84 | 4.10 |
| POS | 170.00 | 170.00 | 73.00 | 73.00 | | 243.00 | 243.00 | 30.04 | 30.04 | 0.00 |
| PTP | 258.00 | 258.00 | 71.91 | 91.91 | | 329.91 | 349.91 | 21.80 | 26.27 | 4.47 |
| SDQ | 506.00 | 506.00 | 185.86 | 205.86 | | 691.86 | 711.86 | 26.86 | 28.92 | 2.05 |
| SJU | 360.00 | 360.00 | 67.45 | 68.95 | | 427.45 | 428.95 | 15.78 | 16.07 | 0.29 |
| SKB | 242.00 | 242.00 | 69.20 | 94.20 | | 311.20 | 336.20 | 22.24 | 28.02 | 5.78 |
| SLU | 136.00 | 136.00 | 55.39 | 85.39 | | 191.39 | 221.39 | 28.94 | 38.57 | 9.63 |
| STT | 344.00 | 344.00 | 59.50 | 79.50 | | 403.50 | 423.50 | 14.75 | 18.77 | 4.03 |
| STX | 344.00 | 344.00 | 59.50 | 79.50 | | 403.50 | 423.50 | 14.75 | 18.77 | 4.03 |
| SVD | | | | | | | | | | |
| SXM | 320.00 | 320.00 | 40.00 | 104.35 | | 360.00 | 424.35 | 11.11 | 24.59 | 13.48 |
| TAB | 170.00 | 170.00 | 68.00 | 111.40 | | 238.00 | 281.40 | 28.57 | 39.59 | 11.02 |

Means same city pairs

Means that fare exist only in one direction or not all

243

## ST MAARTEN (SXM)

| Origin | Fare 2007 | Fare 2008 | Taxes 2007 | Taxes 2008 | LIAT Fuel and S/Charge | Total 2007 | Total 2008 | Taxes as a per cent of Total Fares/2007 | Tax as a per cent of Total Fare/2008 | Increase/Decrease per cent 2008 Over 2007 |
|---|---|---|---|---|---|---|---|---|---|---|
| ANU | 168.00 | 168.00 | 66.80 | 115.15 | | 234.80 | 283.15 | 28.45 | 40.67 | 12.22 |
| AXA | | | | | | | | | | |
| BGI | 345.00 | 345.00 | 103.75 | 155.10 | | 448.75 | 500.10 | 23.12 | 31.01 | 7.89 |
| CUR | | | | | | | | | | |
| DOM | 202.00 | 202.00 | 55.16 | 119.51 | | 257.16 | 321.51 | 21.45 | 37.17 | 15.72 |
| EIS | 136.00 | 136.00 | 47.00 | 91.35 | | 183.00 | 227.35 | 25.68 | 40.18 | 14.50 |
| FDF | | | | | | | | | | |
| GEO | 560.00 | 560.00 | 124.00 | 208.35 | | 684.00 | 768.35 | 18.13 | 27.12 | 8.99 |
| GND | 324.00 | 324.00 | 89.50 | 153.85 | | 413.50 | 477.85 | 21.64 | 32.20 | 10.55 |
| NEV | 192.00 | 192.00 | 89.20 | 123.55 | | 281.20 | 315.55 | 31.72 | 39.15 | 7.43 |
| POS | 378.00 | 378.00 | 104.20 | 168.55 | | 482.20 | 546.55 | 21.61 | 30.84 | 9.23 |
| PTP | 236.00 | 236.00 | 71.91 | 136.26 | | 307.91 | 372.26 | 23.35 | 36.60 | 13.25 |
| SDQ | 460.00 | 460.00 | 178.50 | 242.85 | | 638.50 | 702.85 | 27.96 | 34.55 | 6.60 |
| SJU | 196.00 | 196.00 | 67.45 | 133.30 | | 263.45 | 329.30 | 25.60 | 40.48 | 14.88 |
| SKB | 136.00 | 136.00 | 58.60 | 102.95 | | 194.60 | 238.95 | 30.11 | 43.08 | 12.97 |
| SLU | 250.00 | 250.00 | 68.95 | 158.30 | | 318.95 | 408.30 | 21.62 | 38.77 | 17.15 |
| STT | 188.00 | 188.00 | 59.50 | 103.85 | | 247.50 | 291.85 | 24.04 | 35.58 | 11.54 |
| STX | 180.00 | 180.00 | 59.50 | 103.85 | | 239.50 | 283.85 | 24.84 | 36.59 | 11.74 |
| SVD | 320.00 | 320.00 | 56.00 | 120.35 | | 376.00 | 440.35 | 14.89 | 27.33 | 12.44 |
| SXM | | | | | | | | | | |
| TAB | 0.00 | 378.00 | 0.00 | 203.55 | | 0.00 | 581.55 | 0.00 | 35.00 | 35.00 |

Means same city pairs

Means that fare exist only in one direction or not all

## TOBAGO (TAB)

| Origin | Fare 2007 | Fare 2008 | Taxes 2007 | Taxes 2008 | LIAT Fuel and S/Charge | Total 2007 | Total 2008 | Taxes as a per cent of Total Fares/2007 | Tax as a per cent of Total Fare/2008 | Increase/Decrease per cent 2008 Over 2007 |
|---|---|---|---|---|---|---|---|---|---|---|
| ANU | 316.00 | 316.00 | 84.10 | 144.10 | | 400.10 | 460.10 | 21.02 | 31.32 | 10.30 |
| AXA | | | | | | | | | | |
| BGI | 382.00 | 382.00 | 67.00 | 93.95 | | 449.00 | 475.95 | 14.92 | 19.74 | 4.82 |
| CUR | | | | | | | | | | |
| DOM | | | | | | | | | | |
| EIS | 0.00 | 436.00 | 0.00 | 119.50 | | 0.00 | 555.50 | 0.00 | 21.51 | 21.51 |
| FDF | | | | | | | | | | |
| GEO | 306.00 | 306.00 | 88.40 | 148.40 | | 394.40 | 454.40 | 22.41 | 32.66 | 10.24 |
| GND | 146.00 | 146.00 | 74.20 | 74.20 | | 220.20 | 220.20 | 33.70 | 33.70 | 0.00 |
| NEV | | | | | | | | | | |
| POS | | | | | | | | | | |
| PTP | | | | | | | | | | |
| SDQ | | | | | | | | | | |
| SJU | 208.00 | 0.00 | 68.29 | 0.00 | | 276.29 | 0.00 | 24.72 | 0.00 | -24.72 |
| SKB | 352.00 | 352.00 | 82.70 | 162.70 | | 434.70 | 514.70 | 19.02 | 31.61 | 12.59 |
| SLU | 208.00 | 208.00 | 68.29 | 153.29 | | 276.29 | 361.29 | 24.72 | 42.43 | 17.71 |
| STT | | | | | | | | | | |
| STX | | | | | | | | | | |
| SVD | 170.00 | 170.00 | 51.00 | 111.00 | | 221.00 | 281.00 | 23.08 | 39.50 | 16.42 |
| SXM | 0.00 | 378.00 | 0.00 | 146.85 | | 0.00 | 524.85 | 0.00 | 27.98 | 27.98 |
| TAB | | | | | | | | | | |

Means same city pairs

Means that fare exist only in one direction or not all

Means low season based Q fares

*Note*: All fares are quoted in US dollar and are based on the Q fares for the low season.

# Appendix 4

## Hedging Options

*A Presentation to the Board by Alan Bryon*
*Former LIAT CFO*

23 OCTOBER 2008

## Concepts

- Hedging contracts are based on the price of a futures contract.
- A futures contract is a contract to purchase a fixed quantity at fixed point in time.
- Hedging contracts for aviation fuel (Jet-A1) are done by hedging the NYMEX No. 2 heating oil price.
- Heating oil is the closest oil by-product to Jet-A1 fuel. Therefore Jet-A1 and heating oil prices have high degree of correlation.
- You can't really compare directly the cost per barrel price for oil with the heating oil/ Jet-A1 fuel price. The price varies with the demand for other oil by products.

## Assumptions

- Calculations are based upon hedging 100 per cent of forecast fuel usage for 2009. Total fuel consumption is forecast at 7.8 million US gallons.
- The cost equivalent barrel price is based on 42 gallons per barrel.

## Futures Prices

- As with all financial markets there is an enormous uncertainty in the market currently so we can expect that a significant "risk factor" is included in the futures price.

## Fuel Prices

**Fuel Prices (October 17)**

|  | US Gal | Barrel |
|---|---|---|
| Current Price |  |  |
| Nymex No. 2 heating oil | 2.08 | 87.36 |
| Jet-A1 fuel | 2.15 | 90.3 |
| Calendar 2009 futures price |  |  |
| Nymex No. 2 heating oil | 2.305 | 96.81 |

## Types of Hedging

Two most appropriate types are:

- No cost collar
  Call (Also known as a cap)

## Call Option

- Can be viewed like an insurance policy. If the price is below the call price the option is not exercised and there is no further liability to the company other than the option cost

## Call Option or Cap

Call Option Pricing

| USD Cents | US$ Price Gal. | Barrel | US$ Cost Gal. | US$ Millions 2009 Cost |
|---|---|---|---|---|
| 35 above futures price | 2.655 | 111.51 | 0.28 | 2.18 |
| 75 above futures price | 3.055 | 128.31 | 0.2 | 1.56 |

**Advantages**

- No liability other than cost of option

**Disadvantages**

- Expensive, may add US$2.1 million to operating costs with no return.

# Collar

| No Cost Collar | Floor | Upper |
|---|---|---|
| Bands (price per US gallon) | 1.9755 | 2.655 |
| Barrel Equivalent | 82.971 | 111.51 |

**Costs if Market Price Falls below the Floor Price**

| Market Price Gal. | Barrel | Cost US$ Millions |
|---|---|---|
| 1.90 | 80 | 0.59 |
| 1.79 | 75 | 1.45 |
| 1.67 | 70 | 2.38 |
| 1.55 | 65 | 3.32 |
| 1.43 | 60 | 4.25 |
| 1.31 | 55 | 5.19 |

## Advantages

- No cost unless price falls below floor

## Disadvantages

- High risk if price falls below the floor price
- $80 cost the US$590k
- $60 = US$4.25 million
- Credit assessment required; may require guarantees from shareholder governments
- Sudden and unforeseeable cash flow impact if futures prices drop below floor when counter party will require margin payment to cover potential loss.

# Based on Current Future Price

Fuel Cost Summary Hedging Options and Unhedged Based on a Futures Price of US$96.81

| Average US$ Price BBI | US$ Cost Millions | | | |
|---|---|---|---|---|
| | No Hedge | No Cost Collar | 35 Cents Call | 75 Cents Call |
| 150 | 28.00 | 20.69 | 22.87 | 25.37 |
| 135 | 25.00 | 20.69 | 22.87 | 25.37 |
| 130 | 24.00 | 20.69 | 22.87 | 25.37 |
| 125 | 23.00 | 20.69 | 22.87 | 25.37 |
| 120 | 22.00 | 20.69 | 22.87 | 25.82 |
| 115 | 21.00 | 20.69 | 22.87 | 22.90 |
| 110 | 20.41 | 20.41 | 22.59 | 21.97 |
| 90 | 17.00 | 17.00 | 18.88 | 18.26 |
| 70 | 13.00 | 15.39 | 15.17 | 14.55 |
| 50 | 9.00 | 15.39 | 11.46 | 10.84 |
| Up-front Costs | Nil | Nil | 2.18 | 1.56 |

# Based on Futures Price = US$80

Fuel Cost Summary Hedging Options and Unhedged Based on a Futures Price of US$80/bbl

| Average US$ Price BBI | US$ Cost Millions | | | |
|---|---|---|---|---|
| | No Hedge | No Cost Collar | 35 Cents Call | 75 Cents Call |
| 150 | 28.00 | 17.57 | 19.75 | 22.25 |
| 135 | 25.00 | 17.57 | 19.75 | 22.25 |
| 130 | 24.00 | 17.57 | 19.75 | 22.25 |
| 125 | 23.00 | 17.57 | 19.75 | 22.25 |
| 120 | 22.00 | 17.57 | 19.75 | 22.25 |
| 115 | 21.00 | 17.57 | 19.75 | 22.25 |
| 110 | 20.41 | 17.57 | 19.75 | 21.97 |
| 90 | 17.00 | 17.00 | 19.18 | 18.56 |
| 70 | 13.00 | 13.00 | 15.18 | 14.56 |
| 50 | 9.00 | 12.28 | 11.18 | 10.56 |
| Up-front Costs | Nil | Nil | 2.18 | 1.56 |

# Based on Futures Price = US$70

Fuel Cost Summary Hedging Options and Unhedged Based on a Futures Price of US$70/bbl

| Average USD Price BBI | US$ Cost Millions | | | |
|---|---|---|---|---|
| | No Hedge | No Cost Collar | 35 Cents Call | 75 Cents Call |
| 150 | 28.00 | 15.72 | 17.90 | 20.39 |
| 135 | 25.00 | 15.72 | 17.90 | 20.39 |
| 130 | 24.00 | 15.72 | 17.90 | 20.39 |
| 125 | 23.00 | 15.72 | 17.90 | 20.39 |
| 120 | 22.00 | 15.72 | 17.90 | 20.39 |
| 115 | 21.00 | 15.72 | 17.90 | 20.39 |
| 110 | 20.41 | 15.72 | 17.90 | 20.39 |
| 90 | 17.00 | 15.72 | 17.90 | 18.56 |
| 70 | 13.00 | 13.00 | 15.18 | 14.56 |
| 50 | 9.00 | 10.42 | 11.18 | 10.56 |
| Up-front Costs | Nil | Nil | 2.18 | 1.56 |

*Note:* Assumes collar spread constant

# Spot Fuel Prices

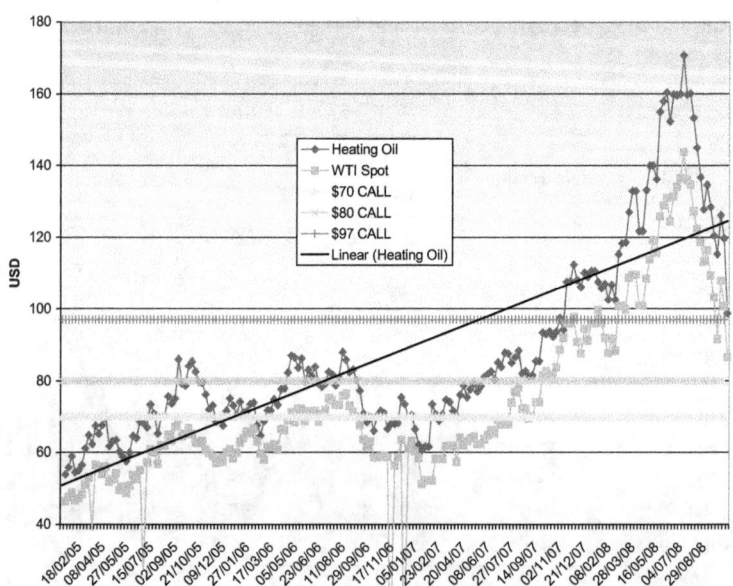

## Accounting Requirements

### COLLAR

- We will be required to account for any potential liability in the year that it first arises.
- This would mean that if the futures price dropped to $80 on December 31 we would need to record the cost of $590k in the 2008 accounts.

### CALL

- Cost of the call will be expensed in the month that the contract matures.

### Disclosure

- Contracts will require disclosure in accounts

### ACTIONS

- Should company adopt a hedging strategy?
- If Yes
    a) No cost collar or call
    b) Price management authorized to contract act? (US$80/bbl or lower?)
    c) Percentage of fuel consumption to hedge

## Other Airline Policies

### SOUTHWEST EXPERIENCE (*Press Report, October 16*)

- Airline known for "Smart Fuel Hedging Strategy"
- Q3 $120 million net loss because of hedging; but saved $1.3 billion for first 9 months of 2008 from hedging.

- Airlines face hefty margin calls against their higher-priced fuel positions.

**Southwest Experience**

- Q4 85 per cent of fuel cost hedged at a cost equivalent value of $62/bbl. Fuel cost in Q4 expect to be $2/gal. Current fuel prices still in excess of this.
- Current fuel hedging contracts valued at $550 Million
- 2009 75 per cent hedged at $73/bbl
- 2010 50 per cent hedged at $90/bbl
- 2011 40 per cent hedged at $93/bbl
- 2012 35 per cent hedged at $90/bbl

**RYANAIR**

- Airline has not hedged in the past but reportedly hedged fuel prices during 2008 at $135/bbl.

# Appendix 5

## Single Caribbean Airspace

*A Paper by Brian Challenger*

Greater clarification is needed about the concept of the "single Caribbean airspace". A distinction should be made between technical measures, for example, for air traffic control and economic policy areas, such as licensing.

The existing example of a single air-space is the single European airspace. This is an initiative where design, management and regulation is harmonized throughout the EU. This is expected to result in safe and efficient use of limited airspace in one of the busiest aviation regions in the world. Airspace management is planned to move away from previous domination by national boundaries to functional airspace blocks.

The single European airspace, while driven by safety as its primary consideration, is also be driven by the needs of the airspace user (for example, for the most direct route) and the need for increasing air traffic. The aim is to use air traffic management more closely aligned to desired flight patterns leading to greater safety, efficiency, and capacity. This merges upper EU airspace into a single space, rather than along national boundaries, with air traffic control based on operational efficiency, not national borders. It also integrates civil and military air traffic management.[1]

While traffic flows in the EU are multidirectional and heavily congested, those in the Caribbean are basically linear following the island chain from north to south with little east–west movement, and are considerably less congested than in the EU.

Within the Caribbean, scope exists at the technical level for minimizing costs of air transport regulation with a substantial effort already underway through CARICOM's Regional Air Safety Oversight System– soon to be replaced by CASSOS. This presently allows the participating Caribbean states to share limited technical expertise. For example, Jamaica is strong on helicopter regulators so that the OECS/Eastern Caribbean Civil Aviation Authority uses these individuals to license and inspect helicopters in our region rather than employing our own. The reverse obtains for the Eastern Caribbean Civil Aviation Authority which is strong on Dash 8 aircraft and can provide this service to Guyana and others. Such an arrangement could conceivably be extended to all CTO members. It should be noted that even the shift from the regional system to CASSOS has taken years to achieve

---

[1]Large areas of restricted airspace due to military purposes have traditionally been a characteristic of European airspace, interfering with the directional flow of aircraft.

and still awaits signature of the required number of states at CARICOM level.

A single airspace from a CTO perspective is unlikely as this would involve incorporation of US, French, Dutch and UK territories. This will have significant political/sovereignty issues.

At the CARICOM level, a single airspace has been conceptualized stretching from Jamaica in the north to Suriname in the south. This would be under the control of a single agency. This will require Caribbean governments to suspend operations of national air traffic and navigation service provider agencies and participating in a single provider agency. CARICOM governments could also take the issue to a higher level by agreeing to suspend the operations of their national CAAs and participate in a single regional CAA that would aim to provide International Civil Aviation Organization standards and recommended practices at the regional level.

Conceivably the single airspace could involve

- A single air traffic management organization
- A single regional civil aviation authority
- Harmonized landing and parking fees
- Harmonized ticket taxes
- Harmonized regulations and standards

At the OECS level harmonization of regulations and standards already obtains and through the Regional Air Safety Oversight System /CASOS there is also movement towards such harmonization, some of which already exists, for example, the OECS legislation and regulations are based on Jamaica which is itself based on the Canadian model.

At the economic level, within the OECS considerable liberalization already exists with fifth freedom traffic rights available to most carriers particularly from the United States, United Kingdom and European community. Conceivably a single airspace could also involve intra-Caribbean cabotage rights, that is, a US carrier could operate between Antigua and Barbuda, or Trinidad and Tobago, or between Kingston and Montego Bay. This has sustainability, employment and other policy concerns but has already been done; for example, Caribbean Star operated uplift between Trinidad and Tobago. Additionally it is unclear how much this will really improve airline operations and profitability since most airlines are interested in point-to-point travel from an economic operational perspective, particularly, at this time of high operational costs.

What is not on the table, as has been recommended in some circles, is for the US FAA to provide safety regulation for the Caribbean. International law places the obligation for safety and regulatory oversight on the state of the operator. The exception to this[2] is where foreign registered aircraft are subject to regulatory oversight by the authorities of the country in which they operate.

The reality is that the United States is presently incapable of adequately meeting its own regulatory needs in the region and is seeking more and more for other states to assist this process under established International Civil Aviation Organization protocols. Similar is the situation for the UK CAA, which is presently struggling to cope with demand in its territories and cooperates with the OECS in this regard and vice versa.

The OECS presently utilizes an extremely liberal regime for all services with costs kept to a minimum. In Antigua and Barbuda, for example, we do not charge for a licence or permit, in contrast to most other international jurisdictions, while in most other OECS states this cost is minimal – in St Kitts this is $1,000 for a permit and there is no fee for scheduled aircraft.

Careful attention is needed, however, to ensure that a US open skies type regime does not allow non-Caribbean carriers to drive Caribbean owned and operated aircraft out of existence. The importance of "having your own" is vital for island states and was mentioned by the Airport Strategy and Marketing Limited consultant at the recent CTO aviation and tourism crisis meeting.

Given the lack of specificity to date as to what is intended for a Caribbean single sky, greater information is needed from CTO as to the nature of the mechanisms involved and as to the benefits and costs that are likely.

---

[2]Convention on International Civil Aviation Article 83 bis.

# Appendix 6

## Caribbean Tourism Organization: Latest Statistics, 2008

**Table 1** Tourist (Stop-over) Arrivals in 2008

| Destination | Period | Tourist Arrivals | Change (%) | | |
|---|---|---|---|---|---|
| | | | Overall | Winter | Summer |
| Anguilla | Jan–Dec | 68,282 | −12.1 | −13.9 | −10.8 |
| Antigua and Barbuda[a] | Jan–Dec | 265,841 | 1.5 | 9.4 | −3.2 |
| Aruba | Jan–Dec | 826,774 | 7.1 | 15.9 | 2.7 |
| Bahamas | Jan–Dec | 1,462,404 | −4.3 | 1.6 | −7.6 |
| Barbados[b] | Jan–Dec | 567,667 | −0.9 | −1 | −0.9 |
| Belize | Jan–Dec | 245,027 | −2.6 | −0.9 | −3.8 |
| Bermuda[a] | Jan–Dec | 263,613 | −13.7 | −10.1 | −14.9 |
| Bonaire | Jan–Dec | 74,342 | 0 | 9.6 | −5 |
| British Virgin Islands[b] | Jan–Dec | 345,934 | −3.4 | −1.1 | −5 |
| Cancun (Mexico)[c] | Jan–Dec | 2,165,320 | 7.1 | 9.5 | 5.6 |
| Cayman Islands | Jan–Dec | 302,879 | 3.9 | 9.5 | 0.3 |
| Cuba | Jan–Dec | 2,348,340 | 9.1 | 14.6 | 5.2 |
| Curaçao | Jan–Dec | 408,942 | 36.4 | 42.9 | 33.6 |
| Dominica | Jan–Dec | 78,481 | 2.6 | −13.6 | 10.9 |
| Dominican Republic[a] | Jan–Dec | 3,979,672 | 0 | 5.6 | −3.4 |
| Grenada[b] | Jan–Dec | 123,770 | −4.1 | −10.6 | −0.4 |
| Guyana[b] | Jan–Dec | 132,776 | 1 | 1.9 | 0.6 |
| Jamaica | Jan–Dec | 1,767,271 | 3.9 | 10.1 | 0.7 |
| Martinique[b] | Jan–Dec | 479,933 | −4.6 | −4.6 | −4.6 |
| Montserrat | Jan–Dec | 7,360 | −5 | −8.4 | −3.3 |
| Puerto Rico[c] | Jan–Dec | 1,320,905 | −2.6 | −3.3 | −2.2 |
| Saba | Jan–Dec | 12,043 | 3.2 | 1.2 | 4.4 |
| St Lucia | Jan–Dec | 295,761 | 2.9 | 9.4 | −0.6 |
| St Eustatius | Jan–Jul | 7,146 | 4 | 1.6 | 7.4 |
| St Kitts and Nevis[b] | Jan–Dec | 106,408 | – | −11.1 | −15.3 |
| St Maarten[a] | Jan–Dec | 475,410 | 1.3 | 5.1 | −1.3 |
| St Vincent and the Grenadines | Jan–Dec | 84,101 | −6.2 | −15.7 | −0.4 |
| Suriname | Jan–Jul | 89,397 | −8.1 | −6 | −10.4 |
| Trinidad and Tobago | Jan–Dec | 430,513 | −4.2 | 5.2 | −9 |
| US Virgin Islands | Jan–Dec | 678,904 | −2.1 | 5 | −6.5 |

[a]Non-resident air arrivals
[b]Preliminary figures
[c]Non-resident hotel registrations only

*Note*: Winter – January to April; Summer – May to December
 Figures are subject to revision by reporting countries.
*Source*: Data supplied by member countries and available as at 21 September 2009.

Table 2a  Tourist Arrivals by Month 2008

| Destination | January Tourists | Change (%) | February Tourists | Change (%) | March Tourists | Change (%) | April Tourists | Change (%) | May Tourists | Change (%) | June Tourists | Change (%) |
|---|---|---|---|---|---|---|---|---|---|---|---|---|
| Anguilla | 6,108 | -17.6 | 7,177 | -6.4 | 8,446 | -14.6 | 6,442 | -16.7 | 6,322 | -8.5 | 5,177 | -14 |
| Antigua and Barbuda[a] | 25,119 | 11.1 | 28,614 | 22.7 | 28,241 | -3.5 | 25,259 | 10.8 | 20,885 | 6.7 | 18,634 | 4.6 |
| Aruba | 71,262 | 20.8 | 73,004 | 22 | 81,204 | 19.1 | 69,889 | 3 | 63,612 | 22.8 | 61,370 | 4.4 |
| Bahamas | 110,503 | 6.6 | 129,001 | 6.8 | 174,681 | -0.8 | 146,273 | -3.3 | 140,943 | 2 | 153,249 | -4.6 |
| Barbados[b] | 48,958 | 4.2 | 54,224 | 10 | 56,027 | 18.3 | 46,330 | -27.4 | 45,342 | -2 | 43,540 | 3.7 |
| Belize | 23,130 | 7.4 | 25,803 | 0.7 | 30,818 | -1.4 | 21,361 | -9.5 | 20,209 | 1.4 | 22,261 | -0.7 |
| Bermuda[a] | 9,320 | -13.1 | 13,524 | 2.5 | 18,885 | -13.8 | 23,557 | -12.1 | 31,102 | -9.8 | 32,796 | -14.5 |
| Bonaire | 6,453 | 12.4 | 7,089 | 2.4 | 7,292 | 1.8 | 7,261 | 24.8 | 5,898 | 5.3 | 6,075 | 6.1 |
| British Virgin Islands[b] | 34,221 | 9.8 | 35,355 | -0.3 | 45,103 | 2.3 | 34,302 | -14.2 | 32,713 | 8.1 | 31,469 | -0.7 |
| Cancun (Mexico)[c] | 189,184 | 8.5 | 202,595 | 11.6 | 231,349 | 11.6 | 205,562 | 6.1 | 183,377 | 10 | 200,400 | 2.8 |
| Cayman Islands | 25,845 | 8.9 | 30,380 | 8.7 | 38,425 | 9.3 | 29,978 | 11 | 25,722 | 9.8 | 27,971 | 8.3 |
| Cuba | 248,446 | 12.3 | 259,832 | 19.2 | 286,145 | 14.3 | 232,668 | 12.7 | 158,824 | 17.4 | 153,727 | 13.9 |
| Curaçao | 29,317 | 33.5 | 33,646 | 54.4 | 35,321 | 55.2 | 30,997 | 29.3 | 26,602 | 31.4 | 26,123 | 28.8 |
| Dominica | 5,561 | -2 | 5,157 | -39.4 | 6,877 | 23.6 | 4,859 | -22.2 | 7,077 | -0.1 | 4,827 | -5.3 |
| Dominican Republic[a] | 391,310 | 4.1 | 413,841 | 11 | 435,779 | 5.6 | 353,782 | 1.4 | 289,402 | 8.1 | 331,871 | 1.2 |
| Grenada[b] | 11,415 | -8.8 | 10,338 | -5.1 | 11,531 | 15 | 9,487 | -34.1 | 9,592 | 3.3 | 10,314 | 25.2 |
| Guyana | 9,062P | 1.4 | 8,885P | 49.9 | 12,626P | -9.7 | 12,139P | -7.2 | 8,286 | -18.1 | 9,244 | -23.4 |
| Jamaica | 142,861 | 10.1 | 156,831 | 18 | 184,267 | 12 | 152,199 | 1.1 | 141,236 | 7 | 161,958 | 3.5 |
| Martinique[b] | 48,622 | -3.1 | 46,709 | -4.9 | 53,399 | 0.5 | 46,170 | -10.9 | 37,580 | 6.8 | 29,084 | -5.8 |

*Table 2a continues*

**Table 2a** Tourist Arrivals by Month 2008 (cont'd)

| Destination | January Tourists | January Change (%) | February Tourists | February Change (%) | March Tourists | March Change (%) | April Tourists | April Change (%) | May Tourists | May Change (%) | June Tourists | June Change (%) |
|---|---|---|---|---|---|---|---|---|---|---|---|---|
| Montserrat | 516 | -10.3 | 581 | 14.8 | 719 | -14.8 | 495 | -17.1 | 481 | -10.4 | 555 | 5.1 |
| Puerto Rico[c] | 121,215 | 1.4 | 130,546 | -0.9 | 147,790 | -4 | 121,561 | -9.1 | 107,755 | -1.3 | 108,420 | -2.1 |
| Saba | 1,101 | 2.2 | 1,132 | -3.5 | 1,193 | 7.3 | 1,114 | -0.9 | 1,124 | 39.8 | 883 | -1.9 |
| St Lucia | 24,958 | 14 | 29,088 | 18.2 | 31,982 | 20.4 | 24,197 | -12.7 | 27,782 | 10.2 | 23,223 | 6.4 |
| St Eustatius | 1,212 | 21.3 | 1,023 | -1.5 | 959 | -11.5 | 940 | -0.6 | 1,098 | 9.6 | 854 | -6.2 |
| St Kitts and Nevis[b] | 10,255 | -16.6 | 10,801 | 4.6 | 12,686 | -13.8 | 9,623 | -15.8 | 8,216 | -18.9 | 10,556 | -5.4 |
| St Maarten[a] | 48,688 | 13.5 | 49,498 | 5.1 | 55,595 | 4.9 | 43,992 | -2.5 | 37,878 | 15.3 | 33,707 | -3.9 |
| St Vincent and the Grenadines | 6,370 | -24.2 | 7,976 | -4.8 | 7,664 | -19 | 6,567 | -14 | 6,131 | -6.8 | 8,020 | 6.4 |
| Suriname | 12,309 | 23.7 | 11,916 | -15.9 | 8,947 | -25.2 | 14,832 | -1 | 11,470 | -1.6 | 10,471 | -15 |
| Trinidad and Tobago | 46,577 | 39.5 | 34,999 | -26.1 | 40,780 | 17 | 37,733 | 4.6 | 29,278 | -15.1 | 30,002 | -15 |
| US Virgin Islands | 64,431 | 7.7 | 66,305 | 10.9 | 81,280 | 2.2 | 67,121 | 0.7 | 58,859 | 5.3 | 62,779 | 1.7 |

[a]Non-resident air arrivals
[b]Preliminary figures
[c]Non-resident hotel registrations only

*Note:* Figures are subject to revision by reporting countries.
*Source:* Data supplied by member countries and available as on 21 September 2009.

Table 2b  Tourist Arrivals by Month – 2008

| Destination | July Tourists | Change (%) | August Tourists | Change (%) | September Tourists | Change (%) | October Tourists | Change (%) | November Tourists | Change (%) | December Tourists | Change (%) |
|---|---|---|---|---|---|---|---|---|---|---|---|---|
| Anguilla | 6,964 | 0.4 | 6,441 | -7 | 1,675 | -11.3 | 2,230 | -18.5 | 4,866 | -19.7 | 6,344 | -13.7 |
| Antigua and Barbuda[a] | 23,883 | 1.8 | 20,972 | -1.3 | 12,211 | -8.8 | 17,159 | -10.4 | 20,662 | -5.9 | 24,022 | -11.1 |
| Aruba | 70,713 | 4.5 | 76,614 | 5.6 | 55,007 | -5.1 | 58,956 | -6.2 | 66,161 | -2.5 | 78,982 | 1.6 |
| Bahamas | 158,836 | 0.1 | 128,137 | -4.9 | 44,297 | -37.1 | 73,883 | -8.4 | 91,685 | -15.1 | 110,916 | -11.1 |
| Barbados[b] | 55,005 | 1.3 | 45,309 | -2.9 | 34,166 | 5.7 | 40,168 | -3.4 | 45,232 | -5.4 | 53,366 | -2.1 |
| Belize | 22,146 | -2.5 | 18,655 | 3 | 8,957 | -20.7 | 11,129 | -9.5 | 17,170 | -9.2 | 23,388 | -2.4 |
| Bermuda[a] | 33,422 | -10.8 | 32,048 | -14.4 | 18,993 | -17.3 | 21,814 | -17.9 | 15,970 | -23.1 | 12,182 | -18.3 |
| Bonaire | 6,223 | -2.6 | 5,687 | 2.3 | 4,510 | -11 | 5,612 | -16.7 | 6,056 | -9.2 | 6,186 | -10.6 |
| British Virgin Islands[b] | 34,805 | 1.7 | 20,817 | -3.6 | 7,949 | -18.5 | 14,209 | -19.9 | 23,125 | -14.9 | 31,866 | -8.8 |
| Cancun (Mexico)[c] | 206,242 | 0.5 | 174,701 | 4.7 | 106,713 | 1.1 | 121,341 | 5.5 | 151,356 | 5.5 | 192,500 | 14.9 |
| Cayman Islands | 30,008 | 11.6 | 21,629 | 11 | 10,330 | -9.8 | 14,710 | -2.6 | 19,731 | -21.8 | 28,150 | -7 |
| Cuba | 185,585 | 8.2 | 167,826 | 8.8 | 104,098 | -12.4 | 124,512 | -0.3 | 180,613 | -1.3 | 246,064 | 5.4 |
| Curaçao | 28,325 | 20.6 | 30,135 | 17.9 | 25,698 | 10.3 | 33,192 | 23.8 | 46,728 | 43.7 | 62,858 | 69.4 |
| Dominica | 9,062 | 1.2 | 7,422 | -1.5 | 3,782 | -8.3 | 12,025 | 54.2 | 4,674 | 29.3 | 7,158 | 13.5 |
| Dominican Republic[a] | 386,690 | -3.6 | 329,636 | -2 | 194,248 | -10 | 209,616 | -10.7 | 268,469 | -5.8 | 375,028 | -6.4 |
| Grenada[b] | 13,294 | 7.9 | 14,713 | -3.3 | 5,828 | -14.6 | 7,978 | -3.9 | 7,999 | -15.3 | 11,281 | -3.4 |
| Guyana | 16,027 | -10.8 | 14,430 | 3.8 | 8,591 | 2.7 | 9,556 | -0.7 | 9,465 | 6.2 | 14,465 P | 68 |

*Table 2b continues*

**Table 2b** Tourist Arrivals by Month – 2008 (cont'd)

| Destination | July Tourists | July Change (%) | August Tourists | August Change (%) | September Tourists | September Change (%) | October Tourists | October Change (%) | November Tourists | November Change (%) | December Tourists | December Change (%) |
|---|---|---|---|---|---|---|---|---|---|---|---|---|
| Jamaica | 185,447 | -5.1 | 142,467 | 4.2 | 92,037 | 2.6 | 106,104 | -1.9 | 122,250 | -1.8 | 179,614 | -0.2 |
| Martinique[b] | 42,079 | -9.4 | 50,902 | -5.6 | 27,321 | -8.1 | 24,410 | 1.7 | 29,623 | 1.2 | 44,034 | -10.8 |
| Montserrat | 763 | 13.4 | 478 | -13.1 | 340 | -16.3 | 473 | 8.7 | 507 | -14.9 | 1,452 | -3.1 |
| Puerto Rico[c] | 113,490 | 0.7 | 114,260 | 4 | 63,690 | -8.2 | 83,986 | -2.6 | 97,589 | -8 | 110,603 | -2.4 |
| Saba | 1,534 | 6.4 | 928 | 5.8 | 532 | -3.1 | 619 | 2.5 | 874 | 2.3 | 1,009 | -12.8 |
| St Lucia | 29,095 | -2.2 | 25,315 | 8.9 | 15,149 | -11.2 | 18,996 | -3.1 | 19,803 | -10.6 | 26,173 | -5.8 |
| St Eustatius | 1,060 | 18.7 | – | – | – | – | – | – | – | – | – | – |
| St Kitts and Nevis[b] | 9,492 | -10.1 | 7,840 | -14 | 5,261 | -15 | 5,422 | -15 | 7,112 | -27.8 | 9,144 | -23.5 |
| St Maarten[a] | 43,162 | 9.7 | 41,291 | 12.6 | 19,273 | -13 | 24,409 | -13.8 | 35,596 | -3.7 | 42,321 | -15.1 |
| St Vincent and the Grenadines | 10,171 | -7.6 | 7,257 | -2.8 | 3,800 | -3.4 | 4,832 | 120.2 | 5,388 | -16.3 | 9,925 | -6.3 |
| Suriname | 19,452 | -12.4 | – | – | – | – | – | – | – | – | – | – |
| Trinidad and Tobago | 47,948 | 12.8 | 36,414 | -6.1 | 26,900 | -7.7 | 30,980 | -3.2 | 29,772 | -17.7 | 39,130 | -19.9 |
| US Virgin Islands | 62,455 | -1.5 | 54,045 | -3.5 | 24,400 | -18.9 | 26,607 | -36.9 | 46,879 | -10.9 | 63,743 | -2.8 |

[a]Non-resident air arrivals
[c]Non-resident hotel registrations only
[b]Preliminary figures

*Note:* Figures are subject to revision by reporting countries.
*Source:* Data supplied by member countries and available as on 21 September 2009.

**Table 3** Tourist Arrivals by Main Market – 2008

| Destination | Period | United States | | Canada | | Europe | | Other | |
|---|---|---|---|---|---|---|---|---|---|
| | | Tourists | Change (%) | Tourists | Change (%) | Tourists | Change (%) | Tourists | Change (%) |
| Anguilla | Jan–Dec | 40,202 | -12.6 | 2,074 | -13.3 | 8,962 | -17 | 17,044 | -7.8 |
| Antigua and Barbuda[a] | Jan–Dec | 84,032 | 6.8 | 13,189 | 25.7 | 110,265 | -4.5 | 58,355 | 2.1 |
| Aruba | Jan–Dec | 537,860 | 3.4 | 32,496 | 26.6 | 73,144 | 8.6 | 183,274 | 15.5 |
| Bahamas | Jan–Dec | 1,176,683 | -6.9 | 114,947 | 14.6 | 93,799 | 7.6 | 76,975 | 0.6 |
| Barbados[b] | Jan–Dec | 131,795 | -1.6 | 57,335 | 8.2 | 251,778 | 0.4 | 126,759 | -6.6 |
| Belize | Jan–Dec | 147,655 | -3.2 | 17,693 | 6.2 | 34,265 | 0.3 | 45,414 | -5.9 |
| Bermuda[a] | Jan–Dec | 189,388 | -17.5 | 27,207 | -2.3 | 35,003 | -2.6 | 12,015 | -2.1 |
| Bonaire | Jan–Dec | 32,267 | 0.6 | 2,024 | 17.9 | 30,768 | -2.1 | 9,283 | 2.2 |
| Cancun (Mexico)[c] | Jan–Dec | 1,679,848 | 6.9 | 130,509 | 11.5 | 213,077 | 1.8 | 141,886 | 14.3 |
| Cayman Islands | Jan–Dec | 240,462 | 3.7 | 18,544 | 6.9 | 21,271 | 5 | 22,602 | 2.7 |
| Cuba[d] | Jan–Dec | – | – | 818,246 | 23.9 | 909,086 | -1.6 | 621,008 | 9.4 |
| Curaçao | Jan–Dec | 43,680 | -5.5 | 7,244 | 5 | 136,747 | 12.6 | 211,271 | 76.7 |
| Dominica | Jan–Dec | 20,458 | -4.7 | 3,310 | 26.8 | 13,179 | 22.7 | 41,534 | -0.4 |
| Dominican Republic[a] | Jan–Dec | 1,092,240 | 1.1 | 635,933 | 8.3 | 1,345,290 | -3 | 906,209 | -2 |
| Grenada[b] | Jan–Dec | 21,479 | -20.8 | 6,211 | 3.2 | 43,047 | 3 | 53,033 | -2.1 |
| Guyana[b] | Jan–Dec | 67,924 | -1.4 | 22,297 | 14.3 | 9,208 | -4.9 | 33,347 | -0.3 |
| Jamaica | Jan–Dec | 1,150,942 | 1.6 | 236,193 | 23.9 | 284,700 | -1.5 | 95,436 | 7.6 |
| Montserrat | Jan–Dec | 1,922 | -8.9 | 395 | 1.8 | 2,333 | -1.4 | 2,710 | -6 |
| Puerto Rico[c] | Jan–Dec | 1,184,769 | -1.4 | 15,936 | -4.8 | 28,673 | -19.7 | 91,527 | -10.5 |

*Table 3 continues*

**Table 3** Tourist Arrivals by Main Market – 2008 (cont'd)

| Destination | Period | United States | | Canada | | Europe | | Other | |
|---|---|---|---|---|---|---|---|---|---|
| | | Tourists | Change (%) | Tourists | Change (%) | Tourists | Change (%) | Tourists | Change (%) |
| Saba | Jan–Dec | 4,456 | -0.2 | 757 | 1.7 | 5,605 | 6 | 1,225 | 4.2 |
| St Lucia | Jan–Dec | 108,596 | -4.3 | 26,279 | 41 | 96,871 | 9.1 | 64,015 | -3.8 |
| St Eustatius | Jan–Jul | 1,663 | -95 | 165 | -94.4 | 3,754 | -47.9 | 1,564 | -90.5 |
| St Kitts and Nevis[b] | Jan–Dec | 62,769 | -8.5 | 6,812 | -3.7 | 9,458 | -35.3 | 27,369 | -16.8 |
| St Maarten[a] | Jan–Dec | 257,912 | 1.6 | 34,055 | 5.3 | 102,713 | 6.6 | 80,730 | -7.1 |
| St Vincent and the Grenadines | Jan–Dec | 24,042 | -9.8 | 6,882 | 2 | 22,302 | -4.9 | 30,875 | -5.9 |
| Suriname | Jan–Jul | 3,026 | 21.3 | 723 | 5.2 | 60,055 | -5.8 | 25,593 | -15.5 |
| Trinidad and Tobago | Jan–Dec | 186,695 | 3.4 | 53,404 | 3.9 | 62,399 | -24.4 | 128,015 | -5.2 |
| US Virgin Islands[c] | Jan–Dec | 672,870 | 9.9 | 8,922 | 48.3 | 15,679 | 5.3 | 34,029 | -26.7 |

[a]Non-resident air arrivals
[b]Preliminary figures
[c]Non-resident hotel registrations only
[d]Unitd States total included in Other

*Note*: U.S.V.I reported figures in this table are hotel registrations whereas they reported stay-over totals as air arrivals; Figures are subject to revision by reporting countries

*Source*: Data supplied by member countries and available as on 21 September 2009.

**Table 4** Cruise Passenger Arrivals – 2008 and 2007

| Destination | Period | 2008 | 2007 | Change (%) |
|---|---|---|---|---|
| Antigua and Barbuda | Jan–Dec | 580,853 | 672,788 | −13.7 |
| Aruba | Jan–Dec | 556,090 | 481,775 | 15.4 |
| Bahamas | Jan–Dec | 2,861,140 | 2,970,659 | −3.7 |
| Barbados | Jan–Dec | 597,523 | 616,354 | −3.1 |
| Belize | Jan–Dec | 597,370 | 624,128 | −4.3 |
| Bermuda | Jan–Dec | 286,409 | 354,024 | −19.1 |
| Bonaire | Jan–Dec | 175,702 | 97,635 | 80 |
| British Virgin Island | Jan–Dec | 571,749 | 575,211 | −0.6 |
| Cayman Islands | Jan–Dec | 1,553,053 | 1,715,666 | −9.5 |
| Cozumel (Mexico) | Jan–Dec | 2,569,433 | 2,488,190 | 3.3 |
| Curaçao | Jan–Oct | 239,208 | 255,985 | −6.6 |
| Dominica | Jan–Dec | 380,941 | 354,515 | 7.5 |
| Dominican Republic | Jan–Dec | 417,685 | 384,878 | 8.5 |
| Grenada[a] | Jan–Dec | 292,712 | 270,323 | 8.3 |
| Jamaica | Jan–Dec | 1,088,901 | 1,179,504 | −7.7 |
| Martinique | Jan–Dec | 87,079 | 71,683 | 21.5 |
| Montserrat | Jan–Dec | 251 | 273 | −8.1 |
| Puerto Rico | Jan–Dec | 1,392,624 | 1,437,239 | −3.1 |
| St Lucia | Jan–Dec | 619,680 | 610,343 | 1.5 |
| St Maarten | Jan–Dec | 1,345,812 | 1,421,906 | −5.4 |
| St Vincent and the Grenadines | Jan–Dec | 11 | 144,555 | −19.3 |
| Trinidad and Tobago | Jan–Dec | 44,042 | 76,741 | −42.6 |
| US Virgin Islands | Jan–Dec | 1,757,067 | 1,917,878 | −8.4 |

[a]Preliminary figures

*Note:* Figures are subject to revision by reporting countries
*Source:* Data supplied by member countries and available as on 21 September 2009.

# Appendix 7

## Caribbean Tourism Organization: Latest Statistics, 2009

**Table 1** Tourist (Stop-over) Arrivals in 2009

| Destination | Period | Tourist Arrivals | Change (%) | | |
|---|---|---|---|---|---|
| | | | Overall | Winter | Summer |
| Anguilla | Jan–Feb | 10,447 | −21.4 | −21.4 | – |
| Antigua and Barbuda[a] | Jan–Jul | 148,767 | −12.9 | −13.6 | −11.8 |
| Aruba[b] | Jan–Apr | 280,269 | −5.1 | −5.1 | – |
| Bahamas | Jan–May | 602,445 | −14.1 | −14.2 | −13.7 |
| Barbados[b] | Jan–May | 229,472 | −8.5 | −7.2 | −14.7 |
| Belize | Jan–Jun | 131,650 | −8.3 | −7.3 | −10.6 |
| Bermuda | Jan–Jun | 107,214 | −17.0 | −21.8 | −12.1 |
| British Virgin Islands | Jan–Mar | 85,964 | −25.0 | −25.0 | – |
| Cancun (Mexico)[c] | Jan–Jun | 1,035,155 | −14.6 | 1.0 | −48.4 |
| Cayman Islands | Jan–Jun | 154,640 | −13.3 | −12.5 | −15.1 |
| Cuba | Jan–May | 1,211,238 | 2.1 | 1.9 | 3.7 |
| Curaçao | Jan–Mar | 94,235 | −4.1 | −4.1 | – |
| Dominica[b] | Jan–Jul | 41,891 | −3.5 | 3.0 | −10.5 |
| Dominican Republic[a] | Jan–Jun | 2,145,957 | −3.2 | −4.8 | 1.0 |
| Grenada[b] | Jan–Mar | 31,741 | −4.6 | −4.6 | – |
| Guyana[b] | Jan–Jun | 61,868 | 2.7 | −1.9 | 13.8 |
| Jamaica | Jan–Jun | 971,191 | 3.4 | 2.0 | 6.2 |
| Martinique[b] | Jan–May | 209,636 | −9.8 | −10.3 | −7.4 |
| Montserrat | Jan–Jun | 2,834 | −15.3 | −11.4 | −24 |
| Puerto Rico[c] | Jan–May | 588,626 | −6.4 | −7.7 | −0.1 |
| Saba | Jan–Jun | 6,554 | 0.1 | 1.4 | −2.9 |
| St Lucia | Jan–Jul | 172,369 | −9.4 | −8.8 | −10.4 |
| St Maarten | Jan–Jun | 235,677 | −12.5 | −13.7 | −9.2 |
| St Vincent and the Grenadines | Jan–Apr | 26,262 | −8.1 | −8.1 | – |
| US Virgin Islands | Jan–Jul | 428,052 | −7.6 | −10.0 | −3.9 |

[a]Non-resident air arrivals
[b]Preliminary figures
[c]Non-resident hotel registrations only

*Note:* Winter–January to April; Summer–May to December; figures are subject to revision by reporting countries
*Source:* Data supplied by member countries and available as on 21 September 2009.

**Table 2a** Tourist Arrivals by Month – 2009

| Destination | January Tourists | January Change (%) | February Tourists | February Change (%) | March Tourists | March Change (%) | April Tourists | April Change (%) | May Tourists | May Change (%) | June Tourists | June Change (%) |
|---|---|---|---|---|---|---|---|---|---|---|---|---|
| Anguilla | 4,958 | -18.8 | 5,489 | -23.5 | — | — | — | — | — | — | — | — |
| Antigua and Barbuda[a] | 22,657 | -9.8 | 24,471 | -14.5 | 23,272 | -18.1 | 22,416 | -11.3 | 17,048 | -18.4 | 16,365 | -12.2 |
| Aruba[b] | 69,616 | -2.3 | 67,384 | -7.7 | 70,430 | -13.3 | — | — | — | — | — | — |
| Bahamas | 93,679 | -15.2 | 110,075 | -14.7 | 143,382 | -17.9 | 133,676 | -8.6 | 121,633 | -13.7 | — | — |
| Barbados[b] | 45,455 | -7.2 | 49,838 | -8.1 | 50,237 | -10.3 | 45,277 | -2.3 | 38,665 | -14.7 | — | — |
| Belize | 22,580 | -2.4 | 22,600 | -12.4 | 26,499 | -14.0 | 22,015 | 3.1 | 17,835 | -11.7 | 20,121 | -9.6 |
| Bermuda | 7,703 | -17.3 | 10,013 | -26.0 | 14,519 | -23.1 | 18,810 | -20.2 | 25,456 | -18.2 | 30,713 | -6.4 |
| British Virgin Islands | 29,514 | -13.8 | 22,570 | -36.2 | 33,880 | -24.9 | — | — | — | — | — | — |
| Cancun (Mexico)[c] | 212,323 | 12.2 | 216,449 | 6.8 | 223,945 | -3.2 | 184,331 | -10.3 | 63,606 | -65.3 | 134,501 | -32.9 |
| Cayman Islands | 23,404 | -9.4 | 26,482 | -12.8 | 31,194 | -18.8 | 27,973 | -6.7 | 21,438 | -16.7 | 24,149 | -13.7 |
| Cuba | 268,114 | 7.9 | 262,985 | 1.2 | 279,199 | -2.4 | 236,261 | 1.5 | 164,642 | 3.7 | — | — |
| Curaçao | 32,457 | 10.7 | 31,712 | -5.7 | 30,066 | -14.9 | — | — | — | — | — | — |
| Dominica[b] | 6,008 | 8.0 | 6,853 | 32.9 | 4,405 | -35.9 | 5,868 | 20.8 | 6,637 | -6.2 | 3,916 | -18.9 |
| Dominican Republic[a] | 382,055 | -2.4 | 387,487 | -6.4 | 406,270 | -6.8 | 342,398 | -3.2 | 296,374 | 2.4 | 331,373 | -0.2 |
| Grenada[b] | 12,772 | 11.9 | 9,383 | -9.2 | 9,586 | -16.9 | — | — | — | — | — | — |
| Guyana[b] | 8,132 | -10.3 | 8,400 | -5.5 | 11,876 | -5.9 | 13,507 | 11.3 | 8,941 | 7.9 | 11,012 | 19.1 |
| Jamaica | 148,886 | 4.2 | 160,282 | 2.2 | 175,929 | -4.5 | 164,090 | 7.8 | 153,443 | 8.6 | 168,561 | 4.1 |
| Martinique[b] | 44,734 | -8.0 | 43,919 | -6.0 | 43,158 | -19.2 | 43,027 | -6.8 | 34,798 | -7.4 | — | — |
| Montserrat | 468 | -9.3 | 502 | -13.6 | 617 | -14.2 | 460 | -7.1 | 395 | -17.9 | 392 | -29.4 |
| Puerto Rico[c] | 116,237 | -4.1 | 117,197 | -10.2 | 128,668 | -12.9 | 118,894 | -2.2 | 107,630 | -0.1 | — | — |
| Saba | 1,178 | 7.0 | 1,119 | -1.1 | 1,193 | 0.0 | 1,115 | 0.1 | 1,013 | -9.9 | 936 | 6.0 |
| St Lucia | 23,051 | -7.6 | 25,262 | -13.2 | 25,938 | -18.9 | 26,326 | 8.8 | 25,292 | -9.0 | 19,706 | -15.1 |
| St Maarten | 44,647 | -8.3 | 42,521 | -14.1 | 41,878 | -24.7 | 41,601 | -5.4 | 33,566 | -11.4 | 31,464 | -6.7 |
| St Vincent and the Grenadines | 6,444 | 1.2 | 6,049 | -24.2 | 7,065 | -7.8 | 6,704 | 2.1 | — | — | — | — |
| US Virgin Islands | 60,679 | -5.8 | 62,225 | -6.2 | 62,585 | -25.0 | 65,738 | -2.1 | 57,571 | -2.2 | 58,110 | -7.4 |

[a]Non-resident air arrivals
[b]Preliminary figures
[c]Non-resident hotel registrations only

*Note:* Figures are subject to revision by reporting countries.
*Source:* Data supplied by member countries and available as on 21 September 2009.

**Table 2b** Tourist Arrivals by Month – 2009

| Destination | July Tourists | July Change (%) | August Tourists | August Change (%) | September Tourists | September Change (%) | October Tourists | October Change (%) | November Tourists | November Change (%) | December Tourists | December Change (%) |
|---|---|---|---|---|---|---|---|---|---|---|---|---|
| Anguilla | – | – | – | – | – | – | – | – | – | – | – | – |
| Antigua and Barbuda[a] | 22,657 | −9.8 | – | – | – | – | – | – | – | – | – | – |
| Aruba[b] | – | – | – | – | – | – | – | – | – | – | – | – |
| Bahamas | – | – | – | – | – | – | – | – | – | – | – | – |
| Barbados[b] | – | – | – | – | – | – | – | – | – | – | – | – |
| Belize | – | – | – | – | – | – | – | – | – | – | – | – |
| Bermuda | – | – | – | – | – | – | – | – | – | – | – | – |
| British Virgin Islands | – | – | – | – | – | – | – | – | – | – | – | – |
| Cancun (Mexico)[c] | – | – | – | – | – | – | – | – | – | – | – | – |
| Cayman Islands | – | – | – | – | – | – | – | – | – | – | – | – |
| Cuba | – | – | – | – | – | – | – | – | – | – | – | – |
| Curaçao | – | – | – | – | – | – | – | – | – | – | – | – |
| Dominica[b] | 8,204 | −9.5 | – | – | – | – | – | – | – | – | – | – |
| Dominican Republic[a] | – | – | – | – | – | – | – | – | – | – | – | – |
| Grenada[b] | – | – | – | – | – | – | – | – | – | – | – | – |
| Guyana[b] | – | – | – | – | – | – | – | – | – | – | – | – |
| Jamaica | – | – | – | – | – | – | – | – | – | – | – | – |
| Martinique[b] | – | – | – | – | – | – | – | – | – | – | – | – |
| Montserrat | – | – | – | – | – | – | – | – | – | – | – | – |
| Puerto Rico[c] | – | – | – | – | – | – | – | – | – | – | – | – |
| Saba | – | – | – | – | – | – | – | – | – | – | – | – |
| St Lucia | 26,794 | −7.9 | – | – | – | – | – | – | – | – | – | – |
| St Maarten | – | – | – | – | – | – | – | – | – | – | – | – |
| St Vincent and the Grenadines | – | – | – | – | – | – | – | – | – | – | – | – |
| US Virgin Islands | 61,144 | −2.1 | – | – | – | – | – | – | – | – | – | – |

[a]Non-resident air arrivals
[b]Preliminary figures
[c]Non-resident hotel registrations only

*Note:* Figures are subject to revision by reporting countries.
*Source:* Data supplied by member countries and available as on 21 September 2009.

**Table 3** Tourist Arrivals by Main Market – 2009

| Destination | Period | United States Tourists | United States Change (%) | Canada Tourists | Canada Change (%) | Europe Tourists | Europe Change (%) | Other Tourists | Other Change (%) |
|---|---|---|---|---|---|---|---|---|---|
| Anguilla | Jan-Feb | 6,771 | -21.8 | 513 | -4.3 | 1,301 | -20.4 | 1,862 | -24.2 |
| Antigua and Barbuda[a] | Jan-Jul | 54,616 | -4.5 | 7,911 | -11.8 | 58,720 | -15.5 | 27,520 | -21.6 |
| Bahamas | Jan-May | 480,998 | -14.9 | 58,155 | -11.2 | 34,689 | -9.6 | 28,603 | -11.9 |
| Barbados[b] | Jan-May | 47,142 | -16.0 | 35,444 | 17.7 | 103,292 | -9.7 | 43,594 | -13.1 |
| Belize | Jan-Jun | 83,613 | -8.1 | 11,179 | -3.9 | 15,833 | -8.0 | 21,025 | -11.6 |
| Bermuda | Jan-Feb | 11,600 | -25.8 | 2,771 | -12.1 | 2,408 | -14.2 | 937 | -25.3 |
| Cancun (Mexico)[c] | Jan-Jun | 773,251 | -16.5 | 86,600 | -2.7 | 107,001 | -7.3 | 68,303 | -17.1 |
| Cayman Islands | Jan-Jun | 125,049 | -13.7 | 10,684 | -10.2 | 10,547 | -10.9 | 8,360 | -13.1 |
| Curaçao | Jan-Mar | 8,884 | -32.3 | 2,822 | -20.2 | 34,824 | 2.3 | 47,705 | 3.8 |
| Cuba[1] | Jan-May | – | – | 567,627 | 11.8 | 387,117 | -9.0 | 256,494 | 1.4 |
| Dominica[b] | Jan-Jul | 11,493 | -9.7 | 1,647 | -3.3 | 7,390 | 11.4 | 21,361 | -4.5 |
| Dominican Republic[a] | Jan-Jun | 605,905 | -2.1 | 461,079 | 4.8 | 649,362 | -9.4 | 429,611 | -2.5 |
| Grenada[b] | Jan-Mar | 5,993 | -1.4 | 5,528 | 16.3 | 11,608 | -16.7 | 11,612 | 4.6 |
| Guyana[b] | Jan-Jun | 33,537 | 11.1 | 10,893 | 4.3 | 4,074 | -7.6 | 13,364 | -12.0 |
| Jamaica | Jan-Jun | 619,070 | -0.2 | 175,365 | 28.3 | 132,929 | -3.4 | 43,827 | -2.2 |
| Montserrat | Jan-Jun | 786 | -17.1 | 200 | -5.7 | 826 | -17.6 | 1,022 | -13.7 |
| Puerto Rico[c] | Jan-May | 531,455 | -6.0 | 8,819 | -9.4 | 14,984 | 7.7 | 33,368 | -16.4 |
| Saba | Jan-Jun | 2,219 | -14.3 | 553 | 22.1 | 3,210 | 14.2 | 572 | -17.3 |
| St Lucia | Jan-Jul | 62,144 | -17.2 | 20,627 | 18.2 | 52,791 | -12.6 | 36,807 | -1.6 |
| St Maarten | Jan-Jun | 136,369 | -12.3 | 18,454 | -13.2 | 49,588 | -5.5 | 31,266 | -22.0 |
| St Vincent and the Grenadines | Jan-Apr | 6,915 | -18.0 | 2,965 | 10.1 | 7,736 | -12.2 | 8,646 | 0.1 |
| US Virgin Islands[c] | Jan-Apr | 270,202 | 1.2 | 4,615 | 44.7 | 7,649 | 20.2 | 10,494 | -4.0 |

[a] Non-resident air arrivals
[b] Preliminary figures
[c] Non-resident hotel registrations only

*Note*: USVI reported figures in this table are hotel registrations whereas they reported stay-over totals as air arrivals; figures are subject to revision by reporting countries; [1] United States total included in "Other"
*Source*: Data supplied by member countries and available as on 21 September 2009.

**Table 4** Cruise Passenger Arrivals – 2009 and 2008

| Destination | Period | 2009 | 2008 | Change (%) |
|---|---|---|---|---|
| Antigua and Barbuda | Jan–May | 415,863 | 344,774 | 20.6 |
| Aruba | Jan–Apr | 343,942 | 327,540 | 5.0 |
| Bahamas | Jan–May | 1,436,165 | 1,307,853 | 9.8 |
| Barbados | Jan–May | 347,789 | 357,497 | -2.7 |
| Belize | Jan–Jun | 365,557 | 337,268 | 8.4 |
| Bermuda | Jan–Jun | 124,553 | 132,143 | -5.7 |
| British Virgin Islands | Jan–Mar | 265,370 | 295,952 | -10.3 |
| Cayman Islands | Jan–Jun | 846,952 | 901,474 | -6.0 |
| Cozumel (Mexico) | Jan–May | 978,385 | 1,245,147 | -21.4 |
| Curaçao | Jan–Feb | 133,592 | 105,551 | 26.6 |
| Dominica | Jan–Jul | 317,117 | 228,445 | 38.8 |
| Dominican Republic | Jan–Apr | 343,779 | 297,674 | 15.5 |
| Grenada[a] | Jan–Jun | 218,533 | 181,162 | 20.6 |
| Jamaica | Jan–Jun | 550,924 | 646,081 | -14.7 |
| Martinique | Jan–Apr | 35,141 | 51,714 | -32.0 |
| Puerto Rico | Jan–May | 618,857 | 755,289 | -18.1 |
| St Lucia | Jan–Jul | 430,682 | 397,115 | 8.5 |
| St Maarten | Jan–Jun | 781,063 | 772,533 | 1.1 |
| St Vincent and the Grenadines | Jan–Apr | 99,607 | 66,689 | 49.4 |
| US Virgin Islands | Jan–Jul | 974,222 | 1,139,031 | -14.5 |

[a]Preliminary figures

*Note:* Figures are subject to revision by reporting countries.
*Source:* Data supplied by member countries and available as on 21 September 2009.

# Appendix 8

Register of Holders of Ordinary Shares in LIAT (1974) Ltd, from 1999 to 2008

# LIAT (1974) LTD
# COMPANY No. 688
# REGISTER OF HOLDERS OF ORDINARY SHARES
# AS AT DECEMBER 31, 1999

| No. | NAMES OF SHAREHOLDERS | SHARES HELD AS AT DECEMBER 31, 1999 | PERCENTAGE OF SHARES |
|---|---|---|---|
| 1 | GOVERNMENT OF ANTIGUA AND BARBUDA | 35,892 | 14.02% |
| 2 | GOVERNMENT OF BARBADOS | 7,500 | 2.93% |
| 3 | GOVERNMENT OF DOMINICA | 3,030 | 1.18% |
| 4 | GOVERNMENT OF GRENADA | 4,545 | 1.77% |
| 5 | GOVERNMENT OF GUYANA | 2,500 | 0.98% |
| 6 | GOVERNMENT OF JAMAICA | 2,500 | 0.98% |
| 7 | GOVERNMENT OF ST. KITTS AND NEVIS | 2,500 | 0.98% |
| 8 | GOVERNMENT OF MONTSERRAT | 3,030 | 1.18% |
| 9 | GOVERNMENT OF ST. LUCIA | 4,545 | 1.77% |
| 10 | GOVERNMENT OF ST. VINCENT & THE GRENADINES | 3,030 | 1.18% |
| 11 | GOVERNMENT OF TRINIDAD AND TOBAGO | 7,500 | 2.93% |
| 12 | ANTIGUA COMMERCIAL BANK | 2,721 | 1.06% |
| 13 | ANTIGUA BARBUDA INVESTMENT BANK | 1,134 | 0.44% |
| 14 | ACB INVESTMENT CO. LTD. | 5,440 | 2.12% |
| 15 | ANTIGUA AND BARBUDA WORKERS UNION | 1,264 | 0.49% |
| 16 | BWIA WEST INDIES AIRWAYS LTD., | 75,755 | 29.58% |
| 17 | CARIBBEAN AIRCRAFT HANDLING | 2,422 | 0.95% |
| 18 | HKH (ANTIGUA) LTD | 38,995 | 15.23% |
| 19 | LEEWARD ISLANDS ENGINEERING ASSOCIATION | 4,000 | 1.56% |
| 20 | LIAT STAFF PROVIDENT FUND | 30,329 | 11.84% |
| 21 | NATIONAL BANK OF DOMINICA | 6,319 | 2.47% |
| 22 | THE REPUBLIC BANK (GRENADA) LIMITED (Formerly NATIONAL COMMERCIAL BANK OF GRENADA | 2,527 | 0.99% |
| 23 | JOAN B. SLACK | 1,264 | 0.49% |
| 24 | STATE INSURANCE CORPORATION | 6,319 | 2.47% |
| 25 | ST. JOHN'S CO-OPERATIVE CREDIT UNION LTD. | 1,000 | 0.39% |
| TOTAL: | | 256,061 | 1.00 |

PERCENTAGE – ISSUED TO AUTHORIZED 34%
AUTHORIZED LAST CHANGED 750,000

# LIAT (1974) LTD
# COMPANY No. 688
# REGISTER OF HOLDERS OF ORDINARY SHARES
# AS AT DECEMBER 31, 2000

| No. | NAMES OF SHAREHOLDERS | SHARES HELD AS AT DECEMBER 31, 2000 | PERCENTAGE OF SHARES |
|---|---|---|---|
| 1 | GOVERNMENT OF ANTIGUA AND BARBUDA | 35,892 | 14.02% |
| 2 | GOVERNMENT OF BARBADOS | 7,500 | 2.93% |
| 3 | GOVERNMENT OF DOMINICA | 3,030 | 1.18% |
| 4 | GOVERNMENT OF GRENADA | 4,545 | 1.77% |
| 5 | GOVERNMENT OF GUYANA | 2,500 | 0.98% |
| 6 | GOVERNMENT OF JAMAICA | 2,500 | 0.98% |
| 7 | GOVERNMENT OF ST. KITTS AND NEVIS | 2,500 | 0.98% |
| 8 | GOVERNMENT OF MONTSERRAT | 3,030 | 1.18% |
| 9 | GOVERNMENT OF ST. LUCIA | 4,545 | 1.77% |
| 10 | GOVERNMENT OF ST. VINCENT & THE GRENADINES | 3,030 | 1.18% |
| 11 | GOVERNMENT OF TRINIDAD AND TOBAGO | 7,500 | 2.93% |
| 12 | ANTIGUA COMMERCIAL BANK | 2,721 | 1.06% |
| 13 | ANTIGUA BARBUDA INVESTMENT BANK | 1,134 | 0.44% |
| 14 | ACB INVESTMENT CO. LTD. | 5,440 | 2.12% |
| 15 | ANTIGUA AND BARBUDA WORKERS UNION | 1,264 | 0.49% |
| 16 | BWIA WEST INDIES AIRWAYS LTD., | 75,755 | 29.58% |
| 17 | CARIBBEAN AIRCRAFT HANDLING | 2,422 | 0.95% |
| 18 | HKH (ANTIGUA) LTD | 38,995 | 15.23% |
| 19 | LEEWARD ISLANDS ENGINEERING ASSOCIATION | 4,000 | 1.56% |
| 20 | LIAT STAFF PROVIDENT FUND | 30,329 | 11.84% |
| 21 | NATIONAL BANK OF DOMINICA | 6,319 | 2.47% |
| 22 | THE REPUBLIC BANK (GRENADA) LIMITED (Formerly NATIONAL COMMERCIAL BANK OF GRENADA | 2,527 | 0.99% |
| 23 | JOAN B. SLACK | 1,264 | 0.49% |
| 24 | STATE INSURANCE CORPORATION | 6,319 | 2.47% |
| 25 | ST. JOHN'S CO-OPERATIVE CREDIT UNION LTD. | 1,000 | 0.39% |
| TOTAL: | | 256,061 | 1.00 |

| | | |
|---|---|---|
| PERCENTAGE – ISSUED TO AUTHORIZED | 34% | |
| AUTHORIZED LAST CHANGED | 750,000 | |

## LIAT (1974) LTD
## COMPANY No. 688
## REGISTER OF HOLDERS OF ORDINARY SHARES
## AS AT DECEMBER 31, 2001

| No. | NAMES OF SHAREHOLDERS | SHARES HELD AS AT DECEMBER 31, 2001 | PERCENTAGE OF SHARES |
|---|---|---|---|
| 1 | GOVERNMENT OF ANTIGUA AND BARBUDA | 35,892 | 14.02% |
| 2 | GOVERNMENT OF BARBADOS | 7,500 | 2.93% |
| 3 | GOVERNMENT OF DOMINICA | 3,030 | 1.18% |
| 4 | GOVERNMENT OF GRENADA | 4,545 | 1.77% |
| 5 | GOVERNMENT OF GUYANA | 2,500 | 0.98% |
| 6 | GOVERNMENT OF JAMAICA | 2,500 | 0.98% |
| 7 | GOVERNMENT OF ST. KITTS AND NEVIS | 2,500 | 0.98% |
| 8 | GOVERNMENT OF MONTSERRAT | 3,030 | 1.18% |
| 9 | GOVERNMENT OF ST. LUCIA | 4,545 | 1.77% |
| 10 | GOVERNMENT OF ST. VINCENT & THE GRENADINES | 3,030 | 1.18% |
| 11 | GOVERNMENT OF TRINIDAD AND TOBAGO | 7,500 | 2.93% |
| 12 | ANTIGUA COMMERCIAL BANK | 2,721 | 1.06% |
| 13 | ANTIGUA BARBUDA INVESTMENT BANK | 1,134 | 0.44% |
| 14 | ACB INVESTMENT CO. LTD. | 5,440 | 2.12% |
| 15 | ANTIGUA AND BARBUDA WORKERS UNION | 1,264 | 0.49% |
| 16 | BWIA WEST INDIES AIRWAYS LTD., | 75,755 | 29.58% |
| 17 | CARIBBEAN AIRCRAFT HANDLING | 2,422 | 0.95% |
| 18 | HKH (ANTIGUA) LTD | 38,995 | 15.23% |
| 19 | LEEWARD ISLANDS ENGINEERING ASSOCIATION | 4,000 | 1.56% |
| 20 | LIAT STAFF PROVIDENT FUND | 30,329 | 11.84% |
| 21 | NATIONAL BANK OF DOMINICA | 6,319 | 2.47% |
| 22 | THE REPUBLIC BANK (GRENADA) LIMITED (Formerly NATIONAL COMMERCIAL BANK OF GRENADA | 2,527 | 0.99% |
| 23 | JOAN B. SLACK | 1,264 | 0.49% |
| 24 | STATE INSURANCE CORPORATION | 6,319 | 2.47% |
| 25 | ST. JOHN'S CO-OPERATIVE CREDIT UNION LTD. | 1,000 | 0.39% |
| TOTAL: | | 256,061 | 1.00 |

PERCENTAGE – ISSUED TO AUTHORIZED         34%
AUTHORIZED LAST CHANGED                  750,000

## LIAT (1974) LTD
## COMPANY No. 688
## REGISTER OF HOLDERS OF ORDINARY SHARES
## AS AT DECEMBER 31, 2002

| No. | NAMES OF SHAREHOLDERS | SHARES HELD AS AT DECEMBER 31, 2002 | PERCENTAGE OF SHARES |
|---|---|---|---|
| 1 | GOVERNMENT OF ANTIGUA AND BARBUDA | 71,784 | 22.32% |
| 2 | GOVERNMENT OF BARBADOS | 7,500 | 2.33% |
| 3 | GOVERNMENT OF DOMINICA | 3,030 | 0.94% |
| 4 | GOVERNMENT OF GRENADA | 4,545 | 1.41% |
| 5 | GOVERNMENT OF GUYANA | 2,500 | 0.78% |
| 6 | GOVERNMENT OF JAMAICA | 2,500 | 0.78% |
| 7 | GOVERNMENT OF ST. KITTS AND NEVIS | 2,500 | 0.78% |
| 8 | GOVERNMENT OF MONTSERRAT | 3,030 | 0.94% |
| 9 | GOVERNMENT OF ST. LUCIA | 4,545 | 1.41% |
| 10 | GOVERNMENT OF ST. VINCENT & THE GRENADINES | 32,626 | 10.15% |
| 11 | GOVERNMENT OF TRINIDAD AND TOBAGO | 7,500 | 2.33% |
| 12 | ANTIGUA COMMERCIAL BANK | 2,721 | 0.85% |
| 13 | ANTIGUA BARBUDA INVESTMENT BANK | 1,134 | 0.35% |
| 14 | ACB INVESTMENT CO. LTD. | 5,440 | 1.69% |
| 15 | ANTIGUA AND BARBUDA WORKERS UNION | 1,264 | 0.39% |
| 16 | BWIA WEST INDIES AIRWAYS LTD., | 75,755 | 23.56% |
| 17 | CARIBBEAN AIRCRAFT HANDLING | 2,422 | 0.75% |
| 18 | HKH (ANTIGUA) LTD | 38,995 | 12.13% |
| 19 | LEEWARD ISLANDS ENGINEERING ASSOCIATION | 4,000 | 1.24% |
| 20 | LIAT STAFF PROVIDENT FUND | 30,329 | 9.43% |
| 21 | NATIONAL BANK OF DOMINICA | 6,319 | 1.97% |
| 22 | THE REPUBLIC BANK (GRENADA) LIMITED (Formerly NATIONAL COMMERCIAL BANK OF GRENADA | 2,527 | 0.79% |
| 23 | JOAN B. SLACK | 1,264 | 0.39% |
| 24 | STATE INSURANCE CORPORATION | 6,319 | 1.97% |
| 25 | ST. JOHN'S CO-OPERATIVE CREDIT UNION LTD. | 1,000 | 0.31% |
| TOTAL: | | 321,549 | 1.00 |

| | |
|---|---|
| PERCENTAGE – ISSUED TO AUTHORIZED | 43% |
| AUTHORIZED LAST CHANGED | 750,000 |

# LIAT (1974) LTD
# COMPANY No. 688
# REGISTER OF HOLDERS OF ORDINARY SHARES
# AS AT DECEMBER 31, 2003

| No. | NAMES OF SHAREHOLDERS | SHARES HELD AS AT DECEMBER 31, 2003 | PERCENTAGE OF SHARES |
|---|---|---|---|
| 1 | GOVERNMENT OF ANTIGUA AND BARBUDA | 112,784 | 24.62% |
| 2 | GOVERNMENT OF BARBADOS | 37,500 | 8.19% |
| 3 | GOVERNMENT OF DOMINICA | 3,030 | 0.66% |
| 4 | GOVERNMENT OF GRENADA | 4,545 | 0.99% |
| 5 | GOVERNMENT OF GUYANA | 2,500 | 0.55% |
| 6 | GOVERNMENT OF JAMAICA | 2,500 | 0.55% |
| 7 | GOVERNMENT OF ST. KITTS AND NEVIS | 2,500 | 0.55% |
| 8 | GOVERNMENT OF MONTSERRAT | 3,030 | 0.66% |
| 9 | GOVERNMENT OF ST. LUCIA | 4,545 | 0.99% |
| 10 | GOVERNMENT OF ST. VINCENT & THE GRENADINES | 98,126 | 21.42% |
| 11 | GOVERNMENT OF TRINIDAD AND TOBAGO | 7,500 | 1.64% |
| 12 | ANTIGUA COMMERCIAL BANK | 2,721 | 0.59% |
| 13 | ANTIGUA BARBUDA INVESTMENT BANK | 1,134 | 0.25% |
| 14 | ACB INVESTMENT CO. LTD. | 5,440 | 1.19% |
| 15 | ANTIGUA AND BARBUDA WORKERS UNION | 1,264 | 0.28% |
| 16 | BWIA WEST INDIES AIRWAYS LTD., | 75,755 | 16.54% |
| 17 | CARIBBEAN AIRCRAFT HANDLING | 2,422 | 0.53% |
| 18 | HKH (ANTIGUA) LTD | 38,995 | 8.51% |
| 19 | LEEWARD ISLANDS ENGINEERING ASSOCIATION | 4,000 | 0.87% |
| 20 | LIAT STAFF PROVIDENT FUND | 30,329 | 6.62% |
| 21 | NATIONAL BANK OF DOMINICA | 6,319 | 1.38% |
| 22 | THE REPUBLIC BANK (GRENADA) LIMITED (Formerly NATIONAL COMMERCIAL BANK OF GRENADA | 2,527 | 0.55% |
| 23 | JOAN B. SLACK | 1,264 | 0.28% |
| 24 | STATE INSURANCE CORPORATION | 6,319 | 1.38% |
| 25 | ST. JOHN'S CO-OPERATIVE CREDIT UNION LTD. | 1,000 | 0.22% |
| TOTAL: | | 458,049 | 1.00 |

| | | |
|---|---|---|
| PERCENTAGE – ISSUED TO AUTHORIZED | 37% | |
| AUTHORIZED LAST CHANGED 2003 | 1,250,000 | |

# LIAT (1974) LTD
# COMPANY No. 688
# REGISTER OF HOLDERS OF ORDINARY SHARES
# AS AT DECEMBER 31, 2004

| No. | NAMES OF SHAREHOLDERS | SHARES HELD AS AT DECEMBER 31, 2004 | PERCENTAGE OF SHARES |
|---|---|---|---|
| 1 | GOVERNMENT OF ANTIGUA AND BARBUDA | 112,784 | 18.38% |
| 2 | GOVERNMENT OF BARBADOS | 136,170 | 22.19% |
| 3 | GOVERNMENT OF DOMINICA | 3,030 | 0.49% |
| 4 | GOVERNMENT OF GRENADA | 4,545 | 0.74% |
| 5 | GOVERNMENT OF GUYANA | 2,500 | 0.41% |
| 6 | GOVERNMENT OF JAMAICA | 2,500 | 0.41% |
| 7 | GOVERNMENT OF ST. KITTS AND NEVIS | 2,500 | 0.41% |
| 8 | GOVERNMENT OF MONTSERRAT | 3,030 | 0.49% |
| 9 | GOVERNMENT OF ST. LUCIA | 4,545 | 0.74% |
| 10 | GOVERNMENT OF ST. VINCENT & THE GRENADINES | 155,126 | 25.28% |
| 11 | GOVERNMENT OF TRINIDAD AND TOBAGO | 7,500 | 1.22% |
| 12 | ANTIGUA COMMERCIAL BANK | 2,721 | 0.44% |
| 13 | ANTIGUA BARBUDA INVESTMENT BANK | 1,134 | 0.18% |
| 14 | ACB INVESTMENT CO. LTD. | 5,440 | 0.89% |
| 15 | ANTIGUA AND BARBUDA WORKERS UNION | 1,264 | 0.21% |
| 16 | BWIA WEST INDIES AIRWAYS LTD., | 75,755 | 12.34% |
| 17 | CARIBBEAN AIRCRAFT HANDLING | 2,422 | 0.39% |
| 18 | HKH (ANTIGUA) LTD | 38,995 | 6.35% |
| 19 | LEEWARD ISLANDS ENGINEERING ASSOCIATION | 4,000 | 0.65% |
| 20 | LIAT STAFF PROVIDENT FUND | 30,329 | 4.94% |
| 21 | NATIONAL BANK OF DOMINICA | 6,319 | 1.03% |
| 22 | THE REPUBLIC BANK (GRENADA) LIMITED (Formerly NATIONAL COMMERCIAL BANK OF GRENADA | 2,527 | 0.41% |
| 23 | JOAN B. SLACK | 1,264 | 0.21% |
| 24 | STATE INSURANCE CORPORATION | 6,319 | 1.03% |
| 25 | ST. JOHN'S CO-OPERATIVE CREDIT UNION LTD. | 1,000 | 0.16% |
| TOTAL: | | 613,719 | 1.00 |

PERCENTAGE – ISSUED TO AUTHORIZED 49%
AUTHORIZED LAST CHANGED 2003 1,250,000

## LIAT (1974) LTD
## COMPANY No. 688
## REGISTER OF HOLDERS OF ORDINARY SHARES
## AS AT DECEMBER 31, 2005

| No. | NAMES OF SHAREHOLDERS | SHARES HELD AS AT DECEMBER 31, 2005 | PERCENTAGE OF SHARES |
|---|---|---|---|
| 1 | GOVERNMENT OF ANTIGUA AND BARBUDA | 169,784 | 25.31% |
| 2 | GOVERNMENT OF BARBADOS | 136,170 | 20.30% |
| 3 | GOVERNMENT OF DOMINICA | 3,030 | 0.45% |
| 4 | GOVERNMENT OF GRENADA | 4,545 | 0.68% |
| 5 | GOVERNMENT OF GUYANA | 2,500 | 0.37% |
| 6 | GOVERNMENT OF JAMAICA | 2,500 | 0.37% |
| 7 | GOVERNMENT OF ST. KITTS AND NEVIS | 2,500 | 0.37% |
| 8 | GOVERNMENT OF MONTSERRAT | 3,030 | 0.45% |
| 9 | GOVERNMENT OF ST. LUCIA | 4,545 | 0.68% |
| 10 | GOVERNMENT OF ST. VINCENT & THE GRENADINES | 155,126 | 23.13% |
| 11 | GOVERNMENT OF TRINIDAD AND TOBAGO | 7,500 | 1.12% |
| 12 | ANTIGUA COMMERCIAL BANK | 2,721 | 0.41% |
| 13 | ANTIGUA BARBUDA INVESTMENT BANK | 1,134 | 0.17% |
| 14 | ACB INVESTMENT CO. LTD. | 5,440 | 0.81% |
| 15 | ANTIGUA AND BARBUDA WORKERS UNION | 1,264 | 0.19% |
| 16 | BWIA WEST INDIES AIRWAYS LTD., | 75,755 | 11.29% |
| 17 | CARIBBEAN AIRCRAFT HANDLING | 2,422 | 0.36% |
| 18 | HKH (ANTIGUA) LTD | 38,995 | 5.81% |
| 19 | LEEWARD ISLANDS ENGINEERING ASSOCIATION | 4,000 | 0.60% |
| 20 | LIAT STAFF PROVIDENT FUND | 30,329 | 4.52% |
| 21 | NATIONAL BANK OF DOMINICA | 6,319 | 0.94% |
| 22 | THE REPUBLIC BANK (GRENADA) LIMITED (Formerly NATIONAL COMMERCIAL BANK OF GRENADA | 2,527 | 0.38% |
| 23 | JOAN B. SLACK | 1,264 | 0.19% |
| 24 | STATE INSURANCE CORPORATION | 6,319 | 0.94% |
| 25 | ST. JOHN'S CO-OPERATIVE CREDIT UNION LTD. | 1,000 | 0.15% |
| TOTAL: | | 670,719 | 1.00 |

PERCENTAGE – ISSUED TO AUTHORIZED     54%
AUTHORIZED LAST CHANGED 2003     1,250,000

## LIAT (1974) LTD
## COMPANY No. 688
## REGISTER OF HOLDERS OF ORDINARY SHARES
## AS AT DECEMBER 31, 2006

| No. | NAMES OF SHAREHOLDERS | SHARES HELD AS AT DECEMBER 31, 2006 | PERCENTAGE OF SHARES |
|---|---|---|---|
| 1 | GOVERNMENT OF ANTIGUA AND BARBUDA | 624,690 | 30.19% |
| 2 | GOVERNMENT OF BARBADOS | 1,006,473 | 48.64% |
| 3 | GOVERNMENT OF DOMINICA | 3,030 | 0.15% |
| 4 | GOVERNMENT OF GRENADA | 4,545 | 0.22% |
| 5 | GOVERNMENT OF GUYANA | 2,500 | 0.12% |
| 6 | GOVERNMENT OF JAMAICA | 2,500 | 0.12% |
| 7 | GOVERNMENT OF ST. KITTS AND NEVIS | 2,500 | 0.12% |
| 8 | GOVERNMENT OF MONTSERRAT | 3,030 | 0.15% |
| 9 | GOVERNMENT OF ST. LUCIA | 4,545 | 0.22% |
| 10 | GOVERNMENT OF ST. VINCENT & THE GRENADINES | 228,311 | 11.03% |
| 11 | GOVERNMENT OF TRINIDAD AND TOBAGO | 7,500 | 0.36% |
| 12 | ANTIGUA COMMERCIAL BANK | 2,721 | 0.13% |
| 13 | ANTIGUA BARBUDA INVESTMENT BANK | 1,134 | 0.05% |
| 14 | ACB INVESTMENT CO. LTD. | 5,440 | 0.26% |
| 15 | ANTIGUA AND BARBUDA WORKERS UNION | 1,264 | 0.06% |
| 16 | BWIA WEST INDIES AIRWAYS LTD., | 75,755 | 3.66% |
| 17 | CARIBBEAN AIRCRAFT HANDLING | 2,422 | 0.12% |
| 18 | HKH (ANTIGUA) LTD | 38,995 | 1.88% |
| 19 | LEEWARD ISLANDS ENGINEERING ASSOCIATION | 4,000 | 0.19% |
| 20 | LIAT STAFF PROVIDENT FUND | 30,329 | 1.47% |
| 21 | NATIONAL BANK OF DOMINICA | 6,319 | 0.31% |
| 22 | THE REPUBLIC BANK (GRENADA) LIMITED (Formerly NATIONAL COMMERCIAL BANK OF GRENADA | 2,527 | 0.12% |
| 23 | JOAN B. SLACK | 1,264 | 0.06% |
| 24 | STATE INSURANCE CORPORATION | 6,319 | 0.31% |
| 25 | ST. JOHN'S CO-OPERATIVE CREDIT UNION LTD. | 1,000 | 0.05% |
| TOTAL: | | 2,069,113 | 1.00 |

PERCENTAGE – ISSUED TO AUTHORIZED　　　41%
OCT. 2007　　　5,000,000

## LIAT (1974) LTD
## COMPANY No. 688
## REGISTER OF HOLDERS OF ORDINARY SHARES
## AS AT DECEMBER 31, 2007

| No. | NAMES OF SHAREHOLDERS | SHARES HELD AS AT DECEMBER 31, 2007 | PERCENTAGE OF SHARES |
|---|---|---|---|
| 1 | GOVERNMENT OF ANTIGUA AND BARBUDA | 624,690 | 30.19% |
| 2 | GOVERNMENT OF BARBADOS | 1,006,473 | 48.64% |
| 3 | GOVERNMENT OF DOMINICA | 3,030 | 0.15% |
| 4 | GOVERNMENT OF GRENADA | 4,545 | 0.22% |
| 5 | GOVERNMENT OF GUYANA | 2,500 | 0.12% |
| 6 | GOVERNMENT OF JAMAICA | 2,500 | 0.12% |
| 7 | GOVERNMENT OF ST. KITTS AND NEVIS | 2,500 | 0.12% |
| 8 | GOVERNMENT OF MONTSERRAT | 3,030 | 0.15% |
| 9 | GOVERNMENT OF ST. LUCIA | 4,545 | 0.22% |
| 10 | GOVERNMENT OF ST. VINCENT & THE GRENADINES | 228,311 | 11.03% |
| 11 | GOVERNMENT OF TRINIDAD AND TOBAGO | 7,500 | 0.36% |
| 12 | ANTIGUA COMMERCIAL BANK | 2,721 | 0.13% |
| 13 | ANTIGUA BARBUDA INVESTMENT BANK | 1,134 | 0.05% |
| 14 | ACB INVESTMENT CO. LTD. | 5,440 | 0.26% |
| 15 | ANTIGUA AND BARBUDA WORKERS UNION | 1,264 | 0.06% |
| 16 | BWIA WEST INDIES AIRWAYS LTD., | 75,755 | 3.66% |
| 17 | CARIBBEAN AIRCRAFT HANDLING | 2,422 | 0.12% |
| 18 | HKH (ANTIGUA) LTD | 38,995 | 1.88% |
| 19 | LEEWARD ISLANDS ENGINEERING ASSOCIATION | 4,000 | 0.19% |
| 20 | LIAT STAFF PROVIDENT FUND | 30,329 | 1.47% |
| 21 | NATIONAL BANK OF DOMINICA | 6,319 | 0.31% |
| 22 | THE REPUBLIC BANK (GRENADA) LIMITED (Formerly NATIONAL COMMERCIAL BANK OF GRENADA | 2,527 | 0.12% |
| 23 | JOAN B. SLACK | 1,264 | 0.06% |
| 24 | STATE INSURANCE CORPORATION | 6,319 | 0.31% |
| 25 | ST. JOHN'S CO-OPERATIVE CREDIT UNION LTD. | 1,000 | 0.05% |
| TOTAL: | | 2,069,113 | 1.00 |

PERCENTAGE – ISSUED TO AUTHORIZED   41%
OCT. 2007                           5,000,000

## LIAT (1974) LTD
## COMPANY No. 688
## REGISTER OF HOLDERS OF ORDINARY SHARES
## AS AT DECEMBER 31, 2008

| No. | NAMES OF SHAREHOLDERS | SHARES HELD AS AT DECEMBER 31, 2008 | PERCENTAGE OF SHARES |
|---|---|---|---|
| 1 | GOVERNMENT OF ANTIGUA AND BARBUDA | 767,890 | 31.18% |
| 2 | GOVERNMENT OF BARBADOS | 1,220,880 | 49.58% |
| 3 | GOVERNMENT OF DOMINICA | 3,030 | 0.12% |
| 4 | GOVERNMENT OF GRENADA | 4,545 | 0.18% |
| 5 | GOVERNMENT OF GUYANA | 2,500 | 0.10% |
| 6 | GOVERNMENT OF JAMAICA | 2,500 | 0.10% |
| 7 | GOVERNMENT OF ST. KITTS AND NEVIS | 2,500 | 0.10% |
| 8 | GOVERNMENT OF MONTSERRAT | 3,030 | 0.12% |
| 9 | GOVERNMENT OF ST. LUCIA | 4,545 | 0.18% |
| 10 | GOVERNMENT OF ST. VINCENT & THE GRENADINES | 264,111 | 10.73% |
| 11 | GOVERNMENT OF TRINIDAD AND TOBAGO | 7,500 | 0.30% |
| 12 | ANTIGUA COMMERCIAL BANK | 2,721 | 0.11% |
| 13 | ANTIGUA BARBUDA INVESTMENT BANK | 1,134 | 0.05% |
| 14 | ACB INVESTMENT CO. LTD. | 5,440 | 0.22% |
| 15 | ANTIGUA AND BARBUDA WORKERS UNION | 1,264 | 0.06% |
| 16 | BWIA WEST INDIES AIRWAYS LTD., | 75,755 | 3.08% |
| 17 | CARIBBEAN AIRCRAFT HANDLING | 2,422 | 0.10% |
| 18 | HKH (ANTIGUA) LTD | 38,995 | 1.58% |
| 19 | LEEWARD ISLANDS ENGINEERING ASSOCIATION | 4,000 | 0.16% |
| 20 | LIAT STAFF PROVIDENT FUND | 30,329 | 1.23% |
| 21 | NATIONAL BANK OF DOMINICA | 6,319 | 0.26% |
| 22 | THE REPUBLIC BANK (GRENADA) LIMITED (Formerly NATIONAL COMMERCIAL BANK OF GRENADA | 2,527 | 0.10% |
| 23 | JOAN B. SLACK | 1,264 | 0.05% |
| 24 | STATE INSURANCE CORPORATION | 6,319 | 0.26% |
| 25 | ST. JOHN'S CO-OPERATIVE CREDIT UNION LTD. | 1,000 | 0.04% |
| TOTAL: | | 2,462,520 | 1.00 |

PERCENTAGE – ISSUED TO AUTHORIZED    49%
Authorized last changed OCT. 2007    5,000,000

# Appendix 9

## LIAT Costs Distribution

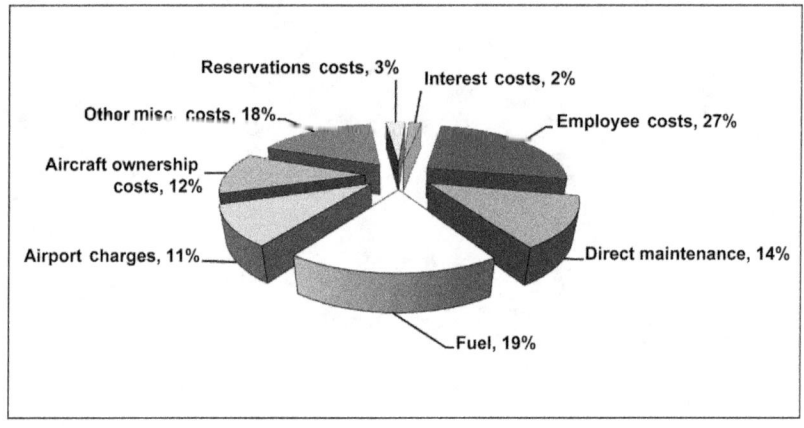

# References

Adams, M., and D. Reed. 2008. Rising costs reshaping air travel across the USA. *USA Today*. 16 May.

Chastanet, A. 2003. Air Jamaica launches Top Class: Rebranding of first-class service offers passengers the ultimate airborne luxury. http://www.airjamaica.com. Accessed 17 June 2003.

Downes, A. 2009. Too big to fail: Economic reality or moral hazard? A global and regional perspective. Lecture to the National Insurance Board of Barbados, Bridgetown. 3 June.

Edwards-Jones, I., and anon. 2005. *Air Babylon*. London: Bantam.

Grossman, D. 2005. Oil fuels the war of attrition. *USA Today*. 18 July.

Holder, J. 2006. Creative branding and transportation: A success strategy for Caribbean airlines. In *Tourism: The driver of change in the Jamaican economy?*, ed. K.O. Hall and R. Holding. Kingston: Ian Randle.

Joyce, A. 2009. Qantas faces "high level of uncertainty". *Financial Times*. 20 August.

Maynard, M. 2008. High fuel costs are squeezing low airfares. *New York Times*. 20 June.

Pilling, M. 2008. Governments cash in on aviation. *Airline Business*. 11 January.

# Index

Advance Passenger Information
    System, 18
Aer Lingus, 192
Air Aruba, 52
Airbus, 7, 31
Air Canada, 157–158, 184
Air Caraibe, 49
Air Dominicana, 2
Air France, 29, 47, 184
Air India, 163
Air Jamaica, 3, 29, 36, 43, 45, 48, 58,
    182–183, 201
  branding factor, 48
  branding of, 7–8
  and decisions about the air
    transportation services, 45
  fleet of, 7
  future viability, 202–203
  losses, 24–25
  ownership, 7–8, 37–38, 197
  performance in 2008, 185
  in promoting Jamaica, 7–8
  services, 7–8
  short-term plans, 208
airline distress syndrome, 62–63
airline industry
  in Caribbean countries, 2–4.
    *See also specific airlines*
  crisis period. *See* crisis period of
    airline industry
  difficulties and complexities, 3–4
  and economic recession of
    2009, 190–193
  in facilitating international
    tourism, 1–2
  financial performance, 27–28
  lessons of 2008 and 2009, 194–195
  during national disaster, 1
  overall net losses, 28–29
  socio-economic development of
    communities, 4
airline seats, conditions satisfying,
    136–137
Air Tran, 22, 156

288    Index

Air Transport Users Council, 23
Alaska Airlines, 23
ALM, 52
Aloha Airlines, 22
American Airlines, 22, 29–30, 47, 133, 155, 184, 194, 203
American Eagle, 49, 124–125, 175
Annual Airline Quality Report, 22–23
Archer, Anthony, 173
Arthur, Owen, 88, 93, 98, 110, 169
Asia Pacific carriers, 29
Association Nacional de Hoteles y Restaurantes (ASONAHORES), 2
ATA Airlines, 22
9/11 attack, 1, 27, 47, 149, 178–179
Ayling, Bob, 47

baggage issues
   Annual Airline Quality Report on, 23
   with Caribbean airline industry, 18–20
   at international airlines and airports, 20–21
Bahamasair, 3, 52, 185
   future viability, 203–204
   historical perspective, 8–9
   losses, 25
   services, 9
Barbados, 2
Barnette, Skip, 87, 91, 93
Beckles, Sir Hilary, xvii
Benjamin, John, 70
Bertrand, Ian, 54
Bird, Lester, 70
Bisignani, Giovanni, 27, 115, 191
Blackman, Jackie, 93
Blais, Roland, 81
BMI, 158–159, 184
Boeing 707-138, 10–11
Boeing 707-320, 11

Boeing 727-100, 10
Boeing 737, 2, 9, 11, 23, 31
Boeing 737-300, 11
Boeing 737-700, 11
Boeing 737-800, 11
Boeing 767, 2
Bombardier Dash 8-300, 11
Bonadie, Burns, 93
Bowen, Brent, 22
branding of an airline, 46–48
Braniff airline, 134
Brazilian carriers, 29
British Airports, 20–21
British Airways, 9, 29–30, 47, 147, 159, 163, 184, 191, 194, 204
British Midland Airways (BMI), 21
British Overseas Airways Corporation (BOAC), 9
British South American Airways (BSAA), 9
British West Indian Airways (BWIA), 3, 36, 43, 48, 52. *See also* BWIA/CAL
   branding factor, 48
   branding of, 10
   fleet, 10–11
   form of CIAH, 54–56
   losses, 25–26
   relationship with CAL, 11
   services, 10
Bros, Cheney, 188
Browne, Oliver, 93, 102
Bryon, Alan, 82, 88, 93
Bushell, Edward, 93
BWee Express, 49, 64, 86
BWIA/CAL, 9–11, 45, 58, 118, 214
   and decisions about the air transportation services, 45
   ownership, 197
BWIA West Indies Limited, 9

Canadian carriers, 29
Canadian economy, 2008, 181
Caribbean airline industry, 2–4
　Annual Airline Quality Report, 22–23
　baggage issues, 18–20
　community carrier, role of, 213–215
　creation of a single CARICOM carrier, 215–216
　financial performance, 23–27
　future viability, 201–208
　government ownership of airlines, 216
　issue of public *vs* private ownership of carriers, 35–37
　on-time performance, 17–18
　operational experiences, 20–22
　private airline sector, 4
　reactions to 2008 crisis, 168–176
　regional air transportation, 43, 209–213
　responsibilities and challenges, 40–41
Caribbean Airlines Limited (CAL), 6, 9–11, 24, 26, 36–37, 45, 48–49, 55, 58, 87, 96–97, 118, 128, 141, 158, 172–174, 183–184, 201, 204, 208
Caribbean Airways, 26, 37, 184–185
　future viability, 204
Caribbean Carrier Consortium, 58, 82
Caribbean Community (CARICOM), 5–6, 10–12, 45, 56, 58–59, 61, 72, 97, 110, 119, 126, 129, 145, 170–173, 194–195, 197, 204, 210–213–216, 212–213, 215–216, 255
Caribbean Development Bank (CDB), 61, 102, 108–112, 115, 145–146, 205, 208, 211, 215
　loan, 108–112, 115
Caribbean functional cooperation strategies, 52–53
Caribbean Hotel Association, 99–100

Caribbean International Airways Holding (CIAH) Company, 53–56
Caribbean Safety and Security Oversight System (CASSOS), 172
Caribbean Single Market and Economy, 45
Caribbean Star, 14, 19, 26–27, 48–49, 58, 63, 71–72, 79, 81
Caribbean Sun, 26–27, 49, 72, 81, 86, 98
Caribbean tourism, performance in 2008
　air transportation factors, 180
　and Canadian economy, 181
　Caribbean advantages, 178–180
　Caribbean Carriers' performance, 183–185
　cruise passenger arrivals, 265
　and Middle East economy, 181
　and North Africa economy, 181
　recovery in cruise passenger traffic, 179–180
　safety and security factors, 178
　source markets of business, 177–178
　stay-over tourists, 178–179, 182
　stop-over arrivals, 258
　tourist arrivals, 259–264
　and UK economy, 181
　and US economy, 180–181
Caribbean tourism, performance in 2009, 189–190
　Caribbean advantage, 193–194
　cruise passenger arrivals, 271
　stop-over arrivals, 267
　tourist arrivals, 268–270
Caribbean tourism reactions, 2008 crisis impact
　CARICOM summit agreements on tourism and air transportation, 171–172

co-op marketing programme, 175
creation of a regional marketing
  fund, 174
functional cooperation between CAL
  and LIAT, 173–174
meeting of LIAT shareholder prime
  ministers, 169–170
meeting of ministers of tourism, 169
safety issues, in air transport, 172–173
steps taken by LIAT, 175–176
Carib Express, 49, 86
CARICOM Petroleum Stabilization
  Fund, 5–6, 11–12, 45, 56, 58–59,
  61, 72, 97
Carter, Jimmy, 130
Cat Airways, 203
Cayman Airways, 3, 35, 52, 185
  fleet, 11–12
  future viability, 204–205
  losses, 25
  ownership, 11, 36
  services, 11
Cayman Brac Airways, 11
Challenger, Brian, 93
Chastanet, Allen, 7
Civil Aeronautics Act of 1938, 131
code-sharing agreement, 50–51
Commonwealth Caribbean Regional
  Secretariat Report, 43
community carrier, 213–215
companion baggage plane, 19
competition, of Caribbean carriers,
  48–50
  vs monopoly, 122–125
Continental Airlines, 133, 184
Continental and Eastern Airlines, 134
Conway, Michael, 37
cooperation
  arguments for, 44
  branding factor, 46–48

challenges, 58–59
code-sharing agreement, 50–51
creation of the Caribbean
  International Airways Holding
  company (CIAH), 53–56
functional, 51–53
material factors, 45–46
by merging, 56–57
psychological factors, 46
reviews, 57–59
types and levels of, 50–56
vs mistrust, 44–45
Court Line, 12, 44
Crandall, Robert, 40, 134–135, 137
Cricket World Cup (2007), 58, 82, 97
crisis period of airline industry
  business travels, 152
  Caribbean carriers' reactions, 168–176
  commissions allowances, cutting on,
    163
  escalation of oil prices, 150–151
  2008 forecast for the global airline
    industry, 150–151
  losses and closures of US carriers, 152
  oil prices, impact, 164–168
  by raising fees on baggage and other
    services, 162–163
  survival strategies, 152–163
  through mergers, 160–162
Cruise Line International Association,
  179
Cullen, Garry, 54, 71–73, 80–82, 86
Cummins, Adrian, 93
CyberSource Corporation, 136

Darby, Mark, 77, 82, 87–88, 93, 98, 173
Dash 8 planes, 13, 17, 19, 64, 83, 116,
  159, 204, 254
DC Dakota, 10

Index    291

DeFreitas-Rait, Karen, 93
Delisle, Frank S., 12
Delta Airlines, 8, 23, 29–30, 48, 133, 156, 194
deregulation, of routes, schedules and fares, 130–135
DHC-6 Twin Otters, 12
disruption in services, 17–18
Dominican Republic, 2
Douglas DC-9-50, 11
Downes, Andrew, 199–201

Eastern Airlines, 133, 194
Eastern Caribbean, airline seats demand *vs* supply, 85–86
Eastern Caribbean (EC) Express, 49
EasyJet, 32, 144–145
economic recession, 2009, 187–188
Edwards, Jennifer, 93
Ellis, Anthony, 93
Emirates Airline, 159

fares, regulations of
  IATA Caribbean report, 145–146
  industry practices, 136–138
  LIAT fare levels, 138–140
  link with oil prices and fuel surcharge, 140–142
  practice of hedging oil prices, 146–148
  setting process through deregulation, 132–135
  taxes and add-ons, 142
  year-on-year comparison for 2007–2008, 226–244
  yield management tool, 135–136
financial performance
  of Caribbean carriers, 23–27
  of international air carriers, 27–29

flight cancellation, 17, 23
Floistad, Chris, 196
Fortuno, Luis, 189
Frank, Sir, 12
Frederick, Vina, 124
Frontier Airways, 22
fuel price, impact on airlines, 27–28
fuel surcharge and airline industry, 140–142
functional cooperation, 51–53

global distribution system (GDS), 33–34, 75, 78, 135, 164
GOL, 29, 83
Golding, Bruce, 37
Goldman Sachs, 28
Gonsalves, Camillo, 93
Gonsalves, Ralph, 71, 80, 88–89, 93, 97, 110, 119, 169
Goodwin, George, 93
Grantley Adams International Airport, 77
Great Depression era, 62
Guyana Airways, 52

Hadeed, Aziz, 70
Hahn Air, 184
Harrigan, Wilbur, 71
Hawker Siddeley 748, 11
hedging oil prices, practice of, 146–148
  accounting requirements, 251
  and airline policies, 251–252
  assumptions, 246
  call option pricing, 247
  collar, 248
  concepts, 246
  fuel prices, 246

hedging oil prices, practice of (*cont.*)
  futures price, 246
  options based on a futures price of US$70, US$80, US$96.81, 249–250
  spot fuel price, 250
  types, 247
Henne, Michael, 93, 99
Holder, Jean, 88
hub and spoke system, 133, 135
Hudson Bombers, 10
human resources, in transportation services, 198
Humphrey, Chester, 71, 93, 119

IATA Operational Safety Audit Programme, 184
Indian airlines, 163–164
Indian Association of Tour Operators, 164
insolvent business, 199–200
international airline taxes and add-ons, 142
International Finance Corporation, 38
the Internet, 34
Island of Dominica, 18

Jamaica Express, 86
Jet Airways, 163
JetBlue, 22, 32, 78, 156

Kingfisher Airlines, 163
KLM, 29
KLM–Air France, 159
Kronenberg, Cyriel, 145

Laker, Freddie, 132
Leeward Islands Airline Pilots Association (LIALPA), 62, 79–80, 118–120
Leeward Islands Air Transport (LIAT), 2–3, 36, 43, 45, 48–49, 52, 58, 172, 201
  airline distress syndrome at, 62–63
  approaches to fuel management, 82–83
  baggage issues, 18–19
  branding factor, 48
  BWIA–LIAT relationship, 12–13
  challenges, 76–80
  code-sharing agreements, 50–51
  combined LIAT–Caribbean Star fleet, 13
  commercial arrangement with Caribbean Star, 63
  commercial arrangement with Grantley Adams International Airport, 77
  and competition, 125–127
  cost distribution, 284
  and decisions about the air transportation services, 46
  employees, 63
  and failure of Speedwing Recovery Plan, 69–73
  fare levels, 138–140, 206, 223–224
  financial position, 64
  financial restructuring, 68–69, 83
  form of CIAH, 54–56
  future viability, 205–208
  general problems of, 64
  government guarantees, 80
  IT restructuring, 66

Leeward Islands Air Transport (LIAT) (*cont.*)
   as legacy carrier model, 75
   longevity factor, 61–62
   losses, 26
   manpower management, 65
   and monopoly status, 113–116, 120–122
   need for new approaches, 82–84
   on-time performance, 17
   ordinary share holders, 273–282
   organizational chart, 66–67
   ownership, 14–15, 36, 38–39, 197–198
   performance in 2008, 183–184
   problems with Navitaire, 78
   relationship with Caribbean Star, 14, 85. *See also* LIAT–Caribbean Star merger
   restructuring strategies, 73–75, 175–176
   role in promoting tourism, 14
   schedule changes, 67
   services, 13–14
   shareholder governments, 61, 63, 72, 80–81
   Shareholders, Board and Management, 220–221
   Speedwing Report and Recovery Plan for, 64–73
   unions of, 62–63
   unit revenues, improvement strategies, 64–65
Leeward Islands Flight Attendants Association (LIFAA), 62–63
legacy carriers, 30
legislations, of air transportation, 130–131
Lehman Brothers, 147–148

LIAT–Caribbean Star merger
   asset purchase deal, 106–112
   beneficial outcomes, 115–117
   CAL's vision of alliance, 96–97
   Caribbean Star/LIAT relationship, 85
   commercial agreement, 98
   committee advisers, 93
   customer services, 120–122
   disagreements between LIAT and LIALPA, 119–120
   discussions for functional cooperation, 86–88
   Eastern Caribbean, airline seats demand *vs* supply, 85–86
   fare levels, 139–140
   financial bail out of LIAT, 89, 101
   initiation, 91–94
   Kingstown agreement, 92
   LIAT's debts, 101–102
   LIAT's financial situation (2006), 88–91
   meeting of shareholders, 88
   negatives of, 117–120
   objectives, 102–106
   operation of planes, 117
   oppositions, 99–101
   options, 104–105
   oversight negotiating committees, 92–93
   pros and cons of winding up and starting over, 106
   share transaction, 105–106
   specifics of the merger proposal, 98–99
   state of industrial relations, 117–120
   statutory amalgamation, 105
   trade union council, 93–94
   unionization of, 96

Lineas Aereas Costarricenses S.A., 11
local ownership of airlines, advantage of, 195–196
Lockheed L 1011-500, 11
Lockheed Lodestar, 10
"Lonely Beaches," 189
losses, of airline industry. *See* financial performance
Lovebird hospitality, 7
low-cost carriers (LCCs), 29, 40, 75–76, 128–129
  attributes of, 31–32
  during 2008 crisis period, 153–154
  global distribution systems and, 32–34
  *vs* legacy carrier model, 34–35
Lufthansa, 22, 30, 47, 147, 158, 163
Lynch, Noel, 88

Manning, Patrick, 37
McCaw, Cameron, 93, 102, 108
McDonnell Douglas MD 83, 11
MD-80 jets, 23
Middle East economy, 2008, 181
Midwest Airlines, 23
Mohamed, Kamaluddin, 43
monopoly status
  and competition of Caribbean carriers, 122–125
  and customer services, 120–122
  of Leeward Islands Air Transport (LIAT), 113–116
Moral Hazard, 200

national security systems, 1
Navitaire, 75–78, 81
Nobles, Bruce, 202

North Africa economy, 2008, 181
Northwest Airlines, 22, 29

Obama, Barack, 187–188, 201
OECS states, 46
oil prices and airline industry, 140–142, 164–168
Oliver, Danny, 81, 86
on-time performance
  Caribbean carriers, 17–18
  of international airlines and airports, 21–22
operational experiences, of international airlines and airports
  Annual Airline Quality Report, 22–23
  loss of baggage, 20–21
  on-time performance, 21–22
Organisation of Eastern Caribbean States (OECS), 12–13
ownership
  advantages, 195–198
  Air Jamaica, 7–8, 36–38
  BWIA, 36
  Cayman Airways, 11, 36
  disadvantages, 199–201
  foreign, 1
  government's position on, 36
  Leeward Islands Air Transport (LIAT), 14–15, 36, 38–39
  public *vs* private ownership of carriers, 35–37

Pan American Airlines, 9, 133–134, 194, 204
People's Express, 134
Petroleum Stabilization Fund, 97

Pineapple Air, 203
preferred partner, 214
Puerto Rico Tourism Company, 175

Quantas, 192
Quikpak service, 14, 64, 66

Regional airlines, 4–5
Regional Aviation Safety Oversight System, 172, 254
regional integration process, to air transportation, 42–44
revenue management. *See* yield management tool
Richards-Anjo, Stacey, 93
Rodgers, Jim, 28
Ryanair, 32, 78, 144, 147, 192, 252

Sabatini, Nicolas, 23
Sabena, 194
Sabre, 75, 77
safety issues, in air transport, 172–173
Sandals hotel chain, 7
Saunders, Philip, 26
Sawyer, Ray, 70
security arrangements and delay issues, 18
Servisair, 144
Singapore Airlines, 8, 35, 163, 191
single Caribbean airspace, 254–256
single Caribbean carrier, 42–43
single European airspace, 254
Skybus, 22
Skywest Airways, 22
social needs, in transportation services, 198

Somavia, Juan, 187
Southern Air, 203
Southwell, Miguel, 93
Southwest Airlines, 22–23, 27, 32, 158
Speedwing Report and Recovery Plan, for LIAT. *See* Leeward Islands Air Transport (LIAT)
Spencer, Baldwin, 88, 93, 110, 169
Spirit Airlines, 29, 32, 155–156, 196, 203
Stanford, Sir Allen, 27, 49, 59, 85–88, 91–92, 96, 98, 100, 102–103, 106–109, 201
Stanford Financial Group (SFG), 88
staycations, 189
Stewart, Gordon "Butch," 7
Surinam Airways, 52
swine flu, 194
Swissair, 194

TAM, 29
Thompson, David, 169
Tobago Express, 11
"too big to fail," rationale for, 199–200
tourism
    airline industry, role in facilitating, 1–2
    and air transportation factor, 180
    Caribbean tourism, 2008 crisis impact, 168–176. *See also* Caribbean tourism, performance in 2008
    and economy factor, 177–181
    intra-Caribbean, 39
    Leeward Islands Air Transport (LIAT), role of, 14
Transportes Aereas Centro-Americano alliance, 52
Travel Agent Association of India, 164

Travel Association Federation of
India, 164
Trinidad and Tobago Air Services, 9

UK economy, 2008, 181
UK government's Air Passenger Duty
Tax, 143–145
unemployment, during 2009 economic
recession, 187–188
United Airlines, 8, 22, 28–29, 133,
147, 156
US Airways, 29, 156–157
US Deregulation Act of 1978, 130
US economy, 2008, 180–181
US Trade and Development Agency
(USTDA), 38

van Eenennaam, Rens, 71
Vickers Viking, 10
Vickers Viscount, 10

Villanueva, Arturo, 2
Virgin Atlantic Airlines, 35–36, 47,
158, 184, 194

Walcott, Sir Frank, 209
Walsh, Willie, 191
Wehby, Don, 37, 202
Welsh, Michael, 89
Western Air, 203
West Indies cricket team, 211
Williams, Eric, 57
Williams, Shirley, 37

yield management tool, 135–136

zero commission policy,
163–164
Zwaig Financial Consultants,
71, 73

www.ingramcontent.com/pod-product-compliance
Lightning Source LLC
Chambersburg PA
CBHW061428300426
44114CB00014B/1593